The Has-Beens and Never-Will-Bes

A Boy's Own Adventure of Australian Cricket and the Raj

Megan Ponsford

CricketMASH

The Has-Beens and Never-Will-Bes

by

Megan Ponsford

Published by CricketMASH

Amstelveen, Netherlands

www. Cricketmash.com

Cover design: Maha @smahaart

ISBN: 978 94-92203 15 1

To the has-beens and never-will-bes

All the bibliographic information has been provided in the notes at the end of each chapter.

CONTENTS

ACKNOWLEDGMENTS

I would like to dedicate this book to the memory of my truly great, great uncle, Tom Leather. I have very fond memories of his silly jokes and tirelessly buoyant personality as the only elder statesman seated, year in and out, on the 'kids' Christmas table. This book about this largely unknown, yet important, chapter in Australian cultural, social and sporting history was written in homage to Tom. I only wish I had earlier probed him, his wife Doll and daughter Wendy on matters pertaining to this research however I possibly would not have devoted close to 15 years to its gestation if I had the luxury of questioning the family. I wish they had known that I would devote a large chunk of my middle age to investigating the conception of Indo-Australia cricket.

I would also like to extend this dedication to my Ponsford relatives, firstly to Grandfather Bill who didn't just encourage my interest in sport but was the loveliest companion when he lived with us when I was a child and my parents worked. His reluctance to discuss his history, especially the potentially controversial chapters of it, has encouraged me to belligerently question, interrogate and probe. Thanks effusively to my parents, Geoffrey and Glenis and their always-accessible sporting bookshelves, refined knowledge of the game, astute memories and unfailing support. Many thanks to my brother Michael, and my sister Rowena, with whom I share a lifetime of sporting spectatorship from my earliest memories of the West Indies Test series in the seventies, to village cricket in Britain and to our continuing regular encounters watching our Demons. I crucially want to acknowledge my children Edoardo and Alessandro, who have endured the long absences of their mother and have been supportive throughout, Baci Baci e Grazie Mille. Edoardo's technical wizardry has been especially vital.

I am enormously grateful for the assistance provided by Keir Reeves, Chris McConville, Jolanta Nowak, Mike Coward, Rahul Mankad, Raj Amarnath, Mark Ray, Thomas Fletcher, Rodney Cavalier, Peter French, the late (great) Raj Singh Dungapur, Mihir Bose, Sharda Ugra, Clayton Murzello, Boria Majumdar, Darshak Mehta, Geoff Lawson, Marcus Couto, Vasant Raiji, Peter Young (Cricket Australia), Ken Jacobs, The Pakistan Cricket Board and ex-chairman Shahryar Khan, Francis Leach, Peter 'Tommy' Hanlon, Waquar Nisar (I follow most cricket literature in spelling the family name as 'Nissar', however Waquar maintains this was a mistake made by English journalists during the 1932 Test), the Salahuddin and Saeed families, Majid Khan, Yayha Ghaznavi, the AFP in Pakistan (Marzio, Danny, Ann and Stavros), Ray Webster, Ken Williams, Brian Stoddart, Rob Pascoe, Rhett Bartlett, Bernard Whimpress, Peter Ebeling, both MCC libraries (Melbourne and Marylebone and their erudite librarians, David Studham and Neil

Robinson), Adam Chadwick, Peta Phillips, Raja Tahir, Najum Latif at the Lahore Gymkhana Museum, Barry Judd, Sean Gorman, Russell Jackson, Dan Eddy, Trevor Ruddell, Abhishek Mukherjee, the Australia-India Council, Raja Randhir Singh, Judith Gibson (the Caulfield Grammar archivist), Cricket Tasmania, the WACA, Patricia Downs, the AGL Shaw Fellowship, Dawn Peel at the Colac Historical Society, Andrew and Penny Torok, Gail Schmidt at the SLV, Andrew May, the incredible hospitality of the Saklanis in Delhi and Dehradun, Brian and Mary in London, Cricket NSW and Colin Clowes. An especially big thanks to the relatives of the Australian cricketers: Pat O'Toole, Cecily Dougan, Kim Innes, Lesley Ryder and siblings; John, Frank and Peter, Jennifer Tilbrook and Ray who shared their archives and their family histories. And lastly to my fabulous friends: Fiona Dalziel, Sarah Tartakover, Fiona Brook, Rosie Kavanavoch, title-maestro Peter Milne, James Kelly, Lydia Marcuzzi, Frank Brunetti and Caroline Ferguson who have all well-and-truly done their bit.

My first visit to India was in 2005 when I travelled with my father. Holidaying with Dad was great, he taught me so much about cricket as we both learnt about Indian culture. We were hosted by Raj Singh Dungapur at the Cricket Club of India and I am indebted to the time, hospitality and opportunities he gave us. This research commenced seriously in 2007 when I was successful in acquiring Australia-India Council funding to finance a research trip to India. On this, my second time in India, I first met my dear friend Vikas Saklani who has been pivotal to all my subsequent Indian adventures. I travelled with my then-new partner and now-husband, intrepid travelling companion, Noel Fermanis. Noel has faithfully accompanied me on many of my research jaunts. Despite being of Greek heritage, and having no interest in cricket, he even donned the whites to play at the Lahore Gymkhana where he faced some pretty serious opposition. A fellowship at the State Library Victoria in 2013 further advanced research.

Finally, enormous gratitude goes to Gideon Haigh and his excellent foreword. I was a little sheepish asking him to do the honours, as he did the same for me in 2003 for my first book Home Ground. Within that time, he's written around 50 books and I've only managed a couple.

I would especially like to thank the patience, mentorship, superlative knowledge and refined intellect of my friend and editor Arunabha Sengupta and his ability to whip this manuscript into shape and expand my repertoire of cricket terminology. His introduction to Adrian Runswick at CricketMASH was invaluable and I'm enormously thankful for the lifeline the publisher has given me.

FOREWORD

by Gideon Haigh

Before Dada, Sourav Ganguly, there was Daddy, as Frank Tarrant was known to the Indian cricket community to whom he was an ambassador to the cricket world. Australian-born, England-made, Tarrant was a cultural intermediary before anyone thought in such terms, and, at last, in Megan Ponsford's excellent book, has a literary testament to his greatest coup.

Megan is not only the granddaughter of Bill Ponsford, run-maker extraordinaire, but the great niece of Tom Leather, who played a handful of games for Victoria in the 1930s. An incongruous presence for many years in Tom's modest suburban unit in Melbourne was a tiger skin - a souvenir, it turned out, of the long-forgotten ensemble of Australian cricketers who Frank Tarrant assembled to tour India in 1935-36. It was the first such tour of its kind, and outside official auspices, disavowed by the authorities and only briefly mentioned by *Wisden Cricketers' Almanack*.

Captivated by the romantic improbability of the expedition, Megan has spent a decade following its historical traces, and recreating its world - the India of the Raj, of the Anglophile Chamber of Princes, of not just Maharajahs but Maharawats, Nawabs, Yuvrajs and Zamindars. At its centre sits Tarrant, who turned a successful career as a county professional for Middlesex into an even more successful career as a factotum of the Maharajahs of Patiala, Jodhpur and Cooch Behar, ostentatious enthusiasts for cricket and racing. Perhaps by virtue of his Australianess, Tarrant had a knack for moving seamlessly between occident and orient, and Megan's cinematic eye suggests that the whole saga is worthy of Save Your Legs treatment: financier of the tour was the Maharajah of Patiala, 'an orientalist prototype: the alluring hero – villain in a Merchant Ivory production'. Tarrant was accompanied on the tour by his wife Eva, a 'not your typical trophy wife', and son Bert, a ne'er-do-well 'ambitiously listed on the Australian electoral role as an "actor".' There were other Australians flourishing improbably in 1930s India, from the actress Mary Ann Evans (who as Fearless Nadia was a star of Indian cinema), to Sydney Cup-winning jockey Ray Wilson (whose saddle-shaped tombstone I recently encountered in my local cemetery). The peripatetic cricket coach Frank Warne was there also, six decades in advance of his namesake.

Megan has unearthed a wonderful variety of primary sources, so that we hear of the cricketers' experiences, as it were, first-hand. The team featured some cricketers of renown including Charlie Macartney, Jack Ryder, Stork Hendry and Ron Oxenham, albeit somewhat past their prime and maybe a little rough round the edges. They played very well too, despite the distractions, the exoticism, the epicureanism, and both: it is hard not to smile at the story of the team trying to souvenir the gold dinner plates of the royal court of Jamnagar before shamefacedly giving them back. They kept politics at arms' length, declining an invitation to meet Gandhi, but kept faith with egalitarian values, declining invitations to join any club that maintained a colour bar. Like many subsequent teams, they had varying health fortunes: Frank Bryant gained weight; Arthur Allsopp spent ten weeks in hospital. They returned at the end with priceless memories and, like Leather, mementos: Ryder a panther skin, Hendry an alabaster model of the Taj Mahal, Ron Morrisby a portrait of the Maharajah of Patiala that for decades surmounted his dining room fireplace and must have intrigued visitors to his Tasmanian family orchard. Tarrant christened his country property Jodhpur Estate, although it proved harder to act the squire in Victoria than in India.

Tarrant, Megan reminds us, blazed his trail in the face of administrative indifference, if not hostility. Macartney called the Australia Board 'cricket Hitlers', which if not as much of an insult in 1935 as it sounds now was still a pretty strong sentiment. Canny chancer that he was, Daddy was well ahead of the curve, sensing the potential tapped in our generation by the Board of Control for Cricket in India and its T20 cash machine. In the same way Kerry Packer anticipates to Lalit Modi, Daddy can perhaps be thought to lead to Dada.

INTRODUCTION – THE CARDBOARD BOX

I come from sporting stock. My grandfather Bill Ponsford was a good cricketer. Actually, he wielded the bat so well over time he became pretty famous and now a stand at the Melbourne Cricket Ground is emblazoned with his name. He was also patient and had the most amazing capacity to concentrate. Bill, unassuming and quite ill-prepared, arrived on the cricket world stage in the 1920s and broke numerous records. If Bradman, who was eight years younger, hadn't subsequently smashed the records that my grandfather had broken he'd now be a national icon. And some digging through my family tree has unearthed a few other Ponsford sports people. It appears that Bill wasn't the only cricketer in the family. Me, I can't catch a ball or run a marathon and yet I still feel a real part of this lineage, if as an informed bystander: watching, interpreting and making sense of forgotten events on the sporting stage.

As a lover of cricket and history, I'm often asked if I'm writing a book on my grandfather. My standard answer is that while I'm proud of his achievements there's another cricket story to tell that's been overlooked. It's about the first Australian cricket tour to India in 1935/36. Despite the cultural and sporting significance of the tour, it didn't and doesn't appear as more than a footnote in historiography. The cricket authorities in Australia washed their hands of any involvement in this brash enterprise. And I dare say, a majority of the sport-loving Australian community even questioned whether following the events in India was permitted, especially considering a Test encounter between Australia and South Africa was taking place concurrently.

This tale doesn't revolve around my grandfather who only plays a minor role in the narrative. It does, however, involve another family member: Grandpa Bill's brother-in-law and my great-uncle, Tom Leather. Convivial, enthusiastic yet lacking sophistication, Tom, alongside the Maharaja of Patiala and Frank Tarrant, are the central characters in this beguiling narrative that commenced with the arrival of a cardboard box.

In 2005 I worked at the Melbourne Cricket Club writing cricket content for the soon-to-open National Sports Museum. Both my great-uncle Tom and my grandfather Bill had also worked at the club. Even my father recalls his job as a schoolboy assisting the overall-wearing staff in the score box changing the tally during Australian Rules football matches. With the ever-changing scores, the weight of the ropes turning the cogs blistered Dad's soft hands. Of course, as a young boy being in the control room of the famous stadium was exhilarating.

On my arrival at the club all the staff seemed to know of me. News rippled that she's the grand-daughter. Some of the old fellows who remembered Bill seemed to like me being there, though I think a few of the younger staff grumbled in hushed tones about nepotism.

Soon after I started, a committee member sheepishly confessed that he had a box of Tom's memorabilia that he thought should be returned to the family. He vaguely explained that, among other cricket goodies, it contained material about the first Australian cricket tour to India in 1935/36. Tom, a promising fast bowler, was on this inaugural tour. He loaned the box to the club in the late 1980s and was told its contents might be used for display at the museum. It wasn't.

The box was delivered to my office as promised. It was a standard-size cardboard storage box. It didn't look all that enticing yet I intuitively sensed its significance, that I was about to discover a discarded yet important chapter in cricket history, family narrative and cultural relations. The sticky tape that had held the box closed was no longer adhesive and it crackled as I rolled it into an uncooperative ball and threw it away.

Opening the cardboard flaps, a stale smell wafted into the room. A framed photograph sat at the top of the box. The glass was grimy and I rubbed it with my finger but it made no difference; perhaps mould was under the glass? It was an official shot of the team on the inaugural cricket tour to India. It was taken in the first week of October 1935 just prior to departure. In the image the Australian cricketers possess an air of rebellion: some have mussed-up hair and look like they have slept in their kit. They are dressed in cricket uniforms or mufti, which resembles sporting apparel but isn't. There are both Test and Sheffield Shield blazers. Assorted caps are worn with bohemian independence. Shirt collars sit in various directions and, like the players, refuse to perform as directed. I sense how these cricketers smelled: a mixture of hair pomade, liniment and body odour. Arthur Allsopp drops his hands into his lap despite the photographer's instruction that they should be folded. He looks back at the snapper with a rebellious smirk that defiantly suggests that he's far more comfortable this way.

Ron Oxenham is recognisable by his heavy brow and precise middle part that divides his dark, brilliantined hair into two carbon-copy halves. In every photograph his part is as straight as lines on a school crossing. Whatever the occasion, regardless of the time of day, his hair is like a centurion helmet.

I'm unsure who the team manager is: he sits in the centre, which is unusual. Typically, the administrator of the team stands to the side yet his placement hints at his importance. He is dressed impeccably in a three-piece suit, yet despite this suggesting he's a man of privilege his meaty hands indicate otherwise. They sit on his splayed legs. (Today it would be called manspreading.) A generous paunch overhangs his waistline and suggests that he's well past his playing days. I later learn this gentleman is tour manager Frank Tarrant: a man who will obsess me for the following decade.

The tour is frequently referred to as the Tarrant Tour and he exudes proprietorial pride. His English friends called him Tarry—he liked the moniker as it had a fraudulent ring of Etonian privilege. His face is pleasant yet lined with tell-tale traces of cigarettes and alcohol and, I later learn, a fair degree of stress too.

This is one of the few images of him where he doesn't wear a hat. Intensely self-conscious about balding, Tarrant usually wears a homburg. I imagine he wore it so he could pass himself off as younger and to integrate with the cricketers and the Sikh community.

A cut-out image of Western Australian Frank Bryant, with his perpetual smile, is crudely pasted on to the team portrait. In the pre-Photoshop age this was the only way a group shot could be orchestrated if the players couldn't all be photographed together. Bryant didn't join the others until they picked him up in Fremantle a few weeks later. He looks like a cheeky rebellious hand puppet that misbehaves, perched as he is on the broad shoulders of Lisle Nagel and Bert Ironmonger.

Promotional team shot, Melbourne. September 1935. Leather archive

On first delving through the box I fear that I'm trespassing, but Uncle Tom's distinctive handwriting on photos of strangers reassures me that as a relative I'm permitted, that I'm not intruding. Family matters.

The position of the framed team portrait in the box signals its importance. Tom has painstakingly noted the names of the players and their state of origin on the back of the frame. He boasts: 'The First Australian Cricket Tour to India.' The first letter of each word is in oversized capitals, big and ornamental in design. Adding emphasis, the word 'First' is underlined multiple times. He then adds 'Approved by the Board of Cricket Control'. I discover later, the official sporting body had nothing to do with the tour yet their approval was necessary.

Tour programmes are scattered throughout the box. The regional cricket clubs created their own distinctive material and, at times, production was rudimentary. The scorecard for the match at the Rajindra Gymkhana Club in Patiala is especially charming. It comprises a crudely drawn map of India with the cities of Bombay, Madras, Calcutta and Patiala identified. A large kangaroo embraces Frank Tarrant, who is wearing his customary hat and smoking a customary cigarette: the two figures dominate the physical representation of India. Frank's son Bert is situated in the pouch of the kangaroo, which encourages him to be viewed as the baby joey of the team despite being older than many of his travelling companions.

Scorecard for match in Patiala. January 1936. Leather archive

Each of the programmes proclaims its event is the most important of the tour and includes coats-of-arms and ostentatious graphics. The bigger cities generate comparatively sophisticated material and advertise the event in a more erudite fashion.

Tom looks especially handsome with his neckerchief falling rakishly over his shoulders. The photographs reveal that he wore it often, on the field to catch his sweat though at other times it seems simply to be an accessory. Maybe it was his good luck talisman, I wonder. An image of a young man in a bathing suit sitting primly under a parasol intrigues me. It is signed: 'To Tom, truly a daring Australian. Robert.' Hmm. Robert looks like a pallid, foppish Pom incongruously placed in an oriental landscape. The tableau suggests a close friendship—my imagination runs rampant.

Another image shows Tom in a Tiger Moth on a joyride above Madras. He has company and I wonder if the unidentified companion is Robert. I hope so. Tom wears aviator goggles and a heavy jacket. He must be unbearably hot when the Tiger Moth lands on terra firma. The handwriting tells me that it's his maiden flight on a plane. His excitement, and his fear, is palpable. Much later in my research, I learn from aviation records that over two years earlier, in 1933, the plane crashed, killing the pilot, and the aircraft was rebuilt from the salvageable parts.

Next, I pluck out an autographed cricket ball that sits on a greening brass plinth. It is a modest souvenir: its base is not much bigger than a matchbox. The ink on the now-faded leather ball has bled over time. The inscriptions are minute and Tom's resolve to include multiple details is evident. I use a magnifying glass to try and decipher the tiny words without success. Perhaps I should appreciate that some details about the ball are indecipherable and will remain a mystery. It's unclear which match the ball comes from and whose hands have gripped it. Ron Oxenham's fingerprints must be all over the ball, as he was the star bowler on tour. I know Tom's prints are there too. I suspect that this memento of the tour sat on Tom's desk at the Maribyrnong munitions factory during the war, and afterwards in his office at the Melbourne Cricket Club. Following his retirement, I suspect the ball was proudly displayed at home—just like his tiger skin, the ultimate trophy from the East that covered the linoleum in Tom's modest Melbourne unit.

The photographs in the box are mostly black-and-white so a dazzling egg-yolk yellow background on the cover of Indian Cricket attracts my attention. An Indian gentleman with a shocking-pink turban is captured in profile, which reminds me of English royalty on postage stamps. He looks majestic with strong features: a regal nose, perfectly arched brows, jet-black coiffured facial hair, glistening lips and a diamond drop earring suspended from his left ear. A coat-of-arms featuring a lion, horse and elephant sits in the bottom right-hand corner of the magazine cover, adding to the programme's opulence. An advertisement for the West End Watch Company along the bottom banner of the cover boasts that the watches are 'shock proof, stain proof and water proof'. I wonder how many average cricket fans could have afforded such a luxury accessory. I doubt many. The man on the cover is identified as the Maharaja of Patiala, the man who privately financed the entire enterprise, almost five months long, and who paid the players handsomely. I'm incredulous.

Official Tour Souvenir. 1935:36. Leather archive

The alluring Maharaja Bhupinder Singh of Patiala appears to be an eccentric man of substantial means and he shines in all the photographs. It's not just his flashing diamonds and pearls; he seems to possess an inner magic as well with his wicked smile and sparkling eyes. Indeed, he hints at rebellion, fun and danger. Maybe it's a cliché but I'm drawn to him as an orientalist prototype: the alluring hero – villain in a Merchant Ivory production.

In another photo, Tom is laughing in the back of a 16-cylinder Rolls Royce, one of many in a fleet owned by the Maharaja. Archives in the box confirm that the potentate customarily kept the same number of prestige vehicles as women in his harem. These figures were fluid and in the mid-1930s it sat around 150. Possession was important to the royal as a symbol of aristocratic entitlement. So, it appears, was symmetry.

I make notes on the contents of Tom's archive and their placement in the box. Seemingly four unofficial Tests were played in Bombay, Lahore, Calcutta and Madras alongside nineteen other games over four months. I record the dramatis personae with my own version of shorthand. As I delve further tour manager Frank Tarrant surfaces as a complex yet compelling creature. Like the Maharaja, Frank has a rebellious streak and after a while I can't decide who has charmed me more. Like a hormone-addled teenager, I spin the bottle, and it lands on Frank.

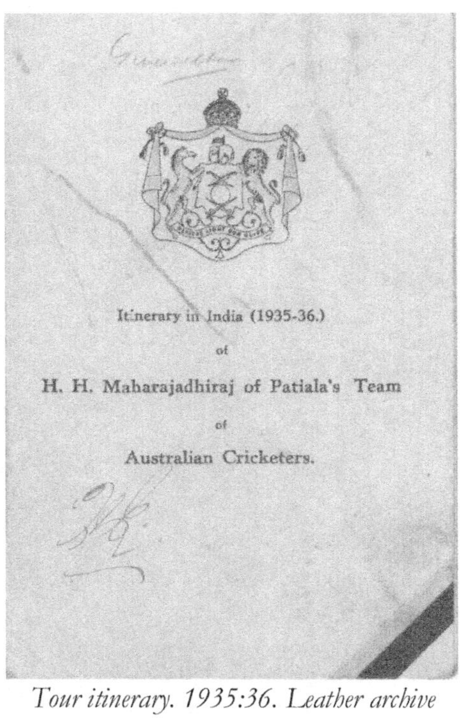

Tour itinerary. 1935:36. Leather archive

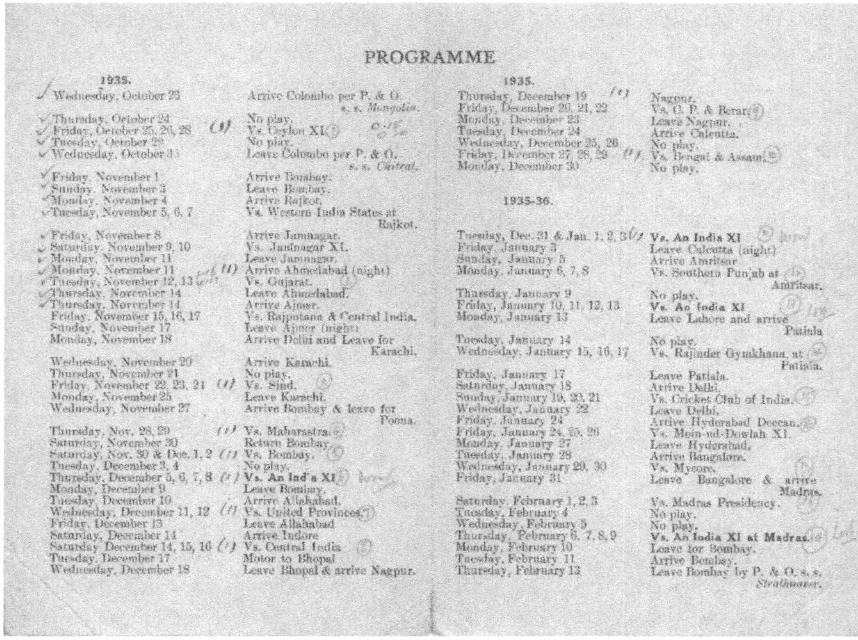

PROGRAMME

1935.	
Wednesday, October 23	Arrive Colombo per P. & O. *s. s. Mongolia.*
Thursday, October 24	No play.
Friday, October 25, 26, 28	Vs. Ceylon XI.
Tuesday, October 29	No play.
Wednesday, October 30	Leave Colombo per P. & O. *s. s. Chitral.*
Friday, November 1	Arrive Bombay.
Sunday, November 3	Leave Bombay.
Monday, November 4	Arrive Rajkot.
Tuesday, November 5, 6, 7	Vs. Western India States at Rajkot.
Friday, November 8	Arrive Jamnagar.
Saturday, November 9, 10	Vs. Jamnagar XI.
Monday, November 11	Leave Jamnagar.
Monday, November 11	Arrive Ahmedabad (night)
Tuesday, November 12, 13	Vs. Gujarat.
Thursday, November 14	Leave Ahmedabad.
Thursday, November 14	Arrive Ajmer.
Friday, November 15, 16, 17	Vs. Rajputana & Central India.
Sunday, November 17	Leave Ajmer (night)
Monday, November 18	Arrive Delhi and Leave for Karachi.
Wednesday, November 20	Arrive Karachi.
Thursday, November 21	No play.
Friday, November 22, 23, 24	Vs. Sind.
Monday, November 25	Leave Karachi.
Wednesday, November 27	Arrive Bombay & leave for Poona.
Thursday, Nov. 28, 29	Vs. Maharastra.
Saturday, November 30	Return Bombay.
Saturday, Nov. 30 & Dec. 1, 2	Vs. Bombay.
Tuesday, December 3, 4	No play.
Thursday, December 5, 6, 7, 8	**Vs. An Ind'a XI**
Monday, December 9	Leave Bombay.
Tuesday, December 10	Arrive Allahabad.
Wednesday, December 11, 12	Vs. United Provinces.
Friday, December 13	Leave Allahabad
Saturday, December 14	Arrive Indore
Saturday December 14, 15, 16	Vs. Central India
Tuesday, December 17	Motor to Bhopal
Wednesday, December 18	Leave Bhopal & arrive Nagpur.
1935.	
Thursday, December 19	Nagpur.
Friday, December 20, 21, 22	Vs. C. P. & Berar.
Monday, December 23	Leave Nagpur.
Tuesday, December 24	Arrive Calcutta.
Wednesday, December 25, 26	No play.
Friday, December 27, 28, 29	Vs. Bengal & Assam.
Monday, December 30	No play.
1935-36.	
Tuesday, Dec. 31 & Jan. 1, 2, 3	**Vs. An India XI**
Friday, January 3	Leave Calcutta (night)
Sunday, January 5	Arrive Amritsar
Monday, January 6, 7, 8	Vs. Southern Punjab at Amritsar.
Thursday, January 9	No play.
Friday, January 10, 11, 12, 13	**Vs. An India XI**
Monday, January 13	Leave Lahore and arrive Patiala
Tuesday, January 14	No play.
Wednesday, January 15, 16, 17	Vs. Rajinder Gymkhana, at Patiala.
Friday, January 17	Leave Patiala.
Saturday, January 18	Arrive Delhi.
Sunday, January 19, 20, 21	Vs. Cricket Club of India.
Wednesday, January 22	Leave Delhi.
Friday, January 24	Arrive Hyderabad Deccan.
Friday, January 24, 25, 26	Vs. Moin-ud-Dowlah XI.
Monday, January 27	Leave Hyderabad.
Tuesday, January 28	Arrive Bangalore.
Wednesday, January 29, 30	Vs. Mysore.
Friday, January 31	Leave Bangalore & arrive Madras.
Saturday, February 1, 2, 3	Vs. Madras Presidency.
Tuesday, February 4	No play.
Wednesday, February 5	No play.
Thursday, February 6, 7, 8, 9	**Vs. An India XI at Madras.**
Monday, February 10	Leave for Bombay.
Tuesday, February 11	Arrive Bombay.
Thursday, February 13	Leave Bombay by P. & O. s. s. *Strathnaver.*

Leather's tour itinerary where he noted wins and losses. 1935:36. Leather archive

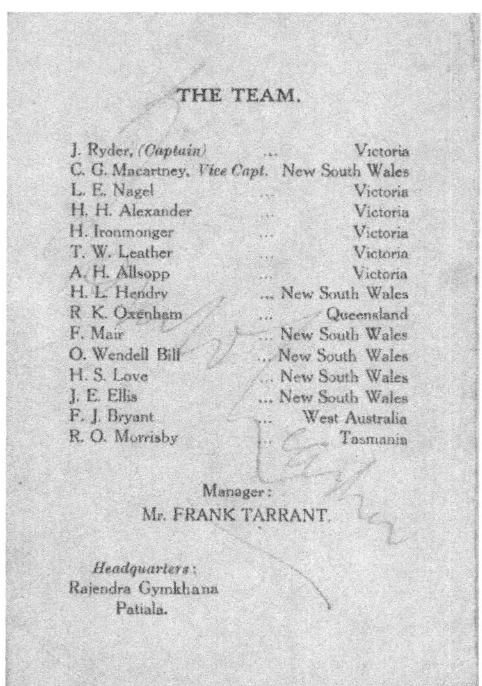

THE TEAM.

J. Ryder, *(Captain)*	Victoria
C. G. Macartney, *Vice Capt.*	New South Wales
L. E. Nagel	Victoria
H. H. Alexander	Victoria
H. Ironmonger	Victoria
T. W. Leather	Victoria
A. H. Allsopp	Victoria
H. L. Hendry	New South Wales
R K. Oxenham	Queensland
F. Mair	New South Wales
O. Wendell Bill	New South Wales
H. S. Love	New South Wales
J. E. Ellis	New South Wales
F. J. Bryant	West Australia
R. O. Morrisby	Tasmania

Manager:
Mr. FRANK TARRANT.

Headquarters:
Rajendra Gymkhana
Patiala.

The selected team to tour India. 1935:36. Leather archive

I find a photograph of Frank (with hat) and a pair of binoculars slung around his neck. A form guide sits in the pocket of his jacket. His cheeky laconic half-smile suggests that he's having a good day punting. I'm getting the idea that he's a connoisseur of horses.

Frank is an ageing sportsman with significant means, and one would imagine the potential to possess a roving eye and yet is frequently pictured with his wife Eva. Eva is not the typical trophy wife. She is small and stocky with a plain yet not unpleasant face, and she frequently wears unflattering designs and prints that accentuate her frame.

The menus make fascinating reading and are beautiful objects. All are printed on quality heavyweight card, often with decorative golden trim, regal insignias and striking Art Deco graphics. They describe a gastronomic cornucopia with influences from India, France, Portugal, England, and even Australia – Peach Melba is served to the cricketers, presumably to make them feel at home.

Some historians argue that anecdotal tales make a vital contribution to history. In an Australian context, it's imperative to challenge the obsession with the Ashes as representing cricket history and to look beyond the venerable history of Donald Bradman and the legendary feats of Shane Warne to gauge a true understanding of the game and its cultural legacy.

And here was a fascinating portal into an unchartered dimension of the history of Australian cricket handed down to me.

I remember being delighted with my discovery that day, though I had no idea that this cardboard box would change my life—igniting over a decade of research, public and private funding, various publications, a PhD and many rewarding jaunts to the UK, India and Pakistan. What I did know was that the contents of Tom's box were significant, that the 1935/36 Australian Cricket Tour of India warranted much closer scrutiny, and that I had now been entrusted with that task.

1 TOUR PREPARATION

Tour manager and retired Australian cricketer Frank Tarrant didn't ever imagine that organising a cricket tour was going to be easy, yet he was unaware of the difficulties that lay ahead. It was early 1935 and Frank was planning the first Australian XI tour to India. Surely, it's worthy of investigation and celebration considering the huge popularity, celebrity and net worth of Indo-Australian cricket today.

The idea was the brainchild of Tarrant and his affluent and influential boss, the Maharaja of Patiala, who gifted the venture £10,000. Together they shared an unbridled enthusiasm for the project and the launch of Indo-Australian cricket. The Maharaja's position on the Indian cricket board, combined with his love of the game, egotistical ambition, political opportunism and his very deep pockets enabled plans to progress. Frank had been the Maharaja's right-hand man in all cricket matters for close to twenty years. Their successful partnership was inspired by the lure of celebrity for the Indian and fortune for the tour manager. Over time their professional arrangement blossomed into friendship.

Frank had been an exceptional all-rounder and was named as one of the five Wisden cricketers of 1908, because of his exceptional 1907 summer in which he scored 1552 runs at 32.33 and captured 183 wickets at 15.70. Despite his undeniable talent, the press and the Australian cricket authorities downplayed his sporting abilities and were suspicious of his wealth made initially through cricket and then by representing Indian royals in business dealings with Britain and Australia. The press delighted in using his initials (FAT) when describing him.[1] Articles hint at him pushing legal boundaries, yet after years of research I don't see him as being lawless. Rather, he was entrepreneurial and certainly made the most of his high-end connections. Simultaneously, he delighted in offending the establishment. Frank fits a common early twentieth century stereotype of a sporting impresario: born into the working class and looking for a way out of a life of factory work and poverty.

At the time, Indian cricket was in its infancy. The national sporting body was new to the Test arena having joined the Imperial Cricket Conference (now the International Cricket Council) in 1926. The official Indian team had participated in four Tests against England: one in England in 1932 and three at home in 1933/34. They were comprehensively defeated in three of them, managing a draw in the other, and were desperate to improve their prospects with the 1936 tour in Britain. The Australians' invitation to India in 1935 was issued to prepare the local team for that later encounter. Compounding the sensitivities were the increasingly mercurial relations between the Indian nationals and the British colonisers. Most suspected that Independence was inevitable, despite staunch British attempts to convince the Empire otherwise, which meant that the central question was when, not if.

From India, Tarrant contacted the Australia Board of Control for International Cricket (now Cricket Australia) in January 1935, about nine months before the Australian team was to depart. Australian cricket administrators rejected initial offers of a tour as they were preoccupied with planning an official Test tour to South Africa scheduled for the same time. They also were not persuaded that 'private tours are always in the best interests of cricket'.[2] Indeed, the minute books from the Australian Board of Control reveal their contemptuous (maybe even culturally dismissive) attitude to the tour. They painstakingly detail protracted meetings where the committee argued over every minute aspect of the tour. This included where games could be played, how the personnel were to be paid and what the team was to be called, caustically even disallowing them to be named an Australian XI.

Initially seventeen famous Australian cricketers, or perhaps more accurately seventeen cricketers residing in Australia, were invited to participate. This was later described as Tarrant's first 'false move' as he invited the players before discussing the matter with the board.[3] The press boasted about the calibre of the would-be team: Woodfull, Ponsford, Bradman, Ryder, Macartney, Grimmett, Richardson, Kippax, O'Reilly, Fingleton, Ironmonger, Love, Hornibrook, Oxenham, Scaife, Nitschke and Alexander. These players were an impressive bunch and would have guaranteed the success of the tour and encouraged significant gate-takings. In the end only five on this list would make it to India nine months later.

The Maharaja was anxious that plans were progressing too slowly, so in late February he dispatched Tarrant to Melbourne to speed up the process. Arriving in Perth on the *Strathnaver*, Tarrant was dismayed to learn that a postal vote by board members had rejected his proposal – the *Argus* shared Tarrant's sentiments calling the board's response 'hostile'.[4]

The tour manager, described by the *Truth* as 'one of the shrewdest men that ever donned the flannels', wasn't easily rebuffed and continued on to Melbourne.[5] Tarrant set up office at *Patiala*, his comfortable residence at 37 Tourello Avenue, Upper Hawthorn and tried to exert some influence over the official cricket body. Previously he'd had the upper hand when it came to influencing authorities in India and he hoped he would have the same success back home. He needed to convince the reluctant board of the merit of the tour and refined his negotiation skills to influence, charm and strategise. In time, he would finesse the art of glad-handing.

Tarrant had frequently been at odds with the cricket establishment. Over his lifetime, he'd taken risks, and this was just another in a long list, yet he was emotionally invested in this one and was determined that it would be a success.

Tarrant had moved to England in 1903 to play cricket on a larger stage. A newspaper article revealed that he had 'given up the hope of ever getting into the first flight of cricketers' in Melbourne.[6] The man himself went on to admit that the move to England had been primarily monetary; he could earn £10 or £12 per week there while only earning £3/10 in Australia: 'I was just 22, married and with one child. I was not keen to leave Australia but the money was good and I was given a chance to play cricket in England, a thing I had always been keen about.'[7]

In the Melbourne Cricket Club archives are two albums meticulously compiled by Tarrant and simply referred to as the Tarrant scrapbooks. They contain artefacts including newspaper articles, letters, photos, sketches, cards and Tarrant's musing on paper. The provenance of many of the items is impossible to identify as frequently the newspaper masthead has been removed. One unidentified newspaper article from the scrapbook confirms that Tarrant had no option but to leave his homeland and states, 'there is little or no scope for the practice of cricket as a professional in Australia'. On 29 November 1907, Tarrant told a *Fitzroy City Press* journalist that he 'confidently urged any good [Australian] cricketer who thought of becoming a professional to go home [England]'.

However, I discovered that Tarrant's rapid exit from Australia wasn't solely motivated by a desire for cricket promotion, as a tiny newspaper entry (not found in the Tarrant scrapbook) reveals that he was also fleeing 'an outstanding debt of £35' to a printer in Melbourne.[8] Despite initially vowing 'that when he had qualified for a county and got regular wages he would settle the debt by the payment of instalments', Tarrant failed to repay the loan for six years.[9] The law eventually caught up with Tarrant and he was summonsed to appear at the Fitzroy Court on 21 February 1908 where he was ordered to repay the loan with costs. The solicitor for the plaintiff knew that Tarrant was leaving for England later that month and, justifiably sceptical that payment would ensue, threatened to take 'legal action to prevent Tarrant leaving Victoria by the boat' on 28 February.[10] Thereafter the paper trail ceases, and payment of the loan cannot be confirmed.

Almost thirty years later, Tarrant's ambition was still evident when the Australian cricket board resisted approving the 1935/36 venture. It all seems rather odd now given that the tour was a private affair, with the Maharaja and Tarrant wholly responsible for finance and planning. Following the snub from the Australian Board of Control, Tarrant judiciously decided not to lure any cricketer in contention for a Test spot in South Africa, and not to disrupt the state competition, the Sheffield Shield. Given that, team selection would need to be more … creative. And both he and the Maharaja knew that Indian cricket fans were starved of international cricket – so any big names, however old, would assist the success of the tour.

Tarrant was also well aware that four and a half gruelling months on the subcontinent required some up-and-coming cricketers with potential and stamina yet to attract the eye of state or international selection, and he announced that he was willing to take 'on tour any young men showing outstanding ability'.[11] Interestingly, he actively sought out other sportsmen. He scoured suburban playing fields in Melbourne to locate an overlooked novice, to entice someone with some talent, any talent, to tour. He even approached Dick Reynolds, the Essendon football clubman, who excelled at the Australian game and had won the Victorian Football League's Brownlow medal the previous year. Reynolds played social cricket in the summer just for a bit of fun and to keep him fit for football. He was also a known name with a public face, which despite having no resonance in India would influence Australia's perception of the tour. The footballer was almost seduced by Tarrant's promise of an adventure but at the last minute rejected the offer following an accident at work at a boot factory in Collingwood where he sliced off the top of his finger.

While Tarrant's plans were taking time to firm the Maharaja had his own setbacks. In late May, following the Silver Jubilee of King George V in London, the Maharaja fell ill in France. He was seriously sick, and rumours circulated that a heart attack was suspected. Hendry wrote that 'A million of his Sikhs were praying for his recovery but not more than we twelve who were scared the trip would be cancelled'.[12] Religious observance and a Parisian cardiologist assisted his recovery and luckily the tour could proceed.

By late July all the parties involved were sick of the argy-bargy. The Australian Board of Control still hadn't approved the final team and Tarrant sent a curt cable to hasten the process and resolve selection:

> Would you please place before your board my application for immediate reconsideration for any or all of the following players in addition to Oxenham – Kippax, Chilvers, Rigg, Woodfull, Ponsford, and Nitschke? I also wish to add for the board's approval two fresh names – Wendell Bill and F. Mair, both of New South Wales. My reasons for this request are that in some cases their own State association has agreed to the players going.
>
> In the case of Victoria the V.C.A. has not raised any official objection. Further, I would stress, judging by the newspaper reports, that public opinion throughout Australians is solidly in favor (*sic*) of all these players being sanctioned by the board. Four of them have retired from first class cricket. I particularly desire Oxenham, Kippax, and Chilvers to complete my team. The Indian Board will meet in Bombay on August 11 to accept or reject the team. I want to get my final three names to India by August 9. I shall be pleased to defray the cost of all telegrams to expedite the decisions.[13]

On 11 August, after months and months of protracted negotiation, the tour was finally approved and the team was named: John 'Jack' Ryder, Charles 'Charlie' Macartney, Henry 'Harry' Alexander, Arthur Allsopp, Oscar 'Wendell' Bill, Francis 'Frank' Bryant, John 'Jack' Ellis, Hunter 'Stork' Hendry, Herbert 'Bert' Ironmonger, Thomas 'Tom' Leather, Hampden 'Hammy' Love, Frederick 'Fred' Mair, Ronald 'Ron' Morrisby, Ronald 'Ron' Oxenham and Lisle Nagel. The reason for the administrators' rejection of New South Welshmen Alan Kippax and Hugh Chilvers is unknown. Eight of the personnel had played Test cricket, though three had only made a fleeting appearance. The rest were largely unknowns. The team ranged in age from twenty to fifty-three and it was a diverse group, really only connected by their love of cricket and an exceptional competence at playing it or rather, in the case of some, having *played* it.

The approved team wasn't the A list that Tarrant had promised, and he worried how would he explain to the Maharaja that he was returning to India with a few famous retired cricket veterans alongside a bunch of unknowns. He did, however, acknowledge that a few of the Australians on their way to a Test encounter in South Africa would have jumped at the chance to have been paid so well. The team travelling to the subcontinent would receive £300, plus £3 spending money per week, which was well above the average yearly wage. Each player would receive the same payment reflecting the egalitarian ethos of the tour though, more than likely, the better-known players were enticed by additional gifts. The Maharaja was, after all, one of the wealthiest men in the world and his ego and deep pockets would ensure the tour was a success.

Tarrant was delighted to have lured two big drawcards: captain Jack Ryder and Charlie Macartney as his deputy. Both had been exceedingly famous Test cricketers. Macartney, aged forty-nine, was a retired sporting superstar and he still held batting world records. However, in 1927, he abruptly retired from first-class cricket and rumours of shell shock following the Great War did rounds. At the time, the physical consequences of WW1 were acknowledged yet the psychological impact of war was frequently overlooked. So, when Charlie unexpectedly signed Tarrant's contract, news of his inclusion on the tour surprised the cricket world and spread like wildfire throughout the Indian cricket community. They were excited by the prospect of seeing Macartney, commonly known by his nickname the 'Governor-General', which reflected his authoritarian persona. Earlier the sharp-witted journalist and former Australian leg-spinning great Arthur Mailey celebrated Macartney's talent in a *Sun* article, writing: 'During my experience in first-class cricket there was no batsman whom I feared more than Macartney. He seemed to call the tune and I danced.'[14]

During the planning stages, Macartney was critical of the Australian board and described them as 'cricket Hitlers'.[15] He later observed, 'Had the Board of Control in Australia favoured the Indian tour, and had desired to help, instead of hinder, the work of Mr. F. A. Tarrant, a much better team would have been selected'.[16]

I'm sure that when Tarrant saw Macartney for the first time in years he was anxious, because the 'greatest batsman in the world' according to the *Sporting Globe* a decade earlier, was barely recognisable.[17] He does look out of shape in the photographs, though I believe his massive hands hadn't lost their capacity to bat, catch, bowl and throw. Macartney seemed undeterred by any notion of being match unfit and fully embraced his role as vice-captain and spokesman. Earlier, with a touch of characteristic hubris, he wrote in the Australian press that he and his team-mates were making history, even if they didn't realise it at the time.[18] Despite Macartney's claims, this tour was overlooked at the time and has subsequently been ignored in sporting history. It's taken over two generations for the realisation to dawn and for the first Indo-Australian cricket encounter to be applauded the due respect it warrants.

Jack Ryder, an attacking batsman, was forty-six years old when he was named captain of the Australian team to tour India. The chieftain still looked physically fit and lean, though his Baggy Green frequently hid his brown hair flecked with silver, and wrinkles were accumulating around his neck possibly from too much sun exposure. He had, after all, spent close to three decades playing cricket. Despite having previously captained the Victorian and Australian teams, the official cricket body had passed on him to lead a touring party.

Like every one of his generation, Jack had experienced the Depression and just about survived. It had been hard, and, in many ways, it still was difficult for him to feed his family. Fortunately, after being put off at a few jobs, the then Attorney General and Minister of Industry, the immensely cricket-loving future Prime Minister Robert Menzies helped find him a position in a Collingwood factory, manufacturing boots. It was helpful having friends in high places! Likewise, this trip and the associated finances fell from the sky at the right time just like the numbers for a winning lotto ticket. And on 5 October a dance at the Collingwood town hall was arranged in his honour: 180 people attended including council and sporting representatives and the Collingwood Cricket Club presented Jack with a wristwatch. *News* reported that the Collingwood City Council considered Ryder to be 'a worthy ambassador' and gifted him two autographs books to have signed by prominent people in India.[19] One he could keep himself and one would be presented to the council on return.

Jack was certainly no greenhorn and had travelled on ocean liners in 1921 and 1926, but this time, unlike England, the destination was exotic and mysterious. For most of the cricketers their knowledge of India started at school with Rudyard Kipling and had a strong imperial bias. Kipling was known as the voice of the Empire and in 1889, he famously proclaimed, 'East is East, and West is West, and never the twain shall meet'. However, the East/West dynamic was changing and by the mid 1930s the two cultures were eliding (sometimes violently) as news of political turbulence and interracial tensions in India dominated the pages of the world news.

Great-uncle Tom was in a very different cricket category from Ryder and Macartney. His captioning of his tour photographs references the immense talent of some of his team-mates, which must have been daunting for the little-known bowler. Despite showing lots of sporting potential, nothing of real consequence had happened for Tom, as employment had been sporadic and inconsequential. His ambition didn't extend beyond wanting to take wickets at club cricket. He'd played football in the winter and a few years earlier was named as the best on ground for the Richmond seconds in a narrow grand final loss to Geelong.[20] Now at twenty-five years of age Tom was weighing up his options: cricket or football? Hopefully both, he imagined. That, he no doubt speculated, might really be the way to manage a decent income. An only child, he loved the camaraderie that came with team sports, however this tour, he knew, would be markedly different from any other sporting jaunts.

Inevitably Tom's parents had shared a similar combination of anxiety and excitement when they immigrated to Australia in 1914 as part of the British diaspora. Around 9000 Scots arrived in Australia that year all seeking a better life and were possibly unaware they were escaping four years of European devastation. Tom's parents fussed over their only child and were immensely proud of his sporting achievements. A young and very shy Doll Ponsford, the younger sister of my grandfather, the famous cricketer Bill, also wanted to spend as much time with Tom before his departure. In late August they had become engaged after meeting at a cricket function. Doll felt that history was repeating itself yet this time she was farewelling her fiancé on an international cricket tour not her brother. She, likewise, was immensely proud.

It appears that Frank Tarrant was too, he gloated to the press that Tom was destined for cricket fame. He revealed, in an interview on tour, that the young cricketer could 'develop into the best fast bowler Australia has had in years'.[21] The Indian publicity machine also promoted the talent of the little known bowler. The August 1935 issue of *Indian Cricket* described Leather as 'Victoria's youthful "cyclone" and to all appearances Australia's Larwood of the future'.[22i] And then it elaborated further:

Indeed, there is no faster bowler in Australia at present. Leather bowls with grim determination and astounding stamina, and makes the ball fly off the pitch in a thrilling manner. To see Tom Leather hurling them down, over after over, like a man possessed is to enjoy one of the greatest thrills of cricket. Yet his bowling is always scrupulously fair: Leather would not hurt a fly. Fairly tall and wiry, with arms and fists of steel, he is also a fine footballer. This is reflected in his dashing fielding.[23]

Leather and Oxenham. Taken sometime on tour. Leather archive.

On 28 September, ten days before leaving, seven of the eight Victorian cricketers, alongside a few willing volunteers, played a practice match against Sandringham (a local suburban team) at the Beach Oval by Port Phillip Bay. Despite the perfect weather, the curator worried about the state of the ground as it barely had time to recover from the football season. The novelty of cricket in early spring, alongside the excitement of seeing the nucleus of an international team, was obvious as the event pulled a crowd of 600 and money raised went towards a new wicket for the club.

Tarrant didn't want to risk any player injury, so the touring personnel were eased into the practice match. His bowlers excelled with Ironmonger taking 3-16. Tarrant participated and managed to take a wicket and a fine catch at first slip, giving Leather his first wicket in the first hour of play. Tarrant's team easily won by forty-nine runs and, according to the press, Nagel played 'the merriest innings of the day'.[24] He scored easily and reached 23 runs in quick time, mostly in sixes, hitting one ball out of the ground, while another ricocheted off a concrete wall and was lost for ten minutes.

The ever-positive Tarrant was especially upbeat about the impending adventure and earlier in a pre-departure interview in the *Barrier Miner* he bragged: 'I am taking a strong team, evidently far stronger than India yet realises'.[25] He went on to declare: 'Fancy calling it a side of 'has beens' and untried colts, as the Calcutta authorities are reported to have done. I will give £100 to Indian charity if the Calcutta team beats mine'. *The Age* wasn't so convinced and described the team as 'The Has Beens and Never Will Bes'.[26]

I fell in love with Frank's enthusiasm and admired the way he fiercely defended the team even when cricket commentators didn't concur. Edward Docker, one of the few cricket historians who reference the tour, wrote in a mischievous yet damning fashion that the team comprised 'superannuated old Test stars and Sheffield Shield discards'.[27]

Whether they were old nor not, the practice game and Frank's enthusiasm excited the players about what was in store and convinced the more experienced that they hadn't forgotten how to play. It seemed they were ready at last to make history as the first Australian XI to tour India.

---

[1] *Sunday Times*, 30 May 1926.
[2] The *Telegraph*, 8 February 1935.
[3] The *Australasian*, 16 March 1935.
[4] 27 February 1935.
[5] The *Truth*, 24 February 1935.
[6] Tarrant scrapbook c.1918–51.
[7] *Sporting Globe*, 29 January 1944.
[8] *Advertiser*, 22 February 1908.
[9] The *Express and Telegraph*, 22 February 1908
[10] *Advertiser*, 22 February 1908.
[11] The *Telegraph*, 26 February 1935.
[12] Hunter Hendry manuscript, nd. Hendry's manuscript was written sometime prior to his death in 1988. It is undated and paginated and is located at the Bradman Museum, Bowral.
[13] The *Daily Standard*, 31July 1935.
[14] 1 December 1933.
[15] The *Truth*, 3 March 1935.
[16] *Newcastle Morning Herald and Miners' Advocate*, 31 August 1935.
[17] *Sporting Globe*, 14 July 1926.
[18] *Newcastle Morning Herald and Miners' Advocate*, 31August 1935.
[19] 22 August 1935.
[20] *The Argus*, 6 October 1930.
[21] *New Call and Bailey's Weekly*, 12 March 1936.
[22] Leather archive.
[23] ibid.
[24] *The Argus*, 30 September 1935.

[25] 13 August 1935.
[26] *The Age*, 11 October 1935.
[27] *History of Indian Cricket* 1976, 103.

2 'WITHOUT A SILVER SPOON IN HIS MOUTH'

Tarrant was 'a man of keen intellect with a flair for business, and by the time he retired from cricket he had reached a stage of moderate affluence. In India he was a financial success, and apparently, as friend of the Maharajah of Patiala, he is in a golden atmosphere'.[1]

But the greatest contribution to the betterment of Indian cricket has been that of Frank Tarrant who made his home in India after having migrated from Australia to England where he played regularly for Middlesex. As a player and as a coach, Tarrant became a legend in Indian cricket and much of the good impression created by the 1932 Indian team in England may be attributed to Tarrant's tutoring.[2]

Frank's early years went according to script. Predetermined by class, cultural lineage and religion, he seemed destined for a life of factory work, devotion and chaste pleasures. Frank was born at home in the then working-class suburb of Fitzroy, Australia on 11 December 1880 to Alfred Francis and Ann Catherine and as clarified by the *Barrier Miner* 'without a silver spoon in his mouth'.[3] Details about Frank's early years are sketchy however Australian Lee Semmens, one of the few cricket historians who have researched Tarrant, asserts that Alfred was a bookmaker – an intriguing fact considering his son Frank's gambling predilection. Yet electoral rolls reveal that from 1903–1924 Tarrant senior was employed as a boot maker. So somewhere along the way, a letter was swapped, and his actual occupation cannot be determined.

Young Frank demonstrated exceptional talent at cricket, no doubt encouraged by his uncle, Ambrose Tarrant, who played the game at a first-class level. Yet, in addition to sporting prowess, Frank also possessed a cunning ambition as outlined in an article in the *Albany Advertiser*:

> More than 30 years ago, when he was a boy coming into prominence at Fitzroy, two junior teams in a Brighton competition had to meet in a final match to decide the winner of a cup. Tarrant happened to be free from cricket at the time, and he was persuaded to play for one of the teams under an assumed name. After the match the district rang with the name of a wonderful new player that this team had discovered.
>
> And no wonder, for Tarrant made a century, and took seven wickets in each innings of the opposing side. Needless to say, his side won. 'I don't know whether the other side have found out about it yet,' says Tarrant; 'but, in any case, it is rather late for them to take any action now'.[4]

In his early twenties, Frank moved to England in 1903 to pursue a cricket career. A few months later his New Zealand born wife, Kathleen [Kate] Moore (sometimes appearing in archives as More) and their son, Loris Bernard Napoleon, joined him. Two subsequent sons, Albert Edward and Francis Alfred, were born two and four years later during their father's tenure at the Middlesex Cricket Club from 1903–07.[5]

The move was opportune for Frank as the cricket culture in Britain could enable the success of a less privileged sportsperson in contrast with the professionally stifling environment of early twentieth century Australia. Tarrant's scrapbook noted: 'there is little or no scope for the practice of cricket as a professional in Australia'. Cricket in Britain was highly hierarchical and codified. However, the system enabled opportunities for the socially and financially disadvantaged professional player.

The amateur/professional divide was, and always has been, murky. Dr W. G. Grace, possibly England's most famous nineteenth century cricketer, made substantial wealth from cricket despite his amateur status. Indian born aristocrat and English amateur cricketer, K.S. Ranjitsinhji (1872-1933) (known as Ranji) noted the shifting status of the professional cricketer in 1897 and proclaimed that, 'a professional in former times was entirely the servant of his club, and in a servant's position'.[6] Ranji identified transformation and claimed that now 'A modern professional who represents his county is partly a servant of the club, partly a servant of the public, and partly a skilled labourer selling his skill in the best market'.

Tarrant recalled his arrival in London: 'I had a tin trunk in which was a clock I had won for taking the bowling honors (sic) at Fitzroy. Round the clock I had wrapped my cricket trousers and the two shirts I possessed. All the money I had was a bad French sovereign'.[7] The ungainly black marble clock weighed 40 pounds and was seemingly a much-cherished possession. The optimistic Tarrant audaciously contacted Pelham 'Plum' Warner, the very influential English cricketer who would lead MCC in Australia in 1903-04, who had casually admired his play in Melbourne when they had met in a cursory fashion at the bowling nets at the Melbourne Cricket Club. Warner had been there as the captain of the touring Lord Hawke's side who visited Australia and New Zealand during the 1902-03 summer. A later article published in the *Barrier Miner* in 1938 provides additional details concerning Tarrant's arrival in London:

> Nearing England, Tarrant began to realise that a 'new chum' in a strange land, he would feel more at home if somebody met him on arrival. The only person he knew in England was 'Plum' Warner. Frank decided to cable him, but not knowing Warner's address, imagined, in some vague way, that he must be the head of a well known patent medicine concern. From Marseilles (France) Tarrant, an innocent abroad, perpetrated a delightful 'howler' in an addled address in the following cable
> **'Mr. Warner, care Warner's Safe Cure, London.-Please meet me on arrival**

> **Himalaya.-Tarrant.'**
> Wrongly addressed, the cable never reached 'Plum' Warner. When the boat berthed at Tilbury Docks, London, Tarrant, scanning the waiting crowd again and again, registered disappointment, then dismay. Warner was not there.[8]

Tarrant's arrival at Lord's cricket ground is described in a manner that is improbable, unashamedly guilty of cultural stereotyping, and verges on malice. Tarrant, is attributed as introducing himself employing demotic idiom, proclaimed, 'Hey, I'm Frank Tarrant . . . come from Australia to play for Middlesex . . .engaged by Mr. Warner'.

Tarrant possessed a winning combination of talent, grit, charm and determination and was successful in acquiring a position on the ground staff at Lord's Cricket Ground. He honed his cricket skills and following the regulatory, two-year, probation period he was selected to play for Middlesex in the English County Championship and became a highly successful all-rounder. Warner captained Middlesex from 1908-20 and frequently opened the batting with Tarrant. The Australian press reported on a match in 1908 when Middlesex played Hampshire and the batsmen put together an opening partnership of 213, Warner was the first wicket to fall after scoring 110 and Tarrant went on the score 157.

Warner's high opinion of Tarrant persisted and in 1912 he selected him in a nominal cricket World Eleven. The other Australians named in the team were Warwick Armstrong, Charlie Macartney [vice-captain of the 1935/36 Australian team in India] and H.V. Hordern. Tarrant was named as a possible candidate for the position of twelfth man. Tarrant was amongst good company as the other potential candidates for the final spot were all celebrated names in cricket history: Victor Trumper, Clem Hill, Frank Woolley and Wilfred Rhodes.

As his celebrity grew, an article in the Tarrant scrapbook identified a shift in Britain's attitude to Tarrant – seemingly coinciding with the indisputable recognition of his superlative cricketing abilities. The article hypothesised that if, 'an All-England eleven had to be selected tomorrow, Frank Tarrant would be the first man chosen'. The article noted that the sentiment was not the fabricated and exaggerated ramblings of the patriotic Australian press but was validated by the 'London correspondent for the Sydney Sun'. Press reportage across the Empire during the early twentieth century demonstrated deference to the British and the prevailing attitude of Tarrant, as an inferior Antipodean, is evidence of this. However, the British press were reassessing Tarrant; 'Nine years ago, when he came to England, he was just an Australian' the journalist claimed. 'Now that he, is the best all-round man in Great Britain he is an "Anglo-Australian"'. Despite the English contempt of Australia and its people, Tarrant, through his display of undeniable talent, was finally accepted or so he imagined.

Over time, the British media were forced to acknowledge Tarrant's abilities yet accredit them to luck. Tarrant is condescendingly described in a Sunday Times article dated 30 May 1926: 'Though Frank rather fittingly answered to his initials, F.A.T., two years ago he was still a bowler of some ability. He interested himself in the turf, took horses to India, gathered in some coin, and is now in Easy-street up Colac way'. Reporting that Tarrant 'gathered in some coin' and is now sitting on 'Easy-street' reinforces the widespread perception of Tarrant as a fortuitous and undeserving fluke. The British and the Australian press refused to acknowledge Tarrant's cricketing genius and were scathing in their criticism of him.

Despite possessing the necessary talent Tarrant was unavailable for Test selection, in any country, due to a change in Marylebone Cricket Club rules that stipulated that a cricketer could not play for more than one country within a calendar year. The penalty for infringing this rule was to be disqualified for two years. Seemingly, Tarrant's itinerant lifestyle precluded him from playing Test cricket. The West Australian observed; 'one of the greatest all-round players the world has known will become historical for the simple reason that he never took part in a Test match'.[9] One of the pioneers of Indian cricket, D. B. Deodhar, wrote of Tarrant; 'Being a rolling stone, however, he never figured in any Test for either Australia or England, though he could have been the first choice".[10] Deodhar's interpretation of Tarrant is typical of Indian homage yet the Western press viewed Tarrant's nomadic lifestyle and financial orientation critically. *The Barrier Miner* outlined Tarrant's remarkable professionalism and explained that, 'No other cricketer, past or present, has capitalised his cricket talent to such purpose and profit as Tarrant: not even Jack Hobbs, former English professional, with his snug sports goods shop in London, nor the amazing Don Bradman, successful Adelaide stockbroker, to whom, as a mere sideline, royalties on cricket material bearing his magic are steadily flowing'.[11] The implicit scorn of the text, even applied to cricketing demigods, reveals the public's condemnation of sporting professionalism.

Research has revealed that Tarrant was equitably rewarded for superlative play however he also possessed a canny ability to favourably negotiate terms and leverage funds from Middlesex. Tarrant returned to Australia to play cricket during the summer of 1907/08. The Australian press reported: 'The health of Frank Tarrant, the ex-Melbourne cricketer, who has performed so well for Middlesex during the past season, is occasioning some concern. With the view of enabling him to recuperate, the Middlesex county club will pay the expenses of the trip to Australia for him'.[12] The British summer of 1907 was easily his best to date and no evidence can be located to suggest that he suffered illness, nor did he demonstrate any signs of lack of match-fitness. Possibly suffering homesickness, Tarrant sensed an opportunity to orchestrate a *gratis* trip to Australia. It appears that he was adept at locating generous financial remuneration and conditions, as the Melbourne Cricket Club minute books reveal that Tarrant had previously contacted them seeking employment for the same season. An entry on 1 November 1907 resolved the matter and pronounced that the question 'of engaging him at £5 per week cannot be entertained'. The reason for this rejection by the Melbourne Cricket Club is not outlined, yet it seems that they wished to distance themselves from him. As customary with Tarrant, his request for £5 per week is overly magnanimous. However, in addition, the conservative Melbourne Cricket Club could not entertain employing an agitator like Tarrant. Instead, he returned to play for his old club, Fitzroy.

The Middlesex minute books reveal that during the meeting of 23 January 1908, 'It was also decided to cable to Tarrant warning him that he might lose his qualification for Middlesex if he played any more 1st class cricket in Australia'. Tarrant would no doubt have evaluated his options as, despite not wanting to offend his English employers, he'd had a superlative season with the bat for Victoria and was a major contributor to their Sheffield Shield victory.[13] Semmens explains, 'It cannot be said of many cricketers that they were the cause of change in the laws or rules, but that is precisely the effect Tarrant had on his return to Australia in 1907-08, to resume his Victorian career'.[14] The reaction caused 'an immediate outcry in England, and in some quarters in Australia'. Public sentiment of Tarrant was savage as his actions were viewed as attempting to destabilise the game: 'Monty Noble, the Australian and New South Wales captain stated that, while he had nothing personal against Tarrant, he was in principle opposed to anyone who had learned his cricket in England playing interstate cricket to the detriment of young cricketers, and he felt it was a bad precedent'. Cricket in Australia during this period was undergoing substantial bureaucratic upheavals. Disunity amongst the Victorian Cricket Association (VCA) and the Melbourne Cricket Club was particularly vitriolic and Tarrant was identified as a potential menace who contributed to the wider story of cricket instability. In many circles, Tarrant's audacity was considered to be tarnishing the reputation of the game.

The Middlesex minute books are equally revealing of Tarrant's ambition and resolve. Correspondence between Tarrant and the Middlesex CC disclose that he frequently requested money from the club and was customarily rewarded. He regularly topped the list of financial recipients. In a club meeting on 19 October 1910 the committee determined that Tarrant would be gifted £100. Other professionals receiving financial remuneration were: J.T Hearne: £50, J.W Hearne: £30, Joe Murrell: £40, Edward Mignon: £30, 'Patsy' Hendren: £30 and George Burton: £10. Tarrant received double the payment of his professional colleagues. During a meeting on 6 November 1912 grants to professionals were again on the agenda and it was determined that Tarrant would receive £65 (£50 had already been paid). Again, Tarrant is gifted significantly more than the next player: J.W Hearne would receive £40. The reason for Tarrant being distributed £50 in advance is not clarified however it appears to have been common practice. Eventually relations between Middlesex and Tarrant soured and the minutes of a meeting on 15 September 1914 detail correspondence between Tarrant and the club quarrelling over his payment for a benefit match and his potential departure to India. The club secretary wrote:

> Dear Tarrant,
> Though the committee felt that you must decide for yourself about accepting the offer of the Maharaja of Patiala, I think there is very little chance of their consenting to you having the game money taken at the Whit-Monday match.
> Mr. Lacey in his letter distinctly pointed out that the benefit was granted before the end of your cricket career because it was thought to be for your advantage, and although I feel sure that the subscribers will be much annoyed and will probably say that they would not have subscribed if they had any idea that you would leave us. I am asking Mr. Leigh to send you a cheque for the donation on the card.
> Yours faithfully,
> (signed) A.J Webbe.

Two years later, an entry in the minute books on 30 November 1916 revealed that there was still ongoing conflict between the parties. The minute books express displeasure in Tarrant's rejection of Britain in favour of India. The club reluctantly agreed to Tarrant's request that some of the benefit money be released to 'purchase goods for the business he is conducting in India'. Even at this late stage, Tarrant was hedging his bets and offered to remain in England if the club could guarantee him an annual remuneration of £300 (he claimed he was to receive £600 from the Maharaja). During a meeting on 31 January 1916, the Middlesex committee concluded: 'It was proposed by Mr. S. S Pawling, seconded by Mr. W.P Harrison, Senr. and carried unanimously that "it is deemed expedient to bring to the notice of the Committee of the M.C.C that the services of Tarrant will no longer be required by the County"'. Tarrant's decision was prescient as first-class cricket was abandoned in England eighteen months later due to the First World War.

Tarrant's connection with Indian cricket eventuated through his friendship with Ranji. They met when Tarrant was employed as a ground bowler at Lord's in 1903/04. On Ranji's recommendation, and due to the fact that he was banned from playing cricket in Australia, Tarrant travelled to the subcontinent each English winter between 1909 and 1914 where he was employed as a cricket coach for the unimaginably wealthy Maharaja of Patiala. Tarrant flourished in this new environment. Paid handsomely for his services, he moved permanently to India in 1914; severing all ties with Middlesex

Cricket Club. Tarrant's relationship with Ranji endured and in 1928 the *Daily News* reported that Tarrant 'took over a number of thoroughbred merino sheep to Ranjisinghi (sic), who is now Maharajah Jamahed (sic) of Nowanagan (sic) formerly, a shining player in the English Eleven'.[15] The journalist, obviously impressed with Ranji's elevation in life, concluded 'now a ruler in India'. Ranji's newfound financial circumstances enabled him to fulfil all his ambitions and he wished to improve the wool in his province and commissioned Tarrant to export fine-grade Australian sheep to assist. I'm sure Tarrant was rewarded a generous commission.

The Ranji Connections

Ranji also introduced his cousin the Maharaja of Jodhpur (rumoured to be the wealthiest man in the world) to Frank. Frank somehow persuaded the royal that he was not just an excellent cricketer but also an experienced negotiator and an equine expert and they established a working relationship buying horses. In 1917, the Maharaja provided Tarrant with £20,000 for a horse-buying spree. Frank purchased Dark Legend which had run third in the Epsom Derby. The Maharaja was so delighted with the acquisition that he gifted Tarrant a further 2000 guineas.[16] The Maharaja loved owning the most successful stable in India, and Frank enjoyed the ensuing fortune. Unfortunately, the Maharaja would die before he achieved the biggest victory in racing across the Empire when Dark Legend won the Viceroy Cup in 1919. Ranji was also responsible for introducing Tarrant to the Maharaja of Patiala. These meetings would prove to be life-changing for Tarrant—seemingly he possessed a canny combination of skill and luck.

An article from the Tarrant scrapbook tilted *Money Made the Gentleman* suggests that obstacles separating the professional from the amateur, for Tarrant, were penetrable. However, it is difficult to ascertain if these boundaries were ever ultimately surmountable and at what cost. The article identified Tarrant's rapid financial gain in India and described his return to London where he wished to entertain his amateur friends; 'Once there they were no longer "Mr." to him, and he ceased to be mere "Tarrant". They quickly lapsed into the form of equality, which is denoted by the use of the Christian name. Frank was no longer a pro'. The status of amateurs and professionals were evolving, and Lord Hawke identified a new classification in the sporting hierarchy that he called the 'gentleman professional'.[17]

In many ways, in India Tarrant occupied the role of the privileged coloniser, however he seemingly preferred the company of the locals and a few British elites were determined to expose him as fraudulent. English captain Douglas Jardine, possibly affronted by Tarrant's popularity with the Indian royalty, his ease with the wider Indian community and his resultant financial gain, objected to the frequency of Tarrant adjudicated Leg Before Wicket rulings in the 1933/34 Test series in India. Following Jardine's condemnation, Worcester amateur J. B Higgins replaced Tarrant as umpire. The Australian press vehemently defended the actions of Tarrant and critiqued Jardine's outburst as a 'cheap sneer', perceiving it as 'utterly deplorable' and 'thoroughly indefensible'. The British public, including English cricket great Jack Hobbs, supported Jardine and the increasing complexity of the broader imperial dynamic intensified.

Despite contrary opinion, Tarrant also had his supporters. The Tarrant scrapbook contains a letter written on Cooch Behar letterhead, the signature is difficult to decipher however it was most likely written by a senior member of the household, possibly the Maharaja himself. The letter illustrates a genuine affection for Tarrant that exceeded the courteous platitudes that are customary for birthday greetings. The author reiterates to Tarrant, 'I cannot give you anything, which would adequately show you my feelings towards you, but I think you know that both myself and my wife would do anything, which is possible for you, and if the necessity arises, & I hope it never may, please let either of us know'. The benevolence espoused and the generosity proposed reveals goodwill between the two however the emphasis on the potential for Tarrant to require the author's assistance highlights the precarious circumstances of his existence and the imploring tone can be interpreted as slightly ominous.

A poem and a limerick located in his scrapbook are further evidence of Tarrant's popularity—the authors of both are unidentified, however they appear to have been written by close contacts. The limerick celebrates the intimate nature of the friendship between Tarrant and the author. The middle sentence proclaimed that 'He's the only true friend' and laments that other friendships cannot compare. The poem is similar in sentiment however it is less blatantly ingratiating and teases Tarrant in a jesting fashion. The poet identifies Tarrant's qualities: financial success, great sporting achievements and the love of a good woman yet the poem describes him as 'verging on the bank of deep despair'. The last stanza reveals the cause of the misery:

You well may ask my trouble, and
I'll now the fact lay bare.
Upon this shining head of mine
I haven't got a HAIR!

Imagery of Tarrant reinforces the sentiment expressed in this poem as he is rarely photographed without his hat, which suggests that he was self-conscious about his balding pate. The wearing of a head covering is another characteristic that unites Tarrant and the Maharaja however both men did so for divergent reasons.

The programme for the cricket match at Patiala in January 1936 is revealing of the egotism of the royal families and their interpretation of their importance to cricket in India and to the history of the game. Their appraisal of cricket history does not extend beyond the contributions of Tarrant, Jardine, a few Indian potentates, some Australian greats and the Maharaja. The final page of the programme is a quiz, which questioned:

1. When Daddy (Frank Tarrant) scored his first century in India?
2. Name Indians who took part in Tests in Australia?
3. Who invented Leg Theory?
4. When did the first English Cricket professional visit PATIALA?
5. Who was the first Ruling Prince in India to play first class Cricket?
6. Name the highest and lowest cricket grounds in the World. Give their heights.
7. What number of runs were scored in Tests in England by Messrs. Woodful (sic) and Bradman?

Referring to Frank Tarrant as Daddy is indicative of the Indian cricket community's perception of him as an experienced veteran who nurtured the growth of the game. In light of evidence to support Tarrant's complex lack of paternalism regarding his own children, the term Daddy is complicated. To a contemporary audience the term Daddy, as applied to Tarrant, is inappropriate in its sycophantic nature and symbolic of an overtly obsequious society. Possibly it was simply bestowed as a joke about Tarrant's age, however the Maharaja would not be affectionately ridiculed in the same way.

Tarrant was a pivotal figure during the early days of Indian Test cricket. In many ways he was a cricket cultural intermediary throughout the British Empire, laying the foundation stone for the development of the game. Tarrant and the Maharaja's ability to acculturate assisted their relationship that evolved from one motivated by mutual advantage to one based on absolute loyalty and affection. Tarrant in an article in his scrapbook proclaimed that he perceived the Maharaja 'as like his father' suggesting that their relationship was sacrosanct. Evaluating this observation, in light of Tarrant's lack of prioritising family and the fact that he was a decade older than the Maharaja, encourages it to be viewed sceptically.

The Tarrant scrapbook provides additional examples verifying Frank's sensitivity. Amongst articles that applaud his sporting prowess are ones that allow us (limited) access to the real Frank Tarrant. He refers to wanting badly to visit Australia, as, he claims, 'I need a holiday'. Tarrant nominates a desire to see some football and his grandchildren as motivations to visit. However possibly nominating a desire to see football first and his grandchildren second is revealing of Tarrant's priorities as he frequently chose sport over family. Tarrant's allegiance to the Patiala family was demonstrated in 1941, after the Maharaja's death. He was urgently summoned to India by Yadvindra Singh, the erstwhile Yuvraj who had now become the Maharaja. An article written after interviewing Tarrant at the Brisbane airport, at a time when plane travel across the Indian Ocean was expensive and uncommon for all bar the elite, read: '"He has simply cabled that he needs my help". Mr Tarrant is keeping a promise he made to the present Maharajah's father many years ago – a promise to go to the child's aid, no matter where he might be'.[18] Tarrant's obligations and commitment seemingly lay with his Indian family rather than his blood relatives.

Due to the portrayal of India as dangerous and exotic, the 1935/36 tour was interpreted with ambivalence and suspicion. The Australian media regularly reinforced the commingling of East and West in terms of what was later described as a 'clash of civilizations'.[19] Likewise, Tarrant's cultural identification was problematic to the West. Tarrant is depicted in the Australian press in a 1935 Table Talk caricature. He is wearing an Indian cricket blazer, western trouser, jumper, shirt and tie and a turban, the unequivocal material marker of racial and religious Otherness that iconizes Sikh identity. The illustration title states, 'Frank Tarrant the man who controlled the Board of Control in the matter of the Australian Cricket team for India'. The copy introduces a tone of xenophobia, cultural essentialism and mistrust: who is this man and how is he able to control the bastion of Englishness, the national cricket board? The illustration portrays Tarrant as an amalgam of cultures, a hybrid identity adhering to neither the exclusive stipulations of Indian or British sensibilities. Despite being Australian born Tarrant's position in India, both literal and figurative, unsettled western tropes. The popular maxim of British Imperialism prevailed that white men were superior in all aspects to their coloured counterparts and Tarrant confused the adage by positioning himself in both camps. Tarrant appointed as team manager, by the Maharaja of Patiala, became the public face of the tour. His role, or at least representations of it, placed the reputation of the expedition, as a serious sporting entity, in jeopardy.

Tarrant represented the Patiala, Cooch Behar and Jodhpur royal families in purchasing thoroughbreds for racing and breeding. The commission on these sales assisted in accruing his wealth. He noted in a press interview: 'At the beginning of each cricket season in England I was in debt. I have made much more money out of racing in a few years than years and years of cricket'.[20] The princely state and the princely family were significant to Frank as the 1929 electoral roll reveals that the Tarrant family lived at *Jodhpur Estate*, a significant country property near Beeac in the agriculturally rich Western District in rural Victoria.[21]

The failed Jodhpur Estate

In the mid-1920s Frank purchased a farm in the Western District, about 160 kilometres southwest from Melbourne, called 'Wilgul' which he promptly renamed 'Jodhpur Estate'. The country property was a status-symbol, a short-lived venture and a conclusive failure. He decorated the house with animal-themed exotic wallpaper suitable for the hill stations in the Punjab yet totally inappropriate for regional Victoria and the locals were shocked by Frank's daring interior design. He left the daily running of the farm to his three sons and newspapers reported on the maltreatment of sheep. The property fell into disrepair, most likely through a lack of expertise and endeavour, and was sold a few years later. Despite this failure, Frank was always intrigued to hear how others succeeded on the land. Of course, at this time Australia was predominantly a sheep, beef, wool and wheat economy.

The Tarrant family seemingly enjoyed the role of enacting the privileged gentry and Frank's scrapbook reveals that he decided 'to settle permanently' at the country property. However electoral records indicate that the Tarrant family's country experiment did not last long as by 1936 family members were back voting in metropolitan Melbourne. This is another example of the Tarrant family narrative of rebirth and reinvention. Most likely, finances accrued from Tarrant's association with the Maharaja of Jodhpur assisted the purchase of the property. Likewise, he named his house in Hawthorn East *Patiala* in tribute to the family. Despite Frank's history of chicanery, he remained indebted to his Indian benefactors and Indian culture.

---

[1] The *Cumberland Argus and Fruitgrowers Advocate* September 12, 1935.

[2] *The Romance of Indian Cricket*, 1968.

[3] 1938, October 22.

[4] April 1, 1935.

[5] Loris is sometimes referred to as Louis and the correct spelling of his name is impossible to determine. Semmens refers to him as Lawrence (most likely his correct full name).

[6] as quoted in Allen 2012, 213.

[7] Tarrant Scrapbook 1918-1951.

[8] October 22, 1938.

[9] June 24, 1912.

[10] 1966, 32.

[11] October 22, 1938.

[12] The *Leader* September 10, 1907.

[13] In gratitude, at the season's end, Tarrant was gifted a gold watch and chain by an appreciative Victorian Cricket Association.

[14] 1991, 6.

[15] May 9, 1928.

[16] *Barrier Miner* October 22, 1938.

[17] Allen 2012, 212.

[18] The *Mercury* January 11, 1941.

[19] Huntington 1996, 22.

[20] *Sporting Globe* May 2, 1923.

[21] The Colac Historical Society records reveal that Tarrant purchased the property in 1925 (then named *Wilgul*). Following the Tarrant family's departure, the property returned to its original name.

3 ON BOARD SS MONGOLIA

The team 'is a combination of real good fellows'[1]

The team departed Melbourne aboard the *SS Mongolia* on October 9. The cricketers were described by the *Daily Commercial News and Shipping List* as 'prominent passengers'.[2] Voyaging by ship in the early twentieth century was an elitist mode of transport as 'ships were associated with the aristocracy and exclusivity, with recreation, leisure, and in particular, a romantic—even erotic—notion of white, (upper) middle-class, luxury travel'.[3] The ragtag Australian cricketers, travelling first class, presumably shared this perception of travel and felt privileged (if also at times undeserving) to be viewed in this opulent light.

Team shot taken after leaving Perth, SS Mongolia. 1935. Leather archive

The *Mongolia* was a combination passenger and cargo ship with four large decks, a swimming pool and a state-of-the-art gym amongst other modern facilities. With the ship described by the press as a 'large floating hotel' and captained by Harry Ramsay Rhodes, an accomplished boatman with forty years of experience at sea, the cricketers were confident they were in capable hands.[4] The players settled into their 'commodious' single-berth cabins, unpacked their luggage and pondered what to do next. It didn't take long for a degree of tedium to set in.

Great mates Harry Alexander and Lisle Nagel set up camp on deckchairs and met a few travelling ladies. Both Victorians, they had made brief Test appearances in the infamous 1932/33 Bodyline series and knew each other well through district cricket and Sheffield Shield. The pair wore distinctive, chic black-and-white brogues while the other cricketers chose more conservative footwear. Evidence reveals that they enjoyed more than a few beers. Author Mike Coward, a contemporary authority on Indo-Australian cricket, notes that the pair drank enthusiastically and 'incurred the wrath of Tarrant before the SS Mongolia reached Fremantle'.[5] They were after all the party boys on the tour and were looking forward to reuniting with like-minded merry-maker Frank Bryant in Perth. Nagel, recognisable by his movie-star looks, pumped chest and athletic physique, towered over the other players. A programme from the Ryder archive introduces Lisle Nagel as 'the giant of the team and a good humoured one too'. Nagel wore his six-foot six-inch frame with pride, he didn't feel the need to shrink to the size of the others. He even looked down on Hunter Hendry who was nicknamed 'Stork' due to his height.

Alexander, known as 'Bull', was Nagel's physical opposite: squat with wavy black hair plastered into shape by glistening wax, a swarthy complexion and a pencil-thin, mobster-esque moustache. He was constantly teased about his waistline – Oxenham even described him in the *Telegraph* as 'podgy'.[6] The West Australian was less derogatory but did observe his 'width of shoulders and breadth of chest'.[7] Alexander was fearless and during the final Test of the Bodyline series he 'achieved a spark of notoriety' when he 'hit Jardine three times in one over'.[8] Following the most aggressive ball of the over, Alexander was rumoured to have gleefully cried out 'I've killed him! I've killed him!'.[9] Alexander was certainly a compelling character who squeezed every last drop of fun out of the tour and enlisted in the Second World War a few years later, motivated by similar sentiments of danger, excitement and again being with the blokes.[10]

Also on board was Oscar 'Wendell' Bill, a stylish batsman who played first-class cricket for New South Wales throughout the first half of the 1930s. The establishment in India was very excited by his arrival as they incorrectly assumed Wendell Bill was a hyphenated surname, denoting he was high society. Midway through the tour in Patiala, Bill was injured when he was struck by a devastatingly fast ball delivered by the demon bowler Mohammad Nissar. It broke his jaw and put an end to not just his innings of 118 but also his cricket in India. Following this injury, he watched from the sidelines and devoted more time to his regular column for *The Sydney Mail* which has filled in many of the missing pieces pertaining to the tour.

Bert Ironmonger turned fifty-three a few months earlier yet much of the tour literature attributes him as being younger. I'm sure the publicity machine acknowledged that shaving a few years off his age was considerably more appealing, as did Bert who didn't correct the misconception, which persisted for much of his career. Yet unfortunately he looked (and felt) his age. Bert was concerned that maybe he wasn't fit enough as he knew that the tour would be physically challenging. Fellow team member, Ron Oxenham called him an 'old warhorse' in print.[11] It was intended as a compassionate gag, yet Bert was offended at being the butt of the younger man's jokes.

Bert worked as a gardener at the St Kilda Botanical Gardens in metropolitan Melbourne and was granted unpaid leave for the tour.[12] He was grateful that his leave had been approved as he didn't want to jeopardise his position—full-time work was hard to come by—however he was equally determined to tour. He bade his family farewell at Melbourne Port and pre-teen daughter Pat was thrilled she made the newspaper and that her father was making history.

Bert had received his first Baggy Green back in 1928 at the grand old age of forty-six years and 237 days, when he was finally named to play against the visiting Poms. (Remarkably, Bert didn't hold the Australian record as the oldest Test player on debut, just pipped at the post by his great mate Don Blackie who was sixteen days older on his inaugural Test outing.) So clearly, Bert had perfected the art of patience. Considering his Test bowling average was 17.97 for his 74 wickets (which is still the sixth best to date if we consider a cut-off of 70 wickets) it didn't seem fair that selectors had routinely ignored him, and perhaps Tarrant was righting their wrongs at last.

Throughout Bert's sporting career, rumours spread that the cricket administrators viewed him as a potential liability and inappropriate as touring stock (especially to Britain) largely because of his suspect bowling action. *The Sun,* an Australian publication, commented in an article about chucking (the outlawed bowling action) that Bert's delivery has 'often been the subject of heated discussion'.[13] Manning Clark, always sensitive to class distinctions, wrote: 'Teams were announced for the Test trial cricket match at the Sydney Cricket Ground in December. Bert Ironmonger was not chosen. That gave the know-alls and the experts in the low-down a field day. Bert Ironmonger, they said, was socially not presentable, not the right sort of man to play for Australia against a team captained by that nice gentleman Arthur Gilligan'.[14] Ironmonger's biography on the Victorian Premier Cricket website provides further evidence and nominates his predilection for swearing as problematic; stating that 'his use of coarse language within the hearing of the Victorian Cricket Association president Canon Hughes is understood to have weighed against him'.[15]

Bert was a left-hand bowler who had lost part of his bowling forefinger as a young man in a chaff-cutting machine accident in rural Queensland. His life was probably saved by his sister who thrust the bleeding hand into a bag of flour. Miraculously, he had perfected bowling spin with four-and-a-half fingers and against all odds he was on the boat and was being paid to play professional cricket.

Likewise, Oxenham hadn't been lucky enough to be the recipient of the selectors' nod to tour. This was queried openly and following the 1935/36 tour, Hendry alluded to it in an article he authored for the *Truth*.

> The reason generally accepted why Ron Oxenham was never given a trip with the Australian Eleven was that he had a peculiar temperament, and was hard to get on with. Well, I can blow those arguments to pieces. Ron was one of the nicest fellows in the party, and never at anytime a wet blanket. How he ever did come to be omitted from the Australian sides to England and South Africa will remain one of the greatest mysteries of Test selections.[16]

My guess is that many in the team didn't quite meet the social standards that Australian cricket at the time appears to have demanded.

In 1935, Ron, a no-nonsense bloke, was one of the best all-rounders from Queensland. English cricketing great Jack Hobbs described him as the most difficult bowler he had faced on the 1928/29 tour. On field Ron bowled with precision, off field he was equally determined. Despite his bravado, he felt anxious on leaving Brisbane. On the first day on the ship Ron wrote of his mixed feelings about the tour and noted that he wandered around 'like a motherless foal', and yet in all of the tour photographs he always looks like an alpha male.[17]

To celebrate his selection Ron's father, a cricket administrator, gifted his son a set of hairbrushes. Twenty-four years earlier, in 1911, his team of charges gave Mr Oxenham senior the set when he was manager of the Queensland team that toured New South Wales. Considering Ron's highly sculptured hairdo throughout the tour, I'm quite sure the styling items were put to good use. In addition to his careful grooming and cricket, Ron jumped at the opportunity to supplement his income further, by contributing articles to the Queensland *Telegraph*. Although he had no journalistic experience, the sixteen articles he penned provide a remarkable insight into the exotic East and are an invaluable record of what actually happened on the first Australian cricket adventure in India.

Ron Oxenham's journalism was candid and he didn't shy away from sensitive information. He stated that the purpose of the tour was to 'erase the unfavourable impressions left by Jardine and his team, with whose methods, apparently, the Indians were disgusted'.[18] Oxenham's observation refers to the Bodyline incidents in Australia in 1932/33 and the following year in India and indicates that anti-imperial ideology was central to the Tarrant tour. Oxenham guaranteed the readers that Tarrant 'will be proud of his Australians in that direction before the tour is ended' which encouraged the tour to be viewed as improving relations between the colony and the dominion at the expense of unity with Britain. In light of Bodyline bowling, and the ill will generated by it, a sense of unease with Britain was developing which encouraged amity between India and Australia. Afterall, the Australians were in India to assist the locals with preparations for their Test encounter with England. Of course, the benevolence between the countries wasn't just a consequence of Bodyline bowling as the Empire was starting to unravel—having reached its pinnacle of area occupied under the Union Jack in 1933. A new world order was in transition with Australia and India both vying to contribute.

The cricketers knew they were in India to assist the selection and development of the national Test team, yet this tour had broader political, racial and cultural implications. They were in India to facilitate and nurture an on-going relationship between the countries using cricket as the conduit. An article in the *Argus* revealed the political overtone of the tour and stipulated that, 'The visit of an Australian cricket team to India is of national importance. We are trying to improve our trade relations with India, and our players would make splendid ambassadors'.[19] A later article, in the same publication, stated that 'the Australian team had not come to win matches but to impart experience'.[20] On the boat, the players became fully cognisant that their roles exceeded those of traditional Australian touring cricketers.

Tarrant spent hours on the *Mongolia* patiently explaining the machinations of Indian cricket and culture and Mike Coward, claimed that he 'would hold the team spellbound with cricket tales of the Raj'.[21]

Frank was concerned how some of the working-class boys would cope with the ritzy social functions. He was aware that many of his charges wouldn't know how to hold a fish knife or how to address the dignitaries so a quick course in high-society manners and etiquette was necessary. Frank had already squabbled with Fred Mair, a working-class battler from Balmain, who refused to attend the welcome-aboard cocktail party, as he didn't want to wear his dinner suit. They argued and Fred's obstinacy rather surprised Frank.

Frank had just over three weeks to get the team in shape and he started on day one. He selected a sports committee from the personnel and the youngest player Ron Morrisby was thrilled he made the cut. A timetable of compulsory physical training was drawn up and distributed to the players. Some mornings Frank would conduct exercise classes on the deck, at other times they were held in the gymnasium which contained all sorts of physical apparatus including rowing machines, exercise bikes and punching-bags. Frank needed to get this group moving and the boys complied, however there were degrees of speed and compliance. He devised age-specific individual exercise regimes that included croquet games, mini-tennis games (more like shuttlecock) and a modified version of cricket played with smaller bats and balls made from rope to avoid injury. Morrisby was delighted when he won the deck quoits completion as he also received a prize of 7/6.

A few minor celebrities were aboard the *Mongolia*, including musicians Margot MacGibbon and her new husband Frederick Jackson. Margot was an Australian violinist who had been awarded a scholarship to the Royal Academy of Music in London in 1927, and there she met Frederick, a pianist and leading choirmaster. They had recently married, and the *Mongolia* was thrilled to have the couple on board, so too was Ron Morrisby. He was seated next to Margot at a function early on the voyage and worried that he would be too overawed to talk. The gracious Margot sensed his anxiety and chatted to him, asking questions about the family orchard in Sandford, Tasmania and his cricket aspirations. They even discussed the up-coming fancy dress party and she promised to lend him a blue dress as Ron and Fred Mair had already decided to go as two little girls in blue. Although they did not win a prize in the fancy dress competition, they thoroughly enjoyed the occasion.

Tarrant was also on the lookout for people he thought it may be advantageous to meet. Mr Seppelt junior was travelling to Europe to visit the vineyards of southern France and Spain. The Seppelt family had purchased Great Western champagne in 1918 and over the next few decades expanded their wine industry in Australia. Tarrant also chatted to Mrs H. E. Currie, the wife of eminent agriculturalist Major Alan Currie, about agrarian initiatives; her husband had not only developed a private hydro-electric scheme and established a renowned horse stud, he was also involved in fine merino wool production and fish breeding. Frank was interested to learn about agriculture and tried to curry favour with the high society that presided over the industry.

Frank's second wife Berlin-born Eva Violet Wilmersdoeffe (sometimes cited as Wilmersdoeffer) was the sole female presence on the cricket tour. They wed in a quick ceremony, soon after she arrived in Melbourne on the Moreton Bay from London in 1931. Before meeting Frank, she'd spent a few years in England working as a domestic having made her way there from post-WW1 Germany. Little is known about how they met, though all reports indicate they were happy in each other's company and were well-suited travelling companions. Eva seemed to relish this new chapter in her life which included frequent travel. Tarrant's scrapbook reveals that they had crossed the Indian Ocean numerous times, so many in fact that Frank had lost count. Circumstances surrounding the death of Frank's first wife Kathleen in 1929 are sketchy and she was not discussed.

At first the team was unsure about Eva. Morrisby, in a letter, remarked that 'Mrs Tarrant travels with the team – she is his second wife but very nice'.[22] Such conservatism would have been soundly challenged later on the tour when Morrisby encountered the Maharaja's numerous wives and his substantial harem!

Eva was very friendly and had a ribald sense of humour that impressed some of the men while shocking others. Short and rotund, she was a bosomy sofa of a woman – to borrow a phrase from one of my favourite authors,

Douglas Stuart. Bill describes her as a 'delightful personality' and admired 'her humour and brightness' which defied the reputation of the dour, serious German.[23] Despite not having children herself, Eva exuded a maternal manner which the younger men appreciated. However, she was outspoken, too, which defied the stereotype of most women at the time. She was well-accustomed to racial and cultural prejudice in the West however in India she surrounded herself with locals and it didn't seem to be an issue there for her. Which I guess is one of the many reasons why she and Frank preferred to spend so much time in India.

As well as Frank being accompanied by Eva, another family member tagged along—his son, Bert. Bert was Frank's middle son and the one who, at this time, was most in need of supervision. The Tarrant boys intermittently worked abroad, assisting their father in various capacities. Throughout the 1930s the brothers ricocheted between India and Australia, but records indicate that they mostly lived at 'Jodhpur Estate', the country property or at 'Patiala', Frank's city residence in Melbourne. In 1935, Loris, the eldest of the Tarrant brothers was employed by the Maharaja of Patiala in India. Now thirty-three, Bert was leaving a volatile marriage, failed entrepreneurial ventures and unpaid gambling debts. He'd tried his hand at various occupations and in 1931 was ambitiously listed on the Australian electoral role as an 'actor'.

Physically Frank and Bert were the spit of each other, with broad physiques, domed foreheads and receding hairlines. The only differences were those etched by time. Tour photographs reveal that they smoked compulsively, both casually dangled their cigarettes between their thumb and their forefinger in the same distinctive way. Often, they wore similar if not identical clothing. The duo was frequently photographed wearing knee-length Macintoshes and a low-slung hat, irrespective of the weather. Outfitted in a similar fashion to how doting mothers dressed twins. Both were chancers, seduced by wealth and the good life, yet at this stage Tarrant was on a high, not so his son.

Bert's role has never been made clear; however, Hendry describes several functions that Bert occupied on tour, including assistant manager, scorekeeper and drinks man. Seemingly it was the latter role that he fulfilled with most ease.

Frank had a friend from Geelong, in rural Victoria, who was the managing director of a whiskey distillery. Corio Whiskey had been available for about five years, although embarking on any commercial venture during the Depression was ambitious. Frank persuaded his friend that Bert could be Corio's salesman in India. Drinking had always been popular with the upper-class living in India. Despite alcohol being prohibitively expensive it was now becoming popular with the middle-class (frequently English educated) locals. And so, two dozen bottles of the affordable Australian spirit were packed into crates as samples for Bert to tempt hoteliers with. In his manuscript, Hunter Hendry wrote that the entrepreneurial venture got off to a bad start: 'Unfortunately for all concerned, it was a fiasco because Bert had drunk the two cases of samples on the voyage!!'

During the two-day journey to Adelaide, the cricketers got a sense of team dynamics. Oxenham quickly decided that they were 'a combination of real good fellows', and he guaranteed that they would give a good account of themselves on the field.[24] However, photographs and other players' writing reveal that the recreational aspects of maritime life seemed to outweigh the players' professional obligations. Despite Tarrant's focus on fitness, education and discipline and the conviction of the press that the cricketers would be 'splendid ambassadors', it was evident that cards, gambling, deckchair naps, flirtation, a good novel and the unrestrained consumption of alcohol and food occupied much of the time on the liner. There was a variance in how the cricketers embraced their sporting and pedagogical obligations and it's fascinating to speculate how they'd cope on the field.

I guess the first match will reveal all.

---

[1] *The Telegraph*, 11 November 1935.
[2] 4 October 1935.
[3] Gowans 2006, 88.
[4] *Sunday Times*, 11 February 1934.
[5] *Cricket Beyond the Bazaar*, 1990, 106.
[6] *The Telegraph*, 11 November 1935.
[7] *The West Australian*, 15 October 1935.
[8] Coleman, *Seasons in the Sun*, 1993.
[9] Bodyline was a bowling technique executed by the English team and refers to a fast delivery being aimed at the batsman with multiple fielders in close on the leg-side. This resulted in the batsman having to choose whether to be hit or to deflect the ball and be caught out by one of the fielders. Cricket laws were subsequently changed to rule it illegal.
[10] Interview with Harry's daughter, Kim Innes.
[11] *The Telegraph*, 11 November 1935.
[12] Letter confirming unpaid leave from the St Kilda City Council sits in the Melbourne Cricket Club Library.
[13] The *Sun* (Sydney), 14 November 1934.
[14] *A History of Australia (Volumes 5 & 6)*, 332.
[15] Victorian Premier Cricket 2006.
[16] April 26, 1936.
[17] *The Telegraph*, 30 September 1935.
[18] *The Telegraph*, 11 November 1935.

[19] 26 July 1935.
[20] 4 January 1936.
[21] *Cricket Beyond the Bazaar*, 1990, 100.
[22] Dougan 2012.
[23] 11 December 1935.
[24] *The Telegraph*, 11 November 1935.

4 'THE DOOR TO INDIA HAS BEEN OPENED'

The SS *Mongolia* pulled into Outer Harbour in Adelaide on 11 October, two days after leaving Melbourne. An icy southerly wind rippled the water and, without much success, the feeble sun tried to break through the gloomy skyline. Hardly cricket weather!

The South Australian Cricket Association arranged a lunchtime function to welcome the team at the South Australian Hotel on North Terrace. Tarrant was delighted (and relieved) as the state body had demonstrated a strong opposition to the tour throughout the planning stage including vetoing the participation of local boy Homesdale Nitschke. Tarrant really wanted Nitschke, a recently retired Test batsman, in the team; yet he was another player that Australian cricket officialdom precluded. In addition to cricket, Nitschke and Tarrant were connected by the world of racing as the South Australian was establishing a successful career as a horse breeder.

Entering the room, Charlie Macartney scanned the crowd and was pleased to see a few big names in the cricket world including the South Australian vice-president, various members of the committee and the state's captain—the great Donald Bradman. The support of these fellows was important. However, according to the October 10 issue of *News*, a few major stakeholders were absent including President Bernard Scrymgour who was 'indisposed' and sent his apologies. Oxenham, in his regular article, observed the ill will generated by the tour: 'there was no little comment among the party when one of the South Australian board members strolled into the function. Everyone knows the attitude the South Australians adopted regarding the tour, and it was very amusing to hear Tarrant in very plain words explain to the gathering why none of their State players were represented in the touring team'.[1]

Following the luncheon, Frank Tarrant was interviewed by the press and promised a successful tour: 'The team is up to expectations, and will win many matches during the tour of India'.[2] He elaborated: 'as soon as I get back from the present tour I will begin negotiations for the visit of an Indian team to Australia in the 1937-38 season'.[3] If he had any doubts about the impending tour and the launch of Indo-Australian cricket, he didn't let on.

A conservative element in the press found Tarrant's unorthodoxy and blatant confidence baffling: 'Some queer statements have been made from time to time relative to Mr F. A. Tarrant's team for India. The latest is the strangest—that he has already selected the elevens to play in the different matches on the tour. Someone is crediting F.T. with omniscience'.[4]

Donald Bradman was keen to meet Ron Morrisby as the batsman's outstanding performances in Tasmanian grade cricket hadn't escaped The Don's notice. Indeed, Ron was a rising star and looked like becoming the next big thing. Ron was up for the meeting, despite being slightly nervous—he'd scrubbed his face so hard it hurt. Don hoped to lure the Tasmanian to Adelaide and suggested that they go for a walk around the Adelaide Oval to inspect the facilities. Ron liked what he saw but realised he'd have to discuss any offer with his parents before he promised a move to South Australia. As Tasmania didn't yet play Sheffield Shield, and wouldn't for another forty-two years, he knew a move interstate was necessary if he wanted to seriously pursue a career in cricket. Still, Ron was pretty chuffed, and he later observed in a letter to his parents, 'Don was a splendid little chap, not a bit stuck-up'.[5]

Ron Morrisby, referred to by the press as a promising young colt, made his debut for Tasmania, aged sixteen, at the Melbourne Cricket Ground on Christmas day 1931. He was a reliable and exciting batsman and still holds many records at club level. Considering his youth and sporting prowess, he was an obvious choice for Frank Tarrant. Ron ended the tour with the third best batting average of 36.8 and fell only 42 short of achieving 1000 runs—always a benchmark of tour success. Ron batted in more innings than the other touring Australians which was no doubt assisted by his youth, vigour and clean-living lifestyle. Ron was the only 1935/36 team member who, following the tour, would again compete against India when the touring Test team played against Tasmania in 1948. He scored 130 and was eventually bowled by Lala Amarnath, a name we will soon become familiar with.

The semblance of respect given to the cricketers by the South Australian authorities didn't extend to their Western Australian counterparts. On arrival on Monday 14 October, Frank requested an interview with the chairman of the cricket council, Mr Harold Rowe. No meeting took place.

Frank had earlier proposed that the team play a one-day game against a local side whilst they were in Perth as he was keen to squeeze in as much practice as possible. He also hinted that maybe the WACA could host a function for the cricketers, which was customary when touring parties departed Australia, as Fremantle was the last stop on Australian soil. On arrival in Perth, Tarrant realised there would be no cricket match or function and the team would be ignored by West Australian cricket officialdom.

Frank Bryant, the sole West Australian, joined the team in Perth. The talented batsman and his two brothers were pivotal in the development of West Australian cricket. Following his playing career, Bryant became involved in the administration of the game and was instrumental in achieving West Australian entry to the Sheffield Shield competition and the WACA ground acquiring Test status. On a personal level, he was an amiable, fun-loving fellow—a role he seemingly perfected in India. Tour images and the players' memoirs reveal that he was routinely the instigator of high jinks. Many photographs capture him with a cigarette in one hand and a glass in the other. Characteristically, a form guide would have been tucked away somewhere too.

The Incognito Cricket Club hosted a luncheon for the visiting team at the United Service Hotel where Bryant had previously been employed as manager. The club treated the team to 'a regal welcome and a hearty adieu'.[6]

Articles appeared in the Australian press criticising the conservatism exhibited by the state cricket authority and their neglect of the travelling XI was denounced. The Sunday Times ran with the headline 'Practically ignored by the W.A.C.A' and described the team's treatment by the cricket board as 'cavalier'.[7] Yet nothing that afternoon could dampen the cricketer's enthusiasm for the adventure that lay ahead. The cricketers refused to be disheartened and lustily celebrated the history they were making—they were after all the first Australian XI to depart from the Australian shores on a cricket tour of India and were being paid a small fortune to do so. Jack Ryder concluded his speech that afternoon by prophesying, 'The door to India has been opened'.[8]

Following the criticism of the board by the press, Mr Rowe back peddled and proposed that the touring team could play a match on their return to Perth. However, no evidence can be found that a match took place five months later. Seemingly, the official cricket authority wanted to distance itself from the Tarrant tour.

The team once again boarded the *Mongolia* and nestled in for the long leg of their journey. It was at this point that Tarrant really got to know his cohort and used this time to identify any problems with tour dynamics—hoping to nip them in the bud. The next stop was Colombo and that was two weeks off. Frank realised that he would have to use the time onboard strategically as he and the Maharaja had significantly invested in the tour: the tour manager emotionally and his boss financially. Frank, used his Roman Catholic connections and, prayed for competitive yet honest cricket on field and racial goodwill and harmony off it. He hoped the tour would prove to be a history-making triumph.

For the most part, ship life was fun. Bill noted that the cricketers found time for 'gay parties' and described ship life as 'very enjoyable'.[9] The team did not include a proficient musician however Arthur Allsopp kept his colleagues entertained, and amused, with his flawed accordion renditions. Other passengers weren't so complimentary and complained about the cacophony emanating from his cabin.

Victorian Jack Ellis, aged forty-four, was one of three wicket keepers on tour. He was another team member who had previously been overlooked for Test selection despite accompanying the Australian team to England in 1926 as the emergency keeper. Unfortunately for him, Bert Oldfield performed well and remained healthy and injury-free, so Ellis missed out on making a Test appearance.

Ellis, known as 'Happy Jack', was an easy-going and popular travel companion. He wasn't the first cricketer to use this nickname as he was possibly given it due to similarities with the legendary early England all-rounder George Ulyett. The official tour programme describes Ellis as a 'successful businessman in Melbourne and is noted for his breezy temperament'—he was voted one of the 'jolliest cricketers' to tour the 'Old Country'. The photograph of Ellis, frequently published in promotional material, portrays him in formal business attire; sitting at a desk surrounded by books implying that he possessed heightened business acumen and epitomised cosmopolitan sophistication. The other players are portrayed in their whites suggesting they identified as cricketers. Seemingly their daytime occupations were of secondary importance. On the Mongolia Ellis contracted influenza and spent three days in bed. This was the only casualty of the voyage. Possibly it provided his team members some respite from his incessant talking as Oxenham maintained that the team 'christened him 3LO'.[10]

In transit, the team read books, played records and commenced their extensive correspondence, as the sole lifeline with home. When they tired of sedentary activities, they played deck quoits, ping-pong and a modified version of tennis—sometimes placing a wager on the outcome. Gambling was endemic in Australian culture in the first half of the twentieth century and shortly after departure, the Australian cricketers, with surplus free time and finances, commenced placing bets on various sporting encounters, taking place on the ship and beyond. The players were delighted by the prospect of any supplementary financial remuneration.

According to Bill, Hendry and Tarrant triumphed in the gambling stakes and he remarked, 'as a matter of fact, these two seemed to be blessed with all the luck' as they appeared to win everything they bet on.[11] Bill observed Tarrant's good fortune on the *Mongolia* Cup race meeting, which 'proved to be a gold mine in disguise for Frank, who cleaned up on every race. Manager's luck!' Oxenham noted that good fortune wasn't with him when he picked *Suspicion* in the *Mongolia* Cup sweep. Starting promisingly, the horse romped home yet just before the finishing line the jockey was tossed off. Oxenham stipulated that the monetary loss wasn't problematic and cavalierly bragged: 'I'll take it out of the £300 allowance, so what's it matter anyway!'[12]

A conversation with Cecily Dougan (Morrisby's daughter) reveals that she is confident her grandparents [Ron's parents] were unaware of the gambling that was routine on tour. The primary material concerning gambling provides further evidence that touring, especially international expeditions, provided a libertarian environment where the tourists could indulge in activities that were less tolerated at home.

An undated and unidentified document from the Bill archive at Cricket New South Wales reveals the bonhomie that typified many activities on the sea journey. The document details the 'Cricket Extraordinary'—a modified cricket match that took place on the 'Sports Deck' between '2.p.m. & 4.p.m.'.

Frederick Gray, a successful manufacturing chemist, was named captain of one team. Gray had devised the importation, or oversaw the production, of a diverse array of scientific innovations into Australia, including the first soda fountain in Sydney, a formula for vanilla ice-cream and a headache powder. He was also a cricket stalwart. With Dr Lesley Poidevin, he inaugurated the Poidevin-Gray Shield, a competition between the district clubs in Sydney. Tarrant was delighted to have the philanthropic entrepreneur alongside him for the journey. Gray was equally thrilled, and the *Referee* described him as a 'hearty enthusiast' and reported that he 'should come back stocked with many tales of Old India'.

The programme describes Bert Tarrant as the 'son of famous Frank Tarrant', which suggests he would play a seemingly lifelong role as subordinate to his father. Bert led the opposing team. He wouldn't play any matches in India, so it is rather surprising that he was named captain. In addition, Bert had a reputation as a Casanova; his biography on the programme concludes with somewhat salacious overtones; 'Connoisseur:—Females understood'.

Tarrant's team comprised four Victorians and Gray's team consisted of four cricketers from his home state of New South Wales. Using geographic cultural representations, Queenslander Ronald Oxenham is named 'the Banana King' and Ron Morrisby is referred to as 'the Tasmanian Devil' with both functioning as 'umpires by special appointment'. The team echoed the orthodox configuration of Australian cricket with the majority of players originating from either New South Wales or Victoria; the highly competitive cricket-dominant states. The southeast mainland dominance of cricket resulted in participants from the minor states being limited to subordinate roles.

The programme outlined the game's guidelines, which adhered to orthodox cricket protocol with an emphasis on rules, teamwork, a strictly devised code of ethics and a highly defined sense of personal and team integrity. The final sentence proposes, 'May the Best Team Win'. In all likelihood the cricket match may not have taken place and the programme was simply concocted as a joke to fill in the numerous spare hours at sea. However, it reinforces the fundamental core values of the game, which emphasise sportsmanship and strictly codified rules.

Yet it wasn't just all cricket and gambling. Travelling frequently doubled as a matchmaking exercise as the cricketers were away from the eyes of disapproving parents or prying neighbours. Despite the majority of the Australian team members being married or engaged, many photographs reveal that they were fixated by prurient intents. In many ways, the cricketers conformed to the reputation attributed to a group of hot-blooded males who spent many hours on tour obsessing about women: some who they left at home, others they had just met or some who they merely viewed on the silver screen. The varying roles of women, the different women encountered and their representation in the decolonisation process materialised as another foreign hurdle that the cricketers attempted to fathom. This dialogue commenced on the ship.

A steady stream of western women journeyed to India for matrimony either as a scheduled matchmaking event or in an unconscious endeavour to meet culturally and financially appropriate partners. A journalist from the *Sydney Morning Herald*, observed that 'Australians as a race travel a great deal, and everyone who has ever set out on a sea voyage knows that shipboard friendships ripen quickly. And with the conviviality of deck sports, long hours spent chatting in a deckchair, or dances under a starlit sky, romance is ever in the air'.[13]

Onboard the Mongolia.. Alexander archive

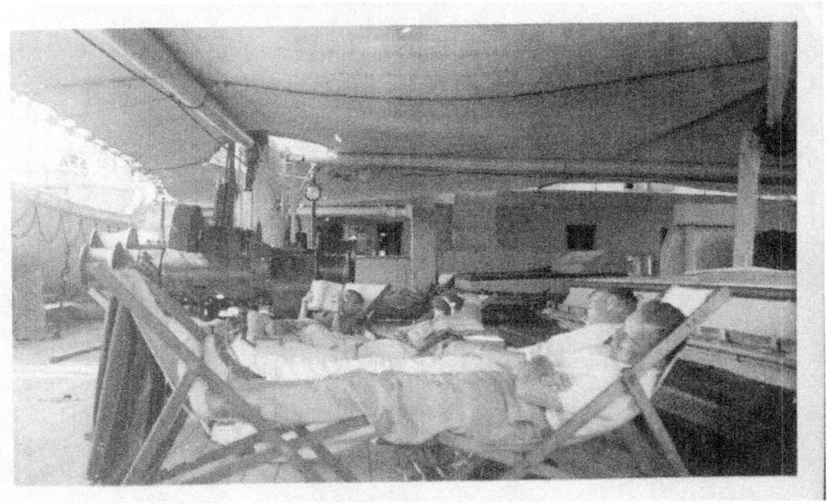

Onboard the Mongolia. Alexander archive

Onboard the Mongolia. Alexander archive

Prior to embarking on the tour, Tom Leather became engaged to my great aunt Doll Ponsford. The more socially sophisticated members of the travelling personnel teased him mercilessly about the highly improbable likelihood of Doll's infidelity whilst he was in India. Apparently, he couldn't cope with being ribbed and the others thought it was highly amusing.

A few photographs survive documenting typical maritime scenes. In one image, bachelor Harry Alexander is caught deep in conversation with an unidentified female. Body language indicates that Alexander is comfortable with his dominance in the situation and even mildly amused by the social exchange. The woman appears somewhat less at ease; she covers her body in a blanket and looks downwards, avoiding eye contact with both Alexander and the unidentified photographer. She doesn't seem to be finding the interaction unpleasant however the image represents orthodox early-twentieth century gender imbalance and behaviour.

Unidentified woman and Alexander on the Mongolia. Alexander archive

Cultural commentators argue that the journey can be as important as the destination. The ship represents transition, in this case travel from the stability of home to the distant unknown. Seemingly activities on the boat were driven by hedonistic desire yet the Australian cricketers also used their time in transit to gain some fitness, reflect on themselves and learn about their destination. The ship as it disconnects itself from land, commences a 'critical transition'.[14] Similarly the inhabitants of the ship, in this case the Australian cricketers, individually transformed during their journey and collectively evolved as a team.

The journey represented a moment of transition in the players' lives, in cricket history, in India's sporting identity, in the history of Australian cricket and in imperial bonds.

It is to Ceylon we now turn.

---

[1] *The Telegraph* November 11, 1935.
[2] *News* October 10, 1935.
[3] *The Advertiser* October 11, 1935.
[4] *Referee* October 17, 1935.
[5] Dougan 2012.
[6] *The Daily News* October 12, 1935.
[7] *Sunday Times* October 20, 1935.
[8] *The West Australian* October 15, 1935.
[9] Bill manuscript 1936–88, 71.
[10] November 11, 1935. 3LO was the callsign of the local ABC radio station in Melbourne.
[11] November 27, 1935.
[12] November 11, 1935.
[13] August 7, 1939.
[14] Rodgers *Feminine Power at Sea* 1984, 2.

5 AN ENCOUNTER WITH AN ELEPHANT

Colombo was the first stopover in the East and the Mongolia pulled into port six hours late. The excited team had dressed formally for their arrival. The gentlemen wore suits, ties and hats and draped overcoats over their arms. I'm unsure if they expected colder weather or maybe even rain? Eva chose a cream dress with a delicate floral print and matching accessories. A captioned photo of the team on deck to commemorate their arrival in Colombo is located in Tom's archive.

Team on arrival in Colombo. October 1935. Leather archive

On disembarking the *Mongolia*, adhering to an Eastern cliché, the cricketers were overwhelmed by oppressive steamy conditions and an enthusiastic crowd gave the team a 'tremendous welcome'. It heralded the team's popularity for the duration of the tour. Bill's first article for the Sydney Mail, noted 'it was with great difficulty that we reached our hotel'.[1]

That afternoon the team went shopping for tropical clothing as they realised such items were a necessity not a luxury. The cricketers especially enjoyed the purchasing of topees, otherwise known as pith helmets, which were routinely worn by, and have become a symbol of, the colonial class in the East. The broad brims of the hat provided protection from the sun and the light-weight material with small holes provided ventilation. There is also a suggestion that the headwear offered the visitors with some protection from the deadeye fast bowlers they would later encounter. As, of course, this was years before helmets became *de rigueur*. The owner of the haberdashery shop recognised the Australian cricketers and, realising that they were good for business, thoroughly fussed over them—cigarettes and cold drinks were on tap. Word got out that the 'famous' cricket team was in the shop and soon a horde gathered. Impressed by such a crowd, the proprietor saw the commercial advantage in having the celebrities in his establishment for as long as possible. He was soon buying ice creams for everyone.

The team had a suite of cars and drivers at their disposal and commenced sightseeing in Colombo. A few of the cricketers purchased tickets for the 'CEYLON, P&O Shore Excursions' and ventured out into the rural areas. This introduction to the East provided the cricketers with sights and experiences that reinforced their expectations. Bill described the 'magnificent drive to Kandy', 'the tropical scenery' and the various types of 'Singhalese' life as 'an eye-opener'. He elaborated: 'Many mysterious temples and village bazaars were explored, and many animals and wild game, were encountered'. Feeling a little ill at ease, Morrisby commented that the Buddhist temple was a 'very strange place'.[2] The slightly prudish Bill was equally tentative and unsure how he should react to the locals walking around shirtless which he described as 'a native custom'.[3]

Startled by cultural differences in Ceylon, the players sought out familiar routines, customs and people. Oxenham caught up with a family contact who had spent some years at his alma mater in Nundah, Queensland. The team was initially impressed by the glamorous globe-trotter, yet later queried the appeal of being nomadic. They also spent time with Jack Daniels, a Victorian jockey based in Colombo. Tarrant, most likely, facilitated the meeting. Oxenham had a meeting with Mr Foenander, a journalist with the Ceylon Observer, who had accompanied the English team during the 1932/33 Test series of Australia. He was 'loud in his praises of the hospitality extended to him by the Australian cricket authorities', yet much to Oxenham's displeasure the one exception was the Queensland Cricket Association. 'I thought what a pity it was that he had gained this impression, for Queenslanders, I think, are renowned the world over for their open-heartedness and their hospitality to visitors,' Oxenham wrote. 'It shows that it would pay the Queensland Cricket Association—which is equally as efficiently managed as any of the Southern associations—to go out of their way to look after these overseas visitors at Test time.'[4]

During their six-day stopover, the team was feted wherever they went. During a visit to St Peter's College, Oxenham and Bryant signed autographs for hours and complained of writer's cramp. Somehow, they summonsed the energy to lead an impromptu cricket training session for the excited students. In appreciation they were gifted a box of cigars with tobacco hand-grown by one of the senior masters from the school. Oxenham was greatly taken with the school's grand buildings and state-of-the-art sporting facilities. However, they were highly bemused to learn that the school experimented with 'open-air' classrooms which educators theorised would provide an environment that was conducive to stimulating the mind.

Luxury hotel, Ceylon. Leather archive.

The team managed to squeeze in some cricket practice to prepare for their first-class match against All Ceylon. The Colombo Cricket Club impressed the Australians, with Bill noting that the 'ground was in a marvellous condition, as green and as true as a bowling green—quite the equal, I should say, of our own Sydney Cricket Ground'.[5] Locals were employed as ground bowlers and Bill commented, 'Our manager declared that should any of these black-skinned Cingalese bowl us out we would have to pay him a rupee (1/6)'. Ron Oxenham wrote of the enthusiasm of these bowlers:

> They gave us wonderful practice, bowling 'flat out' the whole time. The crowd knew all about the arrangement and it was most amusing to hear the barracking. I'm not going to tell how much it cost me, but there were a few of the boys who had to make a cash adjustment at the end of their knock.[6]

Oxenham experimented with bowling wearing his newly acquired topee but found it rather difficult. Indeed, the team 'felt a little strange in them for a time' and Bill observed that when he tried to bowl with one on, he didn't know whether he was going to deliver the ball all right or whether he was 'going to walk over the stumps' and 'decided it was safer to use the cap'.

The first match against All-Ceylon was on 25 October. This was the first time the entire group played together – it was their first big sporting challenge. Allsopp, Love and Alexander missed out on a place in the team and it is feasible that the latter was overlooked due to disciplinary reasons. Bryant was named twelfth man (again, maybe a punitive decision). Heavy rain had fallen the previous evening yet there was no sign of it by the commencement of play and the wicket was surprisingly described by the *Canberra Times* edition on the October 26 as 'fast'. It was a hot day and luckily the rain held off. As was customary, both captains inspected the pitch before the start of play. The rangy Ryder towered over the diminutive Ceylon captain, L. D. S. Gunasekera, and a wag from the crowd joked about them being the 'long and the short of it'.[7]

The locals won the toss and elected to bat first however that was where their good luck ended. The inequity of talent between the teams was obvious.

Tarrant was happy with how his team performed but worried about the stamina of his charges. Frequent water breaks were required. Bill observed that the visitors 'felt the heat intensely'.[8] The umpires carried hand towels so the batsmen could wipe their brows at the end of each over. Dripping with sweat, the towel was wrung out by the umpire and placed into his back pocket.

Oxenham excelled and took 9-18 in the first innings! He shared the bowling duties with Nagel and Leather. In the over following lunch, Oxenham took four wickets including a hat-trick (with the fourth, fifth and sixth balls of the over) – the first ever in representative cricket in Ceylon.[9] It was aptly described by the *Advertiser* as 'sensational'. The local team hung around for another forty minutes but were all dismissed for only 96, which was the then lowest score ever recorded by an All-Ceylon team.

Bill and Hendry opened the batting, and the Australians retained their good form. They scored quickly despite finding visibility difficult, largely because many excited spectators (dressed in white) wanted to be as close to play as possible. A flimsy cord separating the spectators from the players exacerbated the problem. Bill, in particular, had problems distinguishing the outfielders from the crowd though it didn't seem to trouble him as he recorded a century in 130 minutes. He set a cracking pace and was eventually dismissed, caught by Mervyn Kelaart off Ed Buultjens, for 101. The *Sydney Morning Herald* described Bill's game as 'faultless'.[10]

Despite not reaching the heights of Bill and Oxenham, Macartney, the old superstar on tour, was the crowd favourite. The *Australasian* described him as 'the little Dasher'.[11] Buoyed by the enthusiasm of the receptive audience and his growing self-confidence, Macartney batted at number four and made 53. He felt completely invigorated as cheers of the crowd echoed around the ground. At the end of the game, he was carried shoulder-high to the pavilion by a horde of Ceylonese.

Morrisby was dispirited with his score of two. He kept his disappointment to himself but in a letter home he wrote, 'I did not do any good but I am not worrying because we have plenty of matches left. My lbw decision was doubtful because I was given out when the ball struck my outside leg on the legside … But I will get them next time', he promised.[12]

The press emphatically praised the Australians' performance, and the *Truth* nominated the 'Jack Ryder of olden times' as 'the star of the game'.[13] The article maintained that 'Ryder was forceful and cautious by turns, but always masterful'. After scoring 67 he was bowled by Edward Buultjens.

The Australian press were quite disarmed by the sportsmanship of the local team. When a new Australian batsman approached the wicket the opposition players wished him good luck and when he was dismissed, they expressed regret. Nevertheless, the Australians won the game easily by an innings and 127 runs. The players were thrilled with their performance and Oxenham smugly observed that the team cheekily wondered 'what the [Australian] board members will think of us now.'[14]

By any measure, the match was a stunning success though there was an unfortunate suggestion that the Bodyline technique was used by the Australian bowlers. As previously mentioned, Nagel, Ironmonger, Love and Alexander had played in the 1932/33 divisive series and it seems odd that leg-theory bowling was employed in the game.

What actually happened on the day was that Nagel was midway through bowling an over when he was cautioned by fellow team-member Jack Ellis, who suggested his delivery could be misinterpreted given that four fieldsmen were positioned on the leg-side. Nagel was astonished that his bowling tactics might be viewed as unsporting. Likewise, Bill in his newspaper article also scoffed at the suggestion: 'Imagine Nagel bowling "body-line", anyway – and, actually, he couldn't bring the ball up more than stump-high on the perfect wicket'.[15]

Tarrant's Brush with Bodyline

Tarrant also had first-hand experience of leg-theory bowling and was aware that it did not solely take place on Australian soil during the 1932/33 English tour as is now the popular assumption. Bodyline tactics had also been used later in the England-West Indies series in 1933. The West

Indians, spearheaded by Manny Martindale and Learie Constantine, had returned the favour. During that tour, Patsy Hendren used the special cap with three peaks, two of them covering his ears and temples, lined with foam rubber. The "helmet" was designed by his wife Minnie and it is considered the first-time protective headwear was worn. The Englishmen persisted with experimenting with the bowling technique in a later Test encounter in India in 1933/34 (prior to the implementation of rule changes in 1935 and further tweaking took place in 1957 which put a final stop to a Bodyline field) when Tarrant umpired the first two Tests.

Douglas Jardine captained the English team on all these occasions. On being selected as leader on the Australian tour, Rockley Wilson (a Rugby-Cambridge product who played for Yorkshire and was one of Jardine's teachers in Winchester) sagely proclaimed 'We may well win the Ashes, but we may well lose a Dominion'.[16] Unsurprisingly Frank Tarrant, the working-class flashy chancer, and Jardine, the austere silver tail, disliked each other intensely. This animosity commenced on the pitch yet was equally evident over the boundary fence.

In 1933/34 England won two of three Tests, with the middle one a draw. During the second Test in Calcutta, Jardine tendered an official complaint about the frequency of leg-before-wicket rulings made by, the umpire, Tarrant. To placate the English captain, Tarrant was dropped for the third Test. The Australian press inferred that a cultural agenda was evident and wondered if 'it was the fact of Tarrant being an Australian that aroused Jardine's hostility, for the English captain's book on his Australian tour breathed fire and brimstone – against us as a people?'[17] Following the Test series, a vehement public spat between the two ensued for weeks, Jardine insulting Tarrant with the comment, 'cricketers are not considered renowned until they have played in a Test match'. Tarrant had immense ability yet, as previously revealed, had been overlooked for Test selection. Tarrant's scrapbook includes an article that further explains the squabble: Tarrant later protested that unsportsmanlike Bodyline tactics were used by the English to win the Test series in India and claimed that Nobby Clark was bowling at the man – 'a young Maharaja, very popular with the crowd'. The Maharaja was the Yuvraj of Patiala, and when a ball almost knocked the turban off the batsman's head Tarrant (as umpire) interceded and told Jardine that he objected to the bowler's intention and reminded the captain that 'the umpire was the judge of fair and unfair play'. Tarrant, considering his intimacy with the Patiala family and his paranoia about his hair loss, was additionally incensed by Jardine's cultural insensitivity regarding the Maharaja's headwear. The *Truth* reported: 'Jardine is, indeed, the stormy petrel of cricket, and his visit to India has not helped Anglo-Indian relations'.[18]

With the match in Colombo wrapped up in under two days, the Australian team had extra time for sight-seeing. Oxenham described their last day in Colombo as 'a dream day' assisted by receiving a congratulatory cable from the Toombul Cricket Club (where he played) in Queensland, noting 'how quickly news travels these days'.[19] He was indeed proud of his performance and exceedingly happy that he had started 'off the tour so encouragingly' and confessed that Tarrant had earlier told him how concerned he was about 'choosing his team' and worried whether he had enough 'slows'. Tarrant also mentioned his fears to Jack Ellis, who remarked, 'If you've got Oxenham, you won't have to worry about either slows or the fast stuff; he'll get 'em out'. Oxenham was chuffed and wrote, 'Naturally, I felt rather pleased that I was able to come to light so early in the tour; but I do not think I got any more satisfaction out of it than did Jack Ellis. One would almost have thought that he had got the wickets himself, so delighted was he at my success'.

The team spent the afternoon at Queen's House, the Governor's residence and the grandest quarters in the capital city. The imposing two storey white residence was built in 1856 and sat nestled in four acres of tropical garden, overlooking the sea. The acting Governor Sir Graeme Tyrrell, in the absence of Governor Sir Reginald Stubbs who was on leave in Britain, invited the team and hosted them to a wonderful afternoon.

Role playing as colonists, Bill wrote that the players looked 'more like big-game hunters than cricketers in their tropical gear'.[20] Roaming around the 'huge palace and grounds', the tourists' dream materialised when they stumbled across an elephant. Initially fearful, they quickly realised they weren't in danger as the animal was a '"quite" old chap' and then took turns to ride around the estate on its back 'to the accompaniment of loud cheers and the clicking of cameras'.

Following lunch, the players attended a local football match, where Bill admired the 'skill and mastery' of the barefoot players. He observed, 'Their feet must be as hard as their heads, judging by the way both were used'. A farewell dinner at the Cingalese Sports Club followed – from all accounts it was a perfect way to conclude their time in Ceylon. Alcohol was plentiful and the conversation admirable as Bill wrote: 'The English used was perfect and quite overshadowed anything our speakers could produce'. However, it wasn't all praise, as he complained about the complexity of the seating arrangement: 'a plan of the seating is always provided, but so large were the tables and so intricately placed, that we always found it most difficult to find our seats'. This occasion was just a primer for the formality of Indian customs and what lay ahead.

At last, the team boarded the SS *Chitral*, a mailboat, considerably smaller than the Mongolia for the 830-odd nautical miles to Bombay. Oxenham was ambivalent about the stopover and the experience: 'Although our hosts at Colombo were kindness itself, we were not sorry to leave because of the weather,' he explained. 'It started to rain two days before we departed, and it scarcely ceased, making the conditions extremely warm and muggy'.[21] Morrisby was likewise opaque: 'Life is very different here you have no idea what it is like until you see it!!', he wrote home. He did however observe the hospitality bestowed on the team by the locals and noted that 'they can't do enough for you'.[22] Bill's impression of Ceylon was more positive and the editor of the *Sydney Mail* (the newspaper he contributed to) called it 'the enchanted East'.[23]

The *Chitral* rolled around rhythmically in the port as she waited to depart. The motion of the sea was rather off-putting for the imbibers as they had drunk excessively that evening and they hoped that they would be able to keep their curries down. Oxenham was one of the few non-drinkers; indeed, his preferred beverage was tea and his discovery of quality tea had been a profound experience for him: 'After tasting the tea in Ceylon, I arrived at the conclusion that in Australia we do not know what "dinkum" tea is. Never before have I enjoyed "the cup that cheers" more than I did when I sampled it again the day before we left. Fortunately, our ship stocked up at Ceylon'.[24]

The *Chitral* blared its deafening horn and the mailboat coasted through the waves in a westerly direction. The cricketers were psychologically and geographically a step closer to their destination and another step further away from home.

---

1 *The Sydney Mail*, 27 November 1935.
2 Dougan 2012.
3 *The Sydney Mail*, 11 December 1935.
4 *The Telegraph*, 18 November 1935.
5 *The Sydney Mail, 27* November 1935.
6 *The Telegraph*, 18 November 1935.
7 *The Courier-Mail*, 26 October 1935.
8 *The Sydney Mail*, 11 December 1935.
9 26 October 1935.
10 26 October 1935.
11 2 November 1935.
12 Dougan 2012.
13 27 October 1935.
14 *The Telegraph*, 18 November 1935.
15 11 December 1935.
16 *The Age*, 7 November 2002.
17 *Referee*, 22 February 1934.

[18] 18 February 1934.
[19] 18 November 1935.
[20] *The Sydney Mail*, 11 December 1935.
[21] *The Telegraph*, 18 November 1935.
[22] Dougan 2012.
[23] *The Sydney Mail*, 11 December 1935.
[24] *The Telegraph*, 18 November 1935

6 'THE VERY NAUGHTY BOYS OF THE AUSTRALIAN CRICKETING FAMILY'

The first of November was the last day on the ship and the players were aware that they would arrive in Bombay soon and this was the final time for four and a half months where they would be immersed exclusively within Anglo customs. On this day, the sea was 'as smooth as glass' which slightly unnerved the sportsmen. After almost three weeks of being bashed around by turbulent waves the team was unaccustomed to such calm.[1]

The unsettling sensation that Tom Leather had felt on departure in Melbourne was back. Even the veteran traveller Jack Ryder was uncertain if he should feel daunted or excited. He was experiencing an unsettling mishmash of both. Ryder wondered how his team would cope with their inflexible position in the subaltern hierarchy as they would have to acquiesce to an aristocratic class in India with which they had no previous experience beyond some having encountered the few Indian royals doing the rounds on the cricket circuit. The most famous was the Nawab of Pataudi, Iftikhar Ali Khan, who toured Australia playing for England during the Bodyline series in 1932/33. The Australian News observed that 'the Indian potentate, brought visions of Oriental splendor (sic) and wealth'. The newspaper reported that a young University student commented that Pataudi 'reminds me of Coleridge's line in "Kubla Khan"': 'As soon as I saw him I thought – "Beware, beware, his flashing eyes, his floating hair"'.[2] When reporting on India such stereotypes were routinely perpetuated with Western press frequently observing the royal's sexual proclivity, exoticism and their mind-blowing extravagance.

The tourists would have to learn how to negotiate an unfamiliar racial dialogue.

Throughout the journey, team-structure and hierarchy had changed. Tarrant's role as the principal orchestrator and commander grew and simultaneously the Australian Board of Control's authority over the travelling personnel contracted. Now the latter was seemingly non-existent and the churlishness of the Australian board regarding the tour planning felt like a distant, petty, memory.

Cricket was also under transition with a strong professional push—even the rules were being revised. Tarrant sent a wireless message to the Australian press from the *Mongolia* confirming that the contentious LBW law would apply at some matches during the tour as directed by the Indian board.[3] Conversely, the conservative Australian cricket officials had rejected the new rule being implemented on the Test tour of South Africa.[4] Seemingly, even the rules of cricket couldn't be agreed upon and reflected an escalating (and what would become ongoing) battle between the East and the West.

The team was excited about their arrival to the Gateway to India. They had all heard traveller's tales about arriving in Bombay: it was quite unlike the experience of entering other ports, which were usually unimpressive, industrial and rather ugly. With a healthy dose of cabin-fever, the cricketers were disappointed when they realised that they would be tucked up in bed as the ship steered into the harbour. They would have to wait till morning to get the first glimpse of the Empire's Jewel in the Crown.

Despite their excitement, the player's apprehension intensified as they inched closer to Bombay. Frank Tarrant had persistently guaranteed their safety, but the players knew that they would encounter foreign and curious customs of the East, and possibly a bit of danger too. At home, newspaper reports, with sensationalist and histrionic headlines, reminded readers of the political turbulence in India. Not long before departure the *Sydney Morning Herald* reported:

> The important Indian seaport of Karachi has just witnessed deplorable scenes. On Tuesday of last week the burial of a Moslem, executed for murdering a Hindu on sectarian grounds, was made the occasion of a very threatening demonstration. The dangerous situation thus created was not brought to an end until blood had been shed. To save the police from an enraged crowd of nearly 50,000, detachments of the Sussex Regiment, after warnings had been ignored, filed on the mob, killing at least forty and injuring more than a hundred. Regret as one may an occurrence so distressing, it cannot be regarded on its own merits alone as an isolated incident.[5]

More bloodshed was inevitable as Indian independence was looming and, over a decade later, the British would have to pack their bags concluding almost three centuries of rule. In 1935, the cricketers had no idea when it would transpire, and they were even less cognisant of how violent and grievous the process would be. India would witness partition and the birth of two new nations which would later become three. The resultant devastation and bloodshed, caused by the displacement of fourteen million people, could not be imagined.

By comparison interwar Australia was a safe haven.

The final night on the ship was a formal event and the cricketers were dressed in dinner suits. At last, Mair complied. The menu was written in French—Oxenham grumbled. No one appeared to have much of an appetite and they slowly picked over the multiple courses throughout the long night. Macartney usually ate everything in front of him but even he couldn't get through the food. He did however enjoy the *Aloyau de Boeuf* and wondered if they would be eating it in India. Tarrant had informed the team about the culinary restrictions imposed by the various communal groups and suggested that as most Hindus viewed cows as sacred it might be difficult to access beef in India. The team joked how the Indian population would cope with Oxenham's name as it incorporated the two animals that were forbidden for consumption.

While they didn't eat much, they did enjoy the free-flowing alcohol. They foolishly imagined that it may keep their anxiety levels at bay. Tarrant had assured the drinkers that they could imbibe in India, yet they were sceptical as popular sentiment informed that most Indians abstained from alcohol for cultural and religious reasons.

Between courses, the captain of the *Chitral* wished the team an 'enjoyable Tour, Fair Wind and a Safe return'. Everyone in the dining room rose to their feet and applauded the cricketers. The loquacious Tarrant responded in his customary whimsical fashion and spoke about the pride in playing for one's country. He mockingly proposed a toast to the Australian Board of Control. Taking this accolade on face value, the attendees again rose to their feet—heartily clapping. The evening became a congested blur of ebullience—speeches, standing ovations, thunderous applause, raucous laughter, clinking crystal and many of the cricketers drank too much.

Twenty-five-year-old Arthur Allsopp and the younger non-imbibing Ron Morrisby sat together surrounded by half-empty plates, overflowing ashtrays and glasses of various shapes and sizes. Arthur always looked grim lipped in team photographs and is easy to identify by his distinctive broad cheekbones, piercing eyes and a widespread generous nose. The black-and-white shots don't reveal his blonde tips, which apparently lightened the moment he saw the sun. The two cricket hopefuls were entrenched in conversation and were oblivious to the antics of their cohorts.

The two young men were connected by cricket, but little else. Ron's upbringing in Sandford on the leafy outskirts of Hobart hadn't totally shielded him from the harsh realities of the early twentieth century yet it had diluted the experience. Conversely, Allsopp came from the school of hard knocks and had first-hand experience of hardship and prejudice. First-hand experience had cultivated his philosophies and also his street smarts. One story heard on the grapevine was that Allsopp, on failing to find a spot in New South Wales cricket, believed that he might be more successful in Victoria but lacking the funds for train travel, he set out on the over 900 km walk to Melbourne.

Sitting at the dining table with Arthur, Morrisby was consciously aware of the cultural and racial challenges he would soon encounter. Back in Melbourne, Morrisby told Tarrant that his contact with non-whites was limited... well non-existent, he secretly confessed. Frank had laughed it off and dismissed it as an issue of concern. This had rather upset Morrisby who thought Frank was patronising him and he didn't welcome the ridicule.

Maybe Arthur would be more sympathetic, he guessed, despite Morrisby's parents having warned him to steer well clear of the New South Welshman with a rogue reputation.

The inclusion of Arthur, who despite possessing enormous talent had previously been overlooked by selectors, is attributed to Tarrant's fair-minded integrity. Arthur had innate natural sporting talent yet would never make the grade in cricket because, as described by Scascighini and Lawrence, he lacked the 'social graces the powers to be judged necessary'.[6] Following his return to Australia in 1936, Arthur turned his attention to softball possibly inspired by being disillusioned with cricket. Or maybe it was cricket's rejection of him as has been suggested by a family member. He established a formal softball competition in Victoria and in 1991 the *Arthur Allsopp Shield*, the national championship for U16 boys, was named in his honour.

Following the death of his mother in 1923, the Allsopp family found themselves in diminished circumstances. Arthur's father supported them by labouring and intermittent work in the coal mines. His role as sole custodian of six young children was tough. Arthur, the oldest child, was passed around different family members and wound up in 1924, aged sixteen, at the Dr. Parsonage Home for Delinquent Boys in Gosford, New South Wales. He arrived there following a decree from the Children's Court. Specific details about his detention are difficult to locate. However, government records inform that the facility, run by the Child Welfare Department, was 'an industrial school for boys aged 13 to 18 who were committed for "serious offences" or had been deemed "unsuitable for training under the conditions of the Mittagong Farm Home"'.[7]

Allsopp is posthumously suspected of having indigenous blood, which possibly impeded his success although confirmation is not definitive. It is part of folklore, yet Andrew Stark assessed that 'Conclusive evidence proving or disproving these suggestions have not been forthcoming and there is a theory that perhaps a chatter of intergenerational scuttlebutt may have grown out of the fact that members of the family were of colour, and that a false assumption of aboriginality was acquired somewhere along the line'.[8]

Arthur, no doubt, had a disrupted upbringing considering his unorthodox childhood, convoluted racial origins and he quickly gained a reputation as being a ne'er-do-well. Allsopp's bad-boy reputation spread beyond the walls of the cricket administrator's office. Yet Morrisby assured his mother in a letter home, 'Arthur is a great chap, he doesn't drink or smoke so you can tell Dad that Dr. Sprent was wrong when he said he drank too much'.[9]

Sitting at the table surrounded by his fellow team-members engaging in drinking games and other tomfoolery, Morrisby conceded that Arthur was the most rational of the travelling personnel. How wrong his parents had been!

The team's previous interaction with non-Anglos was limited; some of the fellows had played with or against the Queensland bowler Eddie Gilbert and Morrisby knew that if he continued to play cricket, he'd encounter Eddie at some stage too. Eddie, an aboriginal cricketer from the Cherbourg mission, was usually in the press for all the wrong reasons. His bowling action was under constant scrutiny, yet he had received acclaim for flooring Don Bradman with a bouncer and bowling him out for a duck in 1931 in a Sheffield Shield encounter. Eddie bowled faster than anyone at the time.

Late in the evening an unexpected announcement was broadcast over the ship's loudspeaker. The *Chitral* would be docking in a few hours. All passengers quickly returned to their cabins to organise their luggage for arrival.

A uniformed gentleman approached Tarrant and handed him an envelope. The tour manager deftly opened it with a knife then corralled his players, informing them that they were to stay on board the ship and disembark the following day. The official welcome ceremony would be conducted on the deck the next morning at 7.30am. Tarrant urged the team to continue eating and drinking as it would be such a shame for all the delicious food and drink to go to waste. So, in an almost deserted dining room, they picked over the apricot vacherin and macaroons—washed down with some dessert wine.

Shortly after that, the *Chitral* docked.

The Hindu, a premier Indian newspaper, observed that just after midnight many cricket enthusiasts, eager to meet and greet the visiting team, stormed the ship. The journalist noted that the cricket fans were 'agreeably surprised not so much at the vivacity and liveliness of Ryder's team, as by their affability which was entirely a new experience so far as cricket visitors were concerned'.[10] I suspect their friendliness was not solely a uniquely Australian trait but partially a consequence of their intoxication. Incredibly, they somehow managed their official duties faultlessly.

Charlie Macartney was the centre of attention and dutifully responded to requests from the press and the fans. In response to a question, he referred to his wizardry echoing the cliche reputation of the East, which caused a wave of thunderous laughter from the crowd. He hadn't experienced such popularity for years and he lapped it up. Bill and the dapper Nagel, likewise, were crowd favourites. As always, Tarrant was prone to exaggeration and talked-up the talent of the touring sportsmen. He even bragged to a journalist that Oxenham was the 'best all-rounder of all' and the 'coming Bradman of Australia'.[121] It's difficult to imagine that he actually believed these claims as Ron was already in his mid-forties and nearing the end of his playing career and despite being a very able bowler, he was nowhere near analogous to the freakish talent of Bradman who was already a national icon.

Eventually the players found their way back to their cabins and bunked down for the night.

Leather woke with a thumping headache and a nasty feeling of disorientation. He slowly realised that someone was knocking on his door. 'Wake-up Sahib, we're here in Bombay Sir. Would you like some breakfast?' an unknown and foreign voice enquired.

An individual valet had been appointed to the high-profile team members and they would travel with them for the duration of the trip. The B-list had to make do with sharing an attendant. The staff would attend to a variety of needs, including turning back bedding, packing luggage, cleaning shoes, sewing missing buttons and assisting the cricketers on cultural matters or indeed any difficulties that may arise. The bearers had been sent into the cricketers' cabins the previous night and dutifully packed-up their belongings. They had facilitated the luggage through customs and the trunks would be collected on the dock later in the morning. In theory, this was a wonderfully courteous initiative, however the planners didn't realise that this arrangement would lead to the cricketers sleeping in their dinner suits.

It took a few minutes for Tom to fathom where he was and why he woke half dressed in his evening attire. He felt off-colour and couldn't stomach the thought of food yet as he ran his sticky tongue around his spongy gums, he realised that maybe some hydration was necessary, 'A strong cup of tea with four sugars please and do you happen to have any Bex' he called out to the voice behind the closed door.

Tom hadn't grown up with lackeys. He was actually a little uncertain about how he would cope with an ever-present attendant. Surely, he could carry his own luggage, he thought. Last night it had sounded impressive and extravagant yet now he was unsure how he should even address this person. Tom rubbed his feet together and realised that he was only wearing one sock. He hoped he could locate the other. It would be so humiliating meeting the Patiala royalty, cricket officialdom and all the other big knobs wearing one sock and a crumpled dinner suit. He ran his fingers through his unruly hair and then used them to double as a toothbrush. In response to another knock on the door, Tom opened it and came face-to-face with Walgi carrying a cup of hot tea and analgesia. 'Hello Sir, I trust you slept well. Welcome to India', he beamed.

---

[1] *The Telegraph* November 18, 1935.

[2] *News* November 2, 1932.

[3] *The Telegraph* October 21, 1935.

[4] *The Argus* October 11, 1935.

[5] March 27, 1935.

[6] *The O'Farrell Cup: The Quest for the Holy Grail of Riverina Cricket.*

[7] *https://www.findandconnect.gov.au/guide/nsw/NE01149.*

[8] *http://websites.sportstg.com/get_file.cgi?id=35843874.*
[9] Dougan 2012.
[10] November 2, 1935.
[11] *The Hindu* November 2, 1935.

7 BHUPINDER, THE MAGNIFICENT

'cricketer, soldier and idol of his people'[1]

Prior to departure, the touring cricketers knew very little about India, Indian culture and customs and even less about the machinations of Indian cricket. The name Maharaja Bhupinder Singh certainly sounded exotic, but details were scant. In 1990, Mike Coward explained that 'Some members of the [Australian cricket] board had vague recollections of some foreign chap expressing a wish that Woodfull's team play on the Indian subcontinent on their return from England in 1934 but little serious thought had been given to cricket in the mysterious East or to establishing formal ties with India'.[2] The 'foreign chap' was Bhupinder Singh (the Maharaja of Patiala) and during the voyage Tarrant enlightened the travelling personnel about his position in Indian politics, culture and, most importantly, his role in cricket.

Tarrant educated his team about India. During British colonisation, the country was divided into two distinctive zones: two-fifths of the land mass and more than a quarter of its population were governed by the rulers of between 500 and 700 princely states. These principalities ranged in size from large kingdoms that rivalled European countries in territory, revenue or population, to tiny estates whose rulers administered only a few villages. The remaining portion of the country formed British India.

The administrators of British India and the princes constantly bickered with disputes about territory, money and politics. Feasibly, the colonists could have assumed control of the total country following the 1857 mutiny in which they were victorious. However, following the rebellion, laws were implemented to respect the rule of the native princes. To maintain stability, a harmonious relationship between the British and the Indian royal families was desired yet approached with caution. The British were especially circumspect, considering the martial reputation of the royal households as they descended from military rulers. Pragmatically both parties acknowledged that a harmonious relationship was advantageous. A respectful collaboration was necessary to maintain hegemony as the British acknowledged that the 'Indians preferred their old customs, old traditions and old dynasties'.[3] The British implemented sufficient control over the princely states to ensure that the Indian royal families couldn't conquer imperial rule and simultaneously the royals' incomes and privileges were safeguarded. By the start of the twentieth century, the status quo was comparatively peaceful as the British recognised that any threat to their regime would emerge from the nationalist movements not the royal families.

Advancing the history and geography lesson, Frank revealed that despite being only 5,932 square miles, Patiala was one of the wealthiest regions of India due to its immense agricultural resources and the shrewd acquisition of land revenue implemented by the British. By the late nineteenth century, developments in transportation and technology revolutionised the agriculture industry and impacted favourably on the Patiala economy. Crops were shunted from Patiala, and other districts of the Northern Punjab, across India and abroad and the Patiala family profited from the expanding industry. Prosperity led to an autonomous and mutually beneficial relationship between the Patiala family and the British who attributed the ruler a seventeen-gun salute.

The staunchly opportunistic and egocentric Maharaja Bhupinder Singh ruled Patiala with a firm fist. He rewarded honesty and hard work with gifts and benefits and the Australian press described his generosity as 'abounding'.[4] Yet he also had his critics – outlined in a 1930 report titled the 'Indictment of Patiala' which detailed his penchant for luxury and his insatiable sexual appetite alongside his predilection for revenge. A further report was commissioned in 1939 and a description on an India library database (which contains a copy of the document) labels the 'heinous crimes' Patiala committed including 'serious moral turpitude' and murder. Bhupinder was described by Copland, an Australian expert in colonial India, as the 'most formidable and persistent princely adversary'.[5] The potentate was certainly obstinate and inflexible and demanded obeisance. Despite endogenous pressure from the *Akalis* (a Sikh political group), Bhupinder orchestrated the marriage of his daughters to non-Sikhs as he observed the potential benefits from mixed marriages. A similarly ruthless ethos was embraced by Bhupinder and Tarrant to promote Indian cricket.

The Patiala royal family enjoyed a long association with cricket. Bhupinder's father, Maharaja Rajendra Singh (1872–1900), was the earliest sponsor of the game and poured money into it throughout the last decade of the nineteenth century. He imported English professionals for coaching purposes along with other international experts to consult on the building of stadiums and pitch curation. Rajendra also demonstrated a liberal approach to communal and racial inclusion. Inspired by pragmatism and an indomitable desire to succeed, he selected 'a very cosmopolitan eleven at Patiala, which included Sikhs, Hindus, Muslims, Parsis and Christians, at a time when most of the elevens of British India were communal'.[6]

In 1900, Rajendra died prematurely at the age of twenty-eight and was succeeded by his nine-year-old son, Maharaja Bhupinder Singh.

Throughout my research I have met many descendants of the Patiala family. On my first research trip in 2007, I encountered one of Bhupinder's grandson who was confident that I'd heard all the stories about his grandfather's extravagance, yet he knowingly assured me that they were mild compared to the routine excesses of his great-grandfather. Hearing this, his death aged twenty-eight wasn't a surprise.

Fortunately, Bhupinder inherited his father's love for the game alongside an equally benevolent disposition, a ruthless ambition and cricket continued to flourish. Benefitting from the coaching of Yorkshire professionals including Wilfred Rhodes and George Hirst, and combined with some natural talent, he developed into an adequate cricketer, made to look better by frequently being gifted some friendly deliveries.

Bhupinder's generosity, and commitment to nurturing Indian cricket, was immense. In 1928, he donated the Ranji Trophy (a golden Grecian Urn, two foot high and valued at £500) for India's first-class domestic competition and he played a major role in the formation of the Board of Control for Cricket in India. Bhupinder was also instrumental in pioneering the planning of India's first modern cricket arena, Brabourne Stadium, in Bombay, and assisted finance of the Marylebone Cricket Club's first Indian tour in 1926/27. He followed the family tradition by recruiting talented cricket personnel into the stable at Patiala as players, administrators and coaches.

Bhupinder's heir apparent, Yadvindra Singh (the Yuvraj), also demonstrated cricket aptitude as he possessed the necessary temperament and technique. Viewed as the greatest cricketing prospect of the royal lineage, his selection was warranted unlike other cricketing royals. The Yuvraj represented his country respectably in five unofficial 'Tests' and one official Test match.

By the turn of the century, cricket had captured the imagination of other royal families including Natore, Cooch Behar and Dungarpur. They threw money at the game which enabled cricket to further prosper, resulting in the fixturing of formalised matches, the recruitment of players and the implementation of a professional business structure. The role of cultivating the game had shifted from the British army officers and bureaucrats. This transference of responsibility signified the embryonic phase of the Indian custodianship of cricket with locals beginning to occupy positions as stakeholders of the game. The motivation of the royal financiers was partially self-serving as involvement in the game enhanced their social and political reputation and boosted their popularity.

Relations between the royal families and the British became further enmeshed as benefits were bestowed on Indian royals who supported cricket. For example, the Maharaja of Patiala led the All-India team on their first ever tour of England in 1911. Despite a promising start to the tour when he made 47, his excessive indulgences and predilection for English women resulted in him only competing in two more games (scoring 0 and 10). But he did attend the Coronation in London as a special guest in 1911 and was extended an invitation to the Durbar that followed in India. He was also a special royal guest for the Jubilee in 1935 (just before our tour). Bhupinder was also Chairman and Chancellor of the Chamber of Princes from 1926 to 1931 (Ranji took over from 1931 until his death in 1933, underlining the potency of cricketing diplomacy). In 1937, Bhupinder was appointed president of the

Cricket Club of India (CCI) by the administrative board comprising Indians and British. He was rewarded for his seemingly discordant commitment to cricket, imperial rule and to an emerging nationalistic ideology. In 1936, the captain of the Indian Test team that toured England, the Maharajakumar of Vizianagaram, 'Vizzy' received a knighthood. In 1947, overwhelmed by the sentiment of newly acquired Indian sovereignty, Vizzy rejected the title to demonstrate his support of the nationalist administration. In the late nineteenth and early twentieth century, Indian cricket and the royal families were entwined entities.

The close relationship between the royal families and the British was also evident in their military support. During the Indian Mutiny in 1857, many royal households assisted the British. The Patiala family's unconditional support of Britain persisted with their assistance in subsequent conflicts including the Second Afghan war, the Boer war and they provided extensive financial support and manpower in the first and second World Wars.

In 1916, the Maharaja of Patiala played a major role on and off-field as a patron at a First World War cricket fundraiser in Bombay for Lady Willingdon's War Relief Fund. The match between Lord Willingdon's team and All India resulted in an emphatic victory to the Europeans. Tarrant played for Willingdon's team and bowled superbly, taking 15 wickets in two innings. His record in the first innings was brilliant; 19.4-7-35-9. However, cricket wasn't the primary objective as a fundraiser for the war effort followed the match. An article in the Australian *Referee* observed that 'His Highness the Maharajah Ranjitsinghji (sic) of Jamnagar put to auction the bat used by Lord Willingdon' and prefaced the sale with a speech, wherein he applauded the splendid work by the troops at the front. The bidding process was frenetic 'and it was eventually knocked down to the Maharajah of Patiala for 2500rs'. The Maharaja relished this act of his generosity being played out in a public arena with numerous dignitaries in attendance. Akin to other situations where money and power were on the agenda, the Maharaja was victorious.

The Nawabs and Maharajas gave generously to the imperial war effort in 1918 when they were at the peak of their rule yet Bhupinder's commitment of men, money and material was unsurpassed by any state in India. He provided 'floating palaces to serve as hospital ships on the Tigris and Euphrates.'[8]

Support for the war effort endured and another fundraising match took place in 1941, this time for the Second World War. However, enthusiasm for the unconditional support of the war had contracted as the public began to question the rationale of their unreserved commitment to Britain. Not least because Viceroy Lord Linlithgow had declared India, alongside Britain, was at War with Hitler's Germany without consulting a single Indian. Details of the finances accrued cannot be located however the positioning of the Yuvraj of Patiala (in a photograph from the Nisar archive) near the middle of the seated/front row suggests he played a major role in the match and, no-doubt, the fundraising effort.

Fundraising cricket match. Nissar archive

Prior to the visit of the Australian team in 1935, Bhupinder was not just promoting a harmonious relationship with the Mother Country he was already endeavouring to encourage good relations with Australia. In 1925, on behalf of the Indian princes, Bhupinder wrote to the Australian High Commissioner for Britain (ex-prime minister, Sir Joseph Cook) congratulating the Commonwealth on cementing ties between the two great outposts of the Empire.

Bhupinder was educated at Aitchinson College in Lahore, one of five Chiefs' Colleges established to transform errant and indulged little boys into venerable young men. The Chiefs' Colleges (with Mayo College colloquially known as the Eton of the East) were fashioned on the British Public-school model where team sport, specifically cricket, was prioritised to assist with the fostering of physicality and the refining of moral character.

By 1900, the British colonisation of India had reached an apogee and sovereignty would take place just shy of half a century later. Acknowledging the inevitability of self-rule, the Indian royal families questioned the legitimacy of slavishly emulating a British education model. The royal families deemed that their offspring would benefit from being educated in a culturally appropriate environment, one that did not primarily mimic and reinforce

Western values in place of their own.

Viceroy Curzon initiated restructuring the colleges' education system following complaints made by the Gaekwar of Baroda alongside numerous other royals. They were disgruntled by the syllabus and orientation of the education, along with the associated exorbitant costs, and held a protest meeting in 1902 to push for reform at the privileged schools. Initially admission to the schools was restricted to members of the royal families however, following the conference, such stipulations were relaxed, and the colleges welcomed boys from respectable Indian families providing they could finance the exercise. This move was inspired by economic pragmatism and pressure to embrace inclusivity. The education system, like cricket, was increasingly being remodelled and challenged by the locals, with the Patiala family at the helm of the renaissance.

The Patiala royals, like most of the ruling families in India, recognised a need to revise their cultural customs. Having adopted many influences of the British, they wished to pursue their own national identity. The adoption of cricket was one of many influences introduced by the British, yet it was appropriated by the locals and morphed into a slightly different version of the original and has become a major cultural icon of India (and now Pakistan and eventually Bangladesh). Bhupinder led the charge of remodelling, reforming, reinventing and in many ways challenging the foundations of the game.

Physically the Maharaja exhibited a combination of East and West influences. In a caricature from the Ryder's archive, Bhupinder is portrayed as a cultural hybrid—neck down he is depicted as a Western cricketer, immaculately attired in cricket whites and blazer. However, he also wears the distinctive Sikh symbol of the turban and a subtle, but no doubt extraordinarily expensive, drop earring in his left ear. A *tilaka* on his forehead and the style of his distinctive Sikh facial hair also identifies cultural difference.

Alongside cricket, the Patiala family had other interests and pastimes. Some hobbies pre-date British colonisation, yet not all. Despite suffering some financial difficulties throughout the 1920s, Bhupinder continued to spend lavishly on his sporting and diplomatic pursuits, as well as on women, aircraft and cars. Earlier, Rajendra was involved in the revival of equine sports including polo and some evidence suggests his death was attributed to a riding accident, yet details are scant. Bhupinder was equally committed to developing athletics and was voted president of the Indian Olympic Association in 1928. Both Patiala gentleman financed and supported wrestling as a sport that was armed with nationalistic ideals.

In 1912, Ghulam Mohammad Baksh (better known by his ring name the *Great Gama*) was invited into the Patiala enclave as Bhupinder's, well-compensated, official court wrestler after he won the world title in London in 1910 against the Polish champion Stanislaus Zbyszko. Gama, small in stature and weighing far less than his opponents, competed under the Patiala banner in highly popular bouts of national importance. These bouts were highly ritualised events. The wrestlers, dressed in brightly coloured turbans, gold armlets and costumes made from metallic thread were transported to the arena in horse drawn carriages to the beat of rousing drums which stirred the crowd up in a nationalistic frenzy.

Maharaja Bhupinder Singh. Ryder archive

Forty thousand lucky spectators attended the well-promoted re-match against Zbyszko in 1928 arranged by the Maharaja. Gama was again victorious as, unbelievably, he was in all his encounters over a fifty-year career. Post victory, Bhupinder gifted Gama a priceless pearl necklace and later that evening he paraded his star wrestler around the streets of Lahore on his favourite elephant to the delight of the massive crowd. More gifts followed and Gama was the recipient of a silver mace, an entire village and an annual stipend of Rs6000. Gama's success redefined masculinity in the decolonisation process and he became a role-model for the working-classes in the nationalist struggle. Gama attributed his success to his observance of moral self-discipline, a strict physical (uniquely Indian) training routine and a protein-rich diet containing vast quantities of almonds, meat extracts, milk and clarified butter.

Bhupinder also loved cars—his ensemble of British automobiles impressed the visiting Australian team. In 1935/36, the potentate owned 244 Rolls-Royces, matched roughly by the number of concubines in his harem. Bhupinder was also enamoured with jewellery and in 1928 he commissioned the manufacture of the Patiala necklace by Cartier. It comprised 2,930 diamonds including a De Beers diamond which at the time was the seventh largest on record. It disappeared following independence and in recent years the exquisite jewel mysteriously reappeared at a Sotheby's auction in Geneva.

During a match in Delhi between the MCC and Delhi and districts in 1933, play was suspended when a priceless accessory fell from Bhupinder's ear and couldn't be found. Members of both teams were directed to search for the earring on their hands and knees. Disgruntled teams also frequently complained about bowling to the Maharaja as his precious jewels habitually distracted them. However, the Maharaja's costume was not simply worn as a strategy to achieve victory, as Jackson observes: 'Similarly, the dress and jewellery which adorned a ruler and the trappings which surrounded him are not only works of great intrinsic beauty and worth, but more fundamentally are symbolic of the power, status and identity of the ruler'.[9]

Bhupinder's also loved shooting and hunting—spending hours clamouring across his vast country estates to track down and kill wildlife. When he tired, he enlisted the assistance of a Rolls-Royce, decorated with an interior of rose-coloured velvet that was specially designed for the purpose.

One possibly apocryphal story, of which there are many, has become part of folklore. A Rolls-Royce salesman in England rebuffed the Maharaja's desire to purchase a pre-release automobile under the presumption that he wouldn't have the finances. Incensed, when the model became available on the open market, the Maharaja responded by purchasing the fleet, which he modified and used as rubbish trucks in Patiala. He didn't forgive easily and never forgot.

Narratives regarding Bhupinder's profligacies, eccentricities and lavish lifestyle choices proliferated in the popular press. Jaiwant Paul in his 2003 coffee table book describes Bhupinder's voyage to London where he and his entourage of fifty occupied 100 rooms in the Savoy Hotel. It was not uncommon for him to travel with 200 items of luggage, including a silver bathtub for his exclusive use. Hendry's estimation in his manuscript differed as he states that the Maharaja 'had 500 concubines and took 80 to London when attending the King's Jubilee. His suite occupied the whole top floor of the Savoy Hotel'. The numerical accuracy is unimportant, but the presence of the anecdotes demonstrates a Western fascination in Bhupinder's display of extravagance. The public was simultaneously enthralled yet somewhat repulsed by Bhupinder's display of Oriental immoderation.

During a European holiday, in 1935 (prior to the Australian tour), the Maharaja requested a meeting with the German chancellor, Adolf Hitler. Despite initial knock-backs, he was eventually granted ten to fifteen minutes of the Führer's time. It was instant attraction and the two spent three days deep in conversation. At the end of the visit, Hitler gifted the Maharaja a Maybach, a rare and expensive ultra-luxury car. Details regarding the meeting between Hitler and the Maharaja differ in various recounts, however a photograph survives of the two together that Hitler presented to the Indian with a personal dedication which verifies a degree of authenticity of the event.

The politics of both regimes followed similar themes of autonomy however the fundamental philosophical differences were evident. His initiating contact with Hitler (and simultaneously Mussolini) reveals that Bhupinder was intrigued by political machinations. It also signalled his independence from Britain, alongside an aristocratic fascination with fascism itself similar to the contested experience of Edward VIII. By 1935, Hitler had begun to rearm, breaking some of the provisions of the Treaty of Versailles and later in the year he introduced the Nuremberg Laws which declared his anti-Semitic intents. It would have been disadvantageous for Bhupinder's curiosity about the fascist elite to be publicised in British circles as public sentiment was already heralding the malevolence of Hitler's regime. However, seemingly Bhupinder was unperturbed by how others perceived him.

As the *Chitral* manoeuvred into Indian waters, the team knew significantly more about Indian culture, politics and sport. They were also reassured by their growing knowledge of the Patiala family and their significant commitment to cricket in India. Tarrant as tutor on Indian matters was invaluable and without him the team would have had to rely on the misinformation and rumour that circulated in interwar Australia which really just functioned to promote the imperial agenda.

[1] *Albury Banner and Wodonga Express* July 22, 1938.
[2] *Cricket beyond the Bazaar*, 1990, 90.
[3] Pandey 1969, 4.
[4] *Albury Banner and Wodonga Express* July 22, 1938.
[5] 2002, 670.
[6] Cashman 1980, 25.
[7] March 1, 1916.
[8] *Laverton Mercury* August 30, 1919.
[9] 2009, 426.

8 'BON-BOMBAY'

'Welcomed by the Princes at Picturesque Bombay'[1]

The team awoke dishevelled, bleary-eyed and feeling rather worse for wear. They hurriedly readied themselves for the 7.30am welcome on the *Chitral's* deck. Tom felt especially humiliated, self-conscious and sheepish as he ambled along the corridor in his crumpled dinner suit. A throng of cricket fans and the media jostled to be part of the ceremony. Ryder informed a journalist that the team had travelled well, were fit and in good health and were looking forward to shooting some game. Turning his attention to the task at hand, the captain also promised that they were exceedingly eager to get on the pitch and to meet the Indian opposition especially the big stars Major C.K Nayudu, Vijay Merchant and Lala Amarnath. In reply, the scribe told the captain of rumours circulating that the Indian board had decided that the Nawab of Pataudi would captain the Indian team in the unofficial 'Test' encounters. It was news to Ryder and indicative that all wasn't happy in the world of Indian cricket.

The thought of playing cricket made Tom feel nauseous and he was conscious that a miasma emanated from him like a stale bacchanalian aura. It mingled with the distinct melange of Indian odours that had already crept over the rails of the *Chitral*. They were unknown scents to Tom yet later on the tour he would be able to identify them as patchouli oil, henna and turmeric. Weary and hungry, he had fleeting recollections of challenging Lisle Nagel to a fistfight and sculling games with Fred Mair. It was all rather unpleasant and possibly not a great way to start the tour, he acknowledged.

Historically, Tom's antics the previous night were not atypical. Narratives about alcohol excess and travel are embodied in Australian cricket culture typified by Shane Warne, Doug Walters and David Boon and tales of their unbridled, sometimes epic, consumption of beer. Folklore reveals that 'Boonie' won the competition of consumption on a flight from Sydney to London. The diminutive batsman downed fifty-two cans on the close to day-long flight. And it's not just a recent phenomenon as cricketers have always partaken in a drink or three. Tom Wills, a prominent early Australian cricketer and one of the game's forefathers, committed suicide in the throes of alcohol withdrawal in 1880.

The *mise-en-scène* in Bombay was magnificent and helped wake the cricketers. It was early on an Autumn morning, yet the sun already had a savage kick. The crystal-clear water reflected the picture-perfect arch of the Gateway of India. I'm sure the cricketers recalled Kipling's *Kim*: a 'diamond-bright dawn woke men and crow and bullocks'. *Kim*, first published in 1901, regularly featured on the Australian school syllabus and assisted in building the cricketers' understanding of India and her position in the Empire. The team arrived armed with a robust sense of imperial entitlement. I'm unsure if they were aware of the extent that these opinions would be challenged over the ensuing months.

Tom looked out over the Gateway of India and onto a crowded scene of Indian colour and chaos. It was a teeming metropolis, a scene of frenzied activity: Merchants set up shop; some sold sorcery amongst other tourist knick-knacks. A sea of outstretched, dark skinny arms implored the pedestrian traffic to gift alms. Tourists rushed by—they didn't want to be caught gaping. The mayhem and desperation shocked my uncle Tom. He hoped he could cope when he was down there amongst it. In the distance he was happy to see the grand Taj Mahal hotel recognisable by its distinct turrets and arches.

Tom was running slightly late and as he rounded the corner of the *Chitral's* passageway he observed that a crowd had already gathered on the deck. The majority of the cricketers wore last night's dinner suits (goodness knows how the few lucky ones had retrieved their civvies) which contrasted with the sea of colourful turbans and bejewelled metallic tunics.

He could see Frank Tarrant doing what Frank Tarrant did best.

Frank greeted the local dignitaries with a kiss, an embrace and a compliment. Demonstrating the perfect balance of familiarity and respect, he made each person feel special. Gifts were exchanged. Tom could hear exclamations of affection, shrill laughter and raucous backslapping. He could see delight on the faces of everyone involved with the reunion. Frank had lost the anxiety that, at times, accompanied him on the trip. Completely at ease with these people, he was delighted to be back amongst them. Frank spent extra time with one exceptionally tall, immaculately dressed gentleman and presented him with the most extravagantly wrapped gift. Tom wasn't sure but he thought he could see Frank bow. Tom wasn't used to seeing Frank behaving so humbly. The two spoke at length and the Indian passed a scrolled document, secured with a golden ribbon, to the team manager. Tom suspected this man may be the Maharaja yet as the cricketer neared the group, he realised he was too young to be the financier. Frank beckoned Tom and introduced him as 'his star fast bowler'. Tom really wished that Frank would stop bragging about his abilities. However, he realised that he'd have to get used to it.

The tall gentleman was the Maharaja's son, and the team was instructed to address him as the Yuvraj. The crowd was silent, and all eyes were fixed on him as he conducted the welcome ceremony. He apologised that his father had been detained on business and couldn't be present. The Yuvraj's cultivated English accent and elegant cadence surprised Tom – it reeked of privilege. Tom had thought that the Indian would sound more foreign. The Yuvraj directed Frank Tarrant to read aloud the letter written by his father. Frank untied the gold ribbon and cleared his throat; he spoke of the significance of the tour and the merging of the dominion and the colony not just on the field but in a political context as well. He spoke of the great and glorious game of cricket. The Australian cricketers swelled with a sense of importance. The revelry of the previous evening was lost to the solemnity of the welcome. An official surreptitiously slipped Jack Ryder an envelope and instructed him to read it later.

The Yuvraj conducted the official welcome with great aplomb. He took his social obligations seriously in his role of heir apparent. A staff member placed a garland around the cricketers' necks as the Yuvraj introduced them and summarised their successes – not just as cricketers but also as exemplary gentleman. He, or more likely one of his many mignons, had done significant research. The Yuvraj welcomed Macartney back to the centre stage after years of hiatus. The royal was aware that a good speech required a little humour and joked with Morrisby that whilst he would miss Tasmanian apples, he would fall in love with the guavas and pomegranates that India was so famous for. The jewels on his turban sparkled as he commiserated with Tom Leather that he would desperately miss my great aunt as they have recently become engaged, yet he hoped that cricket, an exhilarating social schedule and the glamour of India would compensate.

The ceremony extended well into the morning. The Australians, tired from the arduous journey and the previous night's revelry, realised that they would have to become accustomed to long-winded official functions with an emphasis on pomp, protocol, formality and, maybe a little bit of fraud too.

In attendance was the Nawab of Bhopal who was the president of the Indian Board of Control, the board's secretary Anthony de Mello, a few Sikh royals and various other dignitaries. Each was introduced and invited to the podium to speak. Absent was Dr Kanga who had just resigned from, or was rather strongly coerced to vacate, his position on the Indian cricket board. Newspaper articles observed that his departure had caused a scandal and alluded to it being attributed to 'princely interference'. Edward Docker's publication *History of Indian Cricket* extrapolates that Dr Kanga was upset that the selection of captain to tour England later in 1936 was seemingly restricted to someone whose only real qualification was 'his birth' as Vizzy was soon to be named. Dr Kanga had also grumbled about the Yuvraj being selected as captain during the Australian tour. However, I guess it helped that his father was financing the entire venture and, to be fair, the Yuvraj did demonstrate some talent unlike many other royals. Despite cricket in India aspiring to abide by a meritocratic formula, evidence like this suggests that it still privileged the elite.

Numerous other cricket bureaucrats were in attendance probably due to the fact that they had been urgently called to Bombay to discuss the resignation of Dr Kanga. The Australian cricketers were oblivious to the internal structures and political machinations of Indian cricket, however

Frank Tarrant quietly observed the social exchange and noted who was present and who wasn't. Frank didn't read too much into the Maharaja's absence yet knew that something very important must have kept him away.

Tarrant later described the arrival on Indian soil as a 'riotous reception' and introduced the tour as an event to be lionised.[2] He always portrayed his tour in the most positive light and gloated that a team of dignitaries including the Yuvraj had travelled 1200 miles to attend, press representatives from 'all parts of India' and at least a '1000 cricket enthusiasts' greeted the team. It's difficult to imagine that the *Chitral's* deck could accommodate such a gaggle, but it is nonetheless interesting to have Tarrant's perspective.

Ron Oxenham instantly admired the Yuvraj and described him as handsome, natural and 'indeed a very likeable chap'.[3] The Queenslander felt honoured that the royal had travelled all the previous day to attend the function and following the formalities he would immediately retrace his steps.

After the function, the team faced a battery of cameras. Uncle Tom had never been photographed so much. The cricketers descended the gangplank and were instantly immersed into a typical Indian landscape of rickshaw ranks and paan-stands. A persistent snake charmer tried to lure the tourists into his act. Tom, typical of a Scottish emigree, had a morbid fear of snakes so rebuffed the challenge. Hendry was less hesitant and was actually rather seduced by the display. He observed that the 'deadly cobras have skins like velvet'. Despite the close proximity to the Taj, cars rescued the players from their encounter with the reptiles and ferried them to their accommodation for the next three days.

The first stop was the bar, and the cricketers enjoyed a few bottles of champagne with Prince Pratapsinhji. Seemingly it was an augury of things to come as sparkling wine was drunk to symbolise friendship, affluence and celebration.

The Australian cricketers settled into their rooms at the legendary Taj. Despite being eager to start exploring, Oscar Bill decided he'd make a start on his first column from India for the *Sydney Mail*. It was his first time in the Orient and indeed his first time out of Australia. It was also the first time that he'd agreed to a journalism contract and as a remunerated position, he felt that he should take the responsibility seriously. He sat at the writing bureau in his bedroom and jotted down some notes in his journal. The windows of his room overlooked a magnificent vista. Beyond the chaotic scene of industry and commerce and commuters, the magnificent harbour glimmered, and a flotilla of boats bobbed on the horizon, just like bath toys. The comfort of Bill's wood-panelled room removed him from the outside world and gave him an overwhelming sense of security which considering the terrorist attacks on the hotel over seventy years later now seems rather ironic. He knew it was noisy outside yet the only sound in his room was the crackle as he turned the pages of his journal and the mechanical murmur of the fountainpen as it glided over the paper.

The team's arrival on Indian soil fulfilled the expectations of European's first encounters with the East yet Bill didn't want to bore his readers with observations regarding the heat, the chaos and the odour of the place. He was keen to find beauty in this foreign setting. Bill was surprised how quickly he produced the column and at the end he enticingly added *To be Continued.* He was happy with that. *The Sydney Mail* editor would add his own touches and prefaced Bill's article this way: 'Wendell Bill is writing a story of the Australian's tour for the "Sydney Mail". Obviously the glamour of India has appealed to him, his descriptive touches revealing all the boyish enthusiasm of a youth on his first contact with the enchanted East'. I found it interesting that Bill's appeal was described as boyish considering he was twenty-five years of age. Maybe the editor couldn't believe that a mature mind would find India appealing.

Ron Oxenham, greatly taken by the Taj, gloated 'And what a hotel'. He raved about the facilities in his bedroom which included 'a telephone, writing desk, bathroom, and even an electric clock'. The grandeur of the dining room impressed him, and equally the meals which he described as delicious. Considering the players' latter criticism of the food in India this was surprising.

Taj Mahal hotel, Bombay. 1935_36. Leather archive

Indeed, all the cricketers were pretty awestruck by the five-hundred-bedroom hotel that opened in 1903. Hendry maintained that the hotel was 'known throughout the world as the best in India'. Morrisby, also full of praise, wrote to his parents; 'We stayed at the Taj Mahal Hotel in Bombay–it is the most wonderful building, easily twice the size of any hotel in Australia'. Bill, likewise, was impressed and remarked, 'Soon we found ourselves whisked off through cheering crowds to the famous Taj Mahal Hotel, where we found relief from the heat in enormous ice-cooled rooms'.[4] A month later, Bill hadn't forgotten the comfort of the luxurious facility and wrote, 'It was very pleasant staying at the Taj Mahal Hotel, where ice-cooled dining and dancing rooms made it impossible for one to get hot'.[5] It was the players' first encounter with air-conditioning and they were amazed by its efficiency.

Jack Ryder lay on his bed and opened the envelope he'd been handed at the welcome ceremony. It contained a one-page typed letter on Moti Bagh Palace letterhead – identifiable by the Patiala coat of arms (resplendent with a lion, a tiger and an elephant) on the right-hand top corner. It read:

> Dear Mr. Ryder,
> I extend to you and other members of my Australian team, a most hearty welcome to India. It would have given me great pleasure to receive you all, at the gateway of India, but unfortunately, my engagements made some time ago do not permit my getting away from Patiala at present and I am therefore sending my Yuvraj (heir-apparent) to receive and welcome you on my behalf. I need hardly assure you that the whole of India will welcome you and is looking forward to a really first class display of cricket this season. I wish you the best of luck and a very happy sojourn in India and shall be glad to meet you at the earliest possible opportunity.

The letter reinforced the importance of the journey and, as he read it, Ryder's anxiety about the task at hand heightened. The letter reinforced the Maharaja's significant investment in, not just the team but, the whole venture. Seemingly, tour success was not just crucial for the success of cricket in India but the wider political landscape. Ryder was past his best playing days and the financial recompense was exceedingly handy, yet he hadn't really invested too much thought into the geopolitical significance of the tour.

Armed with callow enthusiasm, Tom Leather and Ron Morrisby wandered around the streets that surrounded the hotel as revealed by a photograph. I'm sure they didn't venture too far. The snap initially isn't that fascinating as it looks like a routine tourist image, yet it subtly hints at the uneasy position of the cricketers within the colonial landscape. The composition of the image emphasises the disassociation of the cricketers from the symbolic architectural façade. The hotel dwarfs the young men in a somewhat foreboding fashion. Typical of novice travellers in a foreign environment, they simultaneously exhibit bravado and hesitation. Tom's fingers firmly wrap-around Ron's upper-arm. I'm sure the physical contact was intended to reassure the younger man, yet the grip looks like it could also hurt. Surely the young men felt a sense of freedom associated with being away from home and removed from the claustrophobia of middle-class Australia, yet they demonstrate ambivalence. A wall functions as a barrier and separates the duo from the hotel grounds behind them. Despite their favourable impressions of the hotel, maybe they can never assimilate with what the Taj represents as they neither belong to the ruling colonial class nor can they culturally align with the colonised masses. I sincerely hope that they were experiencing the joy of travel when the shutter was fired ...yet I'm really not too sure.

Ron and Tom wear suits reflecting the formality and fashion of the era. Ron looks slightly awkward in his light-coloured, double-breasted ensemble. It drapes off his elfin body and I'm reminded of how my sister and I would hang paper dresses on paper dolls. Maybe it's an older-cousin's cast-off – possibly borrowed at the last minute, I imagine. Other photographs reveal that he wore the suit often. Seemingly, he didn't have the option of another one to choose from.

Ron Morrisby and Tom Leather in front of the Taj Mahal hotel, Bombay. Leather archive

Later that afternoon the team convened at the Parsi Cricket Club. Despite feeling fatigued, they were keen to fit in some cricket practice and test out the local conditions. Macartney described the weather as 'exacting' yet it didn't dampen the team's excitement as they donned their whites.[6] Bill estimates that 5000 locals attended the training session (images suggest that Bill overestimated the crowd), yet he noted that the British were noticeably absent. It's remarkable to think that the rag-tag team of cricketers was capable of drawing such a crowd and equally that the colonisers (armed with a self-entitled belief that cricket was an English game) took no interest in the proceedings.

Bill boasted that the cricket fans 'crowded round our nets like bees. It was a miracle that many were not killed or seriously injured, as they stood about seven deep no more than ten yards from our batsmen, despite our warnings as to the danger. Those in front were powerless to evade hard hits, and we all declared afterwards that Indians must be made of steel, as they took many cracks without retreating a yard'.[7] Interestingly, already on day one of the tour, the Australians were admiring the strength and physical resilience of the Indian public, yet their foolishness was also noted. This simultaneously both defied and complied with the reputation of the Asiatic as perpetuated by the West. I'm sure the visiting team would not have realised that their understanding of racial identity would be challenged so soon.

Bombay practice session. 1935. Ryder archive

The cricketers were amazed how the crowd at the cricket matches and in the public arena intuitively congregated into communal and hierarchical groups. Despite adhering to a vastly different set of rules and customs the various communities seemed to cohabit independently, yet functionally and successfully, alongside each other. Unlike racial and cultural codes that defined sport globally, the attitude in India seemed comparatively inclusive and progressive. On the boat, Frank Tarrant had explained to the cricketers that the Bombay cricket competition comprised teams formed on communal lines, each with their own home ground and clubhouse where members could observe their unique set of customs and rules. I'm sure they thought that although, to an extent, Australian society was based on a sectarian divide yet it was nothing like this.

The Parsi gymkhana was a typical colonial building constructed in the boom years around the mid-to-late nineteenth century. In their tour reportage, the Australian tourists describe its impressive facilities. Oxenham immediately felt at-ease with the Parsi community and observed that they were well educated, well-spoken and, typical of a touring sportsman, he noted that the women were especially captivating. The Parsi community had acquired significant wealth due to their ambition, vigorous work ethic and entrepreneurial ways. The Parsi's slightly lighter-coloured skin was used as a feature of assimilation with the British. Historically, the Parsi community had always keenly followed cricket and used it to facilitate leverage in commercial transactions with the British. Indeed, exclusively Parsi teams were the first cricket tourists to depart Indian shores in 1886 and 1888. A tour to Australia in 1893 was touted (yet didn't eventuate). Following their time in the nets, the Australian team adjourned to the lawn surrounding the Parsi clubhouse. They relaxed on garden chairs in the picturesque surrounds under the glorious afternoon sun with drinks in hand.

Parsi rituals intrigued the Australians. In fact, most Western tourist reportage pertaining to India in the early twentieth century observe a fascination with Parsi customs. Bill and Oxenham wrote about Parsi funeral rites, which they found macabre, gruesome and baffling. Devotees believed that cremation or burial of the deceased polluted nature, so following death; the body was placed on a purpose-built structure, known as the Tower of Silence. The corpse was left exposed to be eaten by vultures, kites and crows. Even now, tourist guides schedule a visit to the Tower of Silence as a point of cultural intrigue.

The following afternoon the Australian tourists visited the Muslim Gymkhana. The players were amazed how the communal gymkhanas were positioned in such close proximity. Despite their fierce on field sporting competitiveness and broader philosophical enmity they seemingly demonstrated reciprocity and encouraged pragmatic communal tolerance.

Crowd at the Muslim Gymkhana. 1935. Ryder archive

A photograph from the Ryder archive depicts the afternoon spent at the Muslim Gymkhana, which illustrates the hierarchical nature of 1930s Indian cultural life. High-ranking members of the club and the Australian team are enclosed in a private inner sanctum furnished with wicker chairs, potted plants and crucially some space to move. Languishing in their comfortable chairs, the cricketers are surrounded by the trappings of decadence and luxury. Members of the club orbit around them; keen to be in close proximity with the famous Australian cricketers yet reluctant to intrude. A group of cricketers stand. These are active participants: the tour manager thrusts his arm across numerous people in the crowd to shake an available hand. His broad smile is infectious – he loves this, he loves his role. Captain Jack Ryder and his deputy Alexander are all smiles and stand alongside Tarrant. Bert Tarrant dressed identically to his father (both in homburgs and dark suits), sneaks into the top tier group – cigarette in hand and slightly slouched with a look of grim determination.

Surrounding the comparative calm of the centre stage is a crowd of hundreds or maybe even thousands; mainly wearing white robes with light or dark *taqiyahs*. Patient children queue up and clamour to be involved: pushing their bodies into an invisible barrier that separates them from the cricketers. The older cricket devotees form a wall behind their younger counterparts.

Some stand on tiptoes desperate to get a glimpse of the Australian cricket stars. All eyes are firmly fixed on the team who strangely seem oblivious to the attention.

Each gymkhana ground shared the same spatial dimensions and layout despite having their own vastly distinctive features. They looked like three postage stamps pasted in a row which reminds me of the Melbourne CBD layout with a rigid commitment to symmetry and impartiality. Seemingly, the division of land was executed by an egalitarian draftsperson committed to the concept of communal parity. No mention is made of the players visiting the Hindu Gymkhana, yet I'm confident they did – led by Frank Tarrant's firm commitment to inclusion. The players didn't demonstrate prejudice towards one communal group over another and, despite their avid intrigue, were never demonstratively critical of any cultural custom however unfathomable. I always wonder if Tarrant's philosophies were legitimate or whether he was just a savvy operator who acknowledged the benefits of impartiality. I guess his even-handed embrace was driven by the Maharaja who demonstrated an acceptance of cultural inclusivity and even at times orchestrated the marriage of his daughters to non-Sikhs as he recognised the potential benefits from mixed marriages.

By all accounts it was a wonderful welcome to India and Bill observed, 'Before leaving home we felt certain that we would be well received and well treated in India, but never in our wildest dreams did we imagine that such receptions and such pomp and splendour would be "turned on" for our benefit'.

Despite Bill's enthusiasm about the team's welcome, it had been an exhausting and culturally challenging few days. Alcohol was being downed at a rapid pace and its consumption was already taking its toll. Following dinner, on their final night in Bombay, Alexander and Nagel insisted that the team have 'one last' nightcap following catching a cabaret show at the Taj. Some of the senior boys knew their limitations and declined the offer. They really just wanted to return to their rooms and lay their heavy heads on fine-quality linen. Possibly they needed some quiet time to digest their experiences and to emotionally prepare for what may lay ahead.

---

[1] Oxenham November 18, 1935.

[2] Tarrant scrapbook 1918–51.

[3] November 18, 1935.

[4] December 11, 1935.

[5] January 8, 1935.

[6] *Newcastle Morning Herald and Miners' Advocate* November 19, 1935.

[7] *Sydney Mail* December 11, 1935.

9 WHO WOULDN'T BE A CRICKETER?

It was surprisingly cold at Victoria Terminus on the evening of departure. Tarrant suggested that a chai from a *chaiwallah* might be in order—the players cupped their vessels in an attempt to warm their hands. The steam rising from the boiling brew produced a fine film of moisture on their cheeks.

Construction of the railway station finished in 1888, after a build of almost a decade. Yet despite all endeavours it wasn't completed in time to commemorate the Golden Jubilee of Queen Victoria in 1887. The cricketers were impressed by the grandeur of the massive Italianate Gothic structure with its soaring spires, ornamental arches, ribbed vaulting, gilt work, turrets, domes and gables. Design elements included monkey gargoyles, sculpted elephants and rampart lions in sentinel. However, alongside its aesthetic features, it was also an engineering marvel and accommodated millions of daily commuters. At the time of its construction, it was the largest train station in the world. It demonstrated a perfect combination of imperial ideology, local craftsmanship and the exuberant imagination of unbridled Victorian architectural dreams buttressed by a seemingly endless supply of funds.

The station ambiance conformed to the cliché reputation of India and was abuzz with commuters, noise, colour, chaos and exotic aroma. Trains shunted in and out of platforms every few seconds. It was a logistical nightmare yet somehow it seemed to function: the timetable ran like clockwork which epitomised the regularity and uniformity of the modern colonial state and was proof of British mastery.

The cricketers were waiting for the train to depart for Rajkot on the first leg of their 13,000-mile journey across India. Despite having enjoyed their few days in Bombay they were keen to get moving. The Indian hospitality had been beyond belief, but they were eager to play some cricket.

In the early planning stages, the Maharaja had proposed that the team would journey around the country by aeroplane. It was a grandiose plan and demonstrative of the luxury of the tour. Globally, airline travel was in its infancy and none of the cricketers had been on a plane before and they were excited yet nervous by the prospect of it. Quotes for fares were tallied and, in the end, even the generous and extravagant Maharaja thought the price was too exorbitant. The journey would have to be undertaken by rail.

The cricketers had been appointed Muslim and Hindu bearers who belonged to the Dalit caste of both communities. They would accompany the cricketers throughout the trip. Their role was to function as manservants and advisers yet despite initial wariness and defying racial protocol they, in time, doubled as friends and confidants. The bearers were responsible for transporting the luggage and had packed the cricketers' portable bedding into trunks and loaded all their possessions on to the train. Despite the bearers mostly being small in stature, they were amazingly strong and accomplished the feat hastily and effortlessly. They employed a unique technique of balancing the baggage using almost every muscle of their bodies and managed to carry multiple pieces. The cricketers looked on in awe and marvelled at their speed and strength. Ryder, in a letter to his wife, recounted the process. He imagined that his wife would be impressed by this unusual arrangement as evidence of the servitude of the staff and the cricketer's importance. The Maharaja endeavoured to provide the team with luxury that far exceeded what they had previously experienced and would not be reproduced again on a cricket tour to India for many decades, or maybe ever.

Hendry remarked that the players treated the bearers well and, 'whenever possible', they would give them 'fruit or lollies'. Hendry's manuscript highlights the democratic nature of the tour and he gloated that the cricketers treated the bearers 'in a way they had never experienced before'. Bryant was less egalitarian and observed the servility of the staff noting that they did everything for the team and 'in fact almost thought for' us. He then cheekily added, 'I think I shall bring one home with me'.[1] The bearers were not opposed to the idea and Lalla, Hendry's bearer, 'begged to be taken back' to Australia with them and promised that he would eternally be their 'loyal servant'.

Evidence suggests that the Australian players, being largely egalitarian and unaccustomed to domestic staff, treated their assistants with respect despite unconscious pressure existing from the British Raj to be vigilant in adhering to the rigid social and racial hierarchy which positioned the staff in a role of complete servility. In his memoire, Hendry suspects that most of the bearers were tuberculosis sufferers. Hendry observes the Australian's initial uncertainty about the domestic staff yet, overall, they applauded their services. 'What wonderful servants they were too–all the tales about these Indians being thieves did not apply to our lot. No one lost a rupee, even though like all Australians, we used to empty our pockets of money and leave it on the dressing tables with our watches etc. before retiring'. Early on the trip, Oxenham was a little more circumspect and he noted the team's discomfort with the omnipresent staff and wrote; 'It was the most amusing thing in the world to watch some of the team being dressed by their boys for the first morning or two'.[2] Seemingly, overtime, they grew accustomed to the deferential and close attention they received from the bearers.

Ryder titled this image 'Outside the Tent with Servant at Indore'. Ryder archive.

It was time to board the train, yet Alexander and Nagel couldn't be found. Tarrant ran up and down the platform frantically checking to see if the duo had boarded the wrong cabin. They'd celebrated enthusiastically the previous evening, disobeyed curfew and would miss the train. They'd gone AWOL and god knows where they were—Tarrant was furious as it reflected badly on his ability to manage the team. It also wasn't a good start for the missing pair. The captain of the train intervened and suggested that he would wait for the two stragglers, but Tarrant felt that the duo's racial identity and sporting fame should not disrupt the highly regimented rail system. So instead, they were left to catch the slow train the following morning as punishment for insubordination. Tarrant felt that the visitors should adhere to team rules and in no way should they receive preferential treatment. The bearers had already packed their luggage aboard the train and so the tardy cricketers were left to spend an uncomfortable night in Bombay. The duo complained about being left without a skerrick of clothes, yet they knew that they were in the wrong. Tour rules were broken and Tarrant, as gamekeeper, felt that discipline was necessary to control the team and to reaffirm his position of hegemony. Tarrant hadn't always been so authoritarian and as a younger man had finessed the art of bending societal rules. He was a little surprised that he'd become such an old stickler but knew it was all for the sake of team harmony and tour success.

The first train journey on Indian soil was one to remember. Travelling 450 miles to Rajkot on the Karthia Peninsula railway the players were treated to every conceivable comfort and convenience. They couldn't believe the train's luxurious facilities; the bathrooms even had showers which was a first for the Australians. Oxenham lodged in a carriage with Ironmonger and he joked that it was appropriate as they were both Queensland born and stated 'It was particularly appropriate that the pair of us should be together—It gives us an opportunity to recall memories of so many other trips that we might have had together had we been good-looking enough to tickle the fancy of the Australian selectors!'[3] Obviously it was a sore point, yet in reality it had nothing to do with lacking good looks but rather that the social idiosyncrasies of cricket selection resulted in their previous non-selection.

Bryant and Morrisby on board a train. 1935_36. Alexander archive

The team was surprised by how different the trains were to the ones at home. Macartney described their passenger train as the longest one he had ever seen and counted twenty coaches pulled by one locomotive. He was also surprised that there wasn't a corridor that connected the coaches. So, when the cricketers, who slept in carriages with two bunks, wanted to visit a teammate's carriages they would have to wait until the train stopped at a station and then they'd make a run for it! They weren't prepared to clamber along the train's roof as many of the locals did. Macartney had watched the bearers do it when they assembled the player's bedding and there was definitely an art to it. Mealtimes had to coincide with stopping at a station as the cricketers would make a quick dash for the dining car.

Despite the comfort of the train, this was the first of many tedious long slow journeys. Midway, the cricketers had to change trains to a narrow-gauge railway. Individual states had incompatible rail lines; some argue that this was orchestrated by the British as a means of control. The train eventually pulled into Rajkot nineteen hours later. It did however seem much longer to the already travel-weary cricketers. It wasn't just exhaustion that afflicted the Australians as Bill's December 18 article also noted how culturally confronting the journey had been: 'Many queer sights of Indian life were seen en route—and never have I seen such crowded carriages as this of the third class. People were just herded together like cattle'.

In Rajkot, the team was accommodated in private residences as the organising committee didn't deem the city to have suitable European-style hotels and the Maharaja didn't wish to inflict any substandard conditions on the cricketers. Macartney was billeted with Sir and Lady Latimer at *The Residency* and he bragged that the house was like a palace and that his host 'killed him with kindness'. According to the vice-captain, Sir Latimer was the 'number One man in the state'.[4] Macartney's only complaint was the late nights that he was encouraged to keep as he surmised that they were not conducive to cricket success.

Rajkot signified the real start of the tour as the team commenced their first game on Indian soil. The blistering heat made play difficult and the boys grumbled that the sun was 'furnace-like'.[5] An official from the cricket club assured them that the oppressive weather was atypical for November and promised that it wouldn't last.

The cricketers were having to acclimatise quickly to Indian culture, Indian weather and to the peculiarities of Indian cricket. Bill found the coir matting surface of the wicket especially problematic. He observed: 'I have never seen a wicket so uncertain. Some deliveries rose head-high from good length, some kept down; but the way fast bowlers could break the ball was a revelation, and caused our batsman much concern'.[6] Bill also complained about the 'worst umpiring imaginable'. He claimed: 'Batsman who were obviously out were given not out—and some who were obviously not out were given out'. It was something they would have to get used to as later on the tour another Bill article, published on January 8, even refers to a deaf umpire who officiated with great difficulty.

The players appreciated the local's passion for cricket. Bill's column refers to the 'brown-skinned crowd' and he described them as 'frightfully enthusiastic'; 'terrific howls of delight rent the air when our wickets tumbled'. Numerous royals attended the match, and the Australian team was impressed by their presence and noted that they responded to the cricket in a comparatively sedate manner. Initially the visitors were rather awestruck yet soon got used to being watched by men in bejewelled turbans. Social hierarchy dictated that someone of high rank always captained a local team and in Rajkot the available gent was the Chief of Mandavader otherwise known by his real name: Khan Shri Culammoinuddinkhan. Of course, attempting to pronounce his name caused great hilarity.

The visitors easily won their first game on Indian soil despite the handicap of the 'blinding glare'.[7]

The next stop was Jamnagar which was a fifty-mile journey by train. It was a pleasant and short journey. The visitors were particularly excited to visit the princely state and to meet the royal family, as Jamnagar had a rich cricket history and was the ancestral home of the cricketing great Ranjitsinjhi. The team imagined this would be a highlight of the tour and they were not disappointed.

Arrival at Jamnagar. November 1935. Leather archive

They were welcomed by the Jam Sahib Digvijaysinhji, the nephew of Ranji, at an official ceremony in the station-master's office at the train station. Hendry was instantly impressed by the refined gentleman; 'quiet, kind and warm—Oxford of course—speaking beautifully'.[8] The royal had just returned a few hours earlier from his honeymoon in Europe yet was eager to meet the Australian cricketers. Of course, the visitors sniggered about how many marriages he may have had yet they were chuffed that the Jam Sahib prioritised the meeting. Leather's archive includes a very blurry photograph where the Jam Sahib is out of focus in the foreground and almost unrecognisable. The unidentified photographer seemingly knew nothing about depth of field. I'm surprised the poor-quality photograph made it into Tom's collection, yet I guess my great-uncle valued the experience (and the Jam Sahib) and wanted to forever remember the occasion. Even showing the archive to Indian cricket aficionados over eighty-years later, it's an image that attracts a lot of interest.

The official welcome could be viewed as makeshift, yet Bill set the record straight and described it as 'a magnificent welcome' that 'clean took our breath away'.[9] Photographs reveal that splendidly dressed military escorted the royal through the crowded throng on the platform. The cricketers were realising that despite the seeming chaos of India there was order within the disorder. The cricketers initially thought the horde had turned out to see them but then realised the popularity of the Jam Sahib as he was being mobbed by his people.

Photographs reveals that the team scrubbed up rather well in their best clothes. Everyone looked polished and shipshape in their day suits. Bryant commenced the day wearing a tie, yet images reveal that it soon found its way into his pocket. I imagine that Frank Tarrant wouldn't have been impressed. Eva Tarrant took extra care with her appearance and wore a modern black and white spotted sundress with a fashionable sunhat worn at a jaunty angle. In many images she dresses in dowdy fashion and is always sensibly shod yet in Jamnagar she looks chic and stylish. In contrast to the western dress of the tourists, the Jam Sahib wears a striking light-coloured top that would now be described as a Nehru jacket yet in the 1930s it was a variation of what was called a Jodhpuri suit.

Arrival with Jam Sahib Digvijaysinhji in Jamnagar (Leather incorrectly captioned the Jam Sahib as Ranji's brother but it was his nephew). November 1935. Leather archive

Arrival scene at Jamangar. November 1935. Leather archive

Bill, in his December 18 column, noted of the reception: 'A prince could not have been welcomed with more ceremony—red carpets were down, garlands of beautiful flowers were thrown around our necks, many bouquets were presented to us, and accompanied by Prince Pratapsinhji, nephew of the world-famous Ranjitsinhji, we drove off to the palace through a regiment of horse guards'. The procession of golden carriages wound their way around the streets of the city which were lined by devotees, estimated at 30,000, desperate to get a glimpse of the top-brass and the visiting cricketers. The team followed the carriages in convertible cars: Nagel, Ellis, Alexander and Bryant travelled together, and one imagines that conversation involved devising the social schedule with an objective of maximum pleasure as these four were quickly gaining a reputation as being the party boys on tour.

Arrival scene at Jamangar. November 1935. Leather archive

Bryant, Alexander, Nagel and Ellis arrive in style at the palace in Jamnagar. November 1935. Alexander archive

The players were accommodated in facilities built for the Viceroy when he visited the royal palace. Oxenham was over-the-moon with the accommodation at their own 'palace' and he confessed 'no words of mine can adequately describe [the setting]. Our rooms, with their exquisite pictures and furnishings left us utterly speechless. And this, we understand, is the guest house, kept only for visitors! In the garage there is accommodation for 180 cars. I chose a "Rolls" for my first ride. They have a club house, with every convenience—tennis courts, swimming pool; in fact, everything for which one could wish. After each day's cricket you can imagine how enjoyable it was to step into a car, and within a few minutes to be splashing in beautifully cool water'.[10] Bill also claims he was speechless on arrival, as the palace was 'too magnificent and colossal to describe in mere words'.[11]

It's interesting to note that Hendry was greatly impressed with the priceless art collection as I imagine his fine-art knowledge was limited. Ranji collected sporting paintings and curated his own private art gallery. A portrait of the revered Australian cricketer Victor Trumper, who died prematurely at only thirty-seven years of age, was hung in a prime position and adjacent was a painting of Charlie Macartney. How chuffed he must have been! The palace also contained a library which the players were told held every book on cricket ever published.

Jack Ryder and Jack Ellis were secretly shown the bedroom where Ranji died by the Jam Sahib. They described it as a solemn moment. The room was preserved just as it was when Ranji was alive—his clothes, boots and his cherished personal possessions were all there, neatly arranged, as though ready for him when he returned.

Another highlight of Jamnagar was also a much-anticipated first for the tour. The cricketers were treated to a shooting expedition. Big game hunting was a popular pastime for the elite in India and the team couldn't wait to be invited on a shikar. They returned to the palace with six deer, numerous big birds and what they described as a dingo; most likely it was an Indian pariah dog. It appears that none of the cricketers showed much promise in the shooting stakes and they joked that as shots they made good fisherman. Ironmonger proved to be particularly inept and Bill claimed that he 'shot three legs off a black buck—and yet it ran away'.[12] Times have changed since then; shooting a black buck in 1998 resulted in a messy court case for the Bollywood superstar Salman Khan.

Despite enjoying the luxury of Jamnagar, Hendry's manuscript alludes to feeling uncomfortable with the entitlements and he observed that 'some of our chaps took too much advantage of his [the Jam Sahib's] generous hospitality when allowed to order champagne etc. ad lib during the nights in our flats'. However, it's important to remember that Hendry's manuscript was written decades after the event and it's likely that he didn't appraise his travelling companions, nor the excesses bestowed on them, so critically at the time. A contemporary sensibility permeates his delayed interpretation of events.

The team played their second match in India at Ranji's superb cricket ground where they met a Jamnagar side. They especially appreciated the work of the curator who produced a top-notch wicket which was impressive considering the non-first-class status of the match.

Despite the comforts of Jamnagar and the superiority of the wicket, the list of casualties stated to accumulate: Leather (a carbuncle on his toe), Hendry (a heavy cold) and Ryder were unable to play. Ryder explained his absence in a letter to his wife: 'I was indisposed, well I was a little bit off in the tummy just before our Jamnagar match, although I was fit to play, but Frank Tarrant thought I was due for a spell, so don't get excited when I'm not playing as we must all take our turn'. Jack affectionately concluded, 'So don't you go worrying about your little honey'.

During the game, Macartney was in fine form before misfortune hit. On reaching 106, he had to retire due to a groin injury which would prevent him from playing for a number of weeks. The game ended in a draw. It was fitting that the veteran Macartney won the best-on-field award for his century and was gifted a gold cigarette case by the Jam Sahib. Oxenham enviously estimated it was worth between £50 and £70 and joked he would have tried a bit harder if he knew such a valuable gift was to be awarded to the best player.

From all accounts, the team lustily celebrated on their last night (November 10, 1935) in Jamnagar at *Vibha Villas* in fine style. Seventy guests, presumably the cream of the city, were invited by the Jam Sahib to partake in the celebrations. The royal orchestra was tucked out of sight and played jazz throughout the evening. Ryder thought it rather incongruous that jazz was played at such a formal event, however he interpreted it as a courteous gesture to entertain the guests with contemporary western music. The guests enjoyed an extravagant twelve-course dinner where they ate off golden cutlery with jewel-encrusted crockery. They had never seen a dinner setting with so many pieces including cruets and finger bowls. Oxenham (as he frequently did) estimated its worth at £30,000. Yet he acknowledged that the estimation was at least ten years old! Macartney, also impressed by the crockery at Jamnagar and the predominance of western food, wrote: 'On the Sunday evening the Jam Sahib gave us an official State banquet, and for the first time we saw the gold plate service in use. Many of us have often heard of the gold plate, but here it was in reality. The sight of those two immense tables with every article upon them consisting of gold, was one which will not easily be forgotten. The banquet was served in European style, with only one Indian dish (curry), and topped by a very nice speech by the Maharajah of Nawanagar'.[13] Ron Morrisby, in a letter to his family, described the last night at the Palace, 'they gave us a banquet everything on the table was solid gold even the plates. It was a beautiful sight but of course the 9 course dinner did not taste any better'.[14] Surprisingly Morrisby was critical as the banquet comprised mainly Western fare including: oysters, roast turkey, asparagus and ham.

A menu from the Jamnagar banquet serves not only as a curio of the evening but also reveals larger cultural patterns that expose an embrace of ethnic difference. The Indian component of the banquet is classified simply as Jamnagar dishes. The culinary specifics of the Indian food are not identified beyond regional idiom. Using region as a descriptor stipulates that the origin of the food is the sole distinguishing feature of the dish. This is revealing of the Indian narrative and its historic foundation as a country divided into autonomous provinces with a diverse range of peoples, languages, customs and cultural practices. Historically, Indian culinary tradition was oral in transmission so elaborate descriptors are generally not incorporated into titles of dishes. Conversely, western dishes traditionally disclose their ingredients and sometimes their preparation and process. Elaborate epicurean descriptions are a relatively recent phenomenon.

Peach Melba was served as the second-last course—as a tribute to the famed Australian singer, Dame Nellie Melba, who passed away four years prior to the tour. Melba embodied a deeply proud sense of Australian nationalism and stated, 'If you wish to understand me at all, you must understand first and foremost that I am an Australian'.[15] This sentiment, in all likelihood, was shared by the cricketers.

The lack of pretence in the description of the food at Jamnagar suggests that the catering staff lacked the sophistication of the Cricket Association of Bengal and Assam, where they dined later on the tour, and where the menu is detailed in French. However, it also reflects that the different regions were culturally unique. The Bengal and Assam menu also contained an accolade to the Australian diva however this time it appeared as *Pêches Melba*. The French translation of the dish illustrates a sophisticated gesture within a social hierarchy where foreign (in this case French) terminology was considered fashionable and as an attribute of prestige. The various cultural influences as evidenced by the menus (including Indian, British, French and even Australian foods and preparations) reveal the increasingly globalisation of the 1930s.

Despite conscientious efforts to entertain the tourists in a lavish fashion in Jamnagar, Tarrant observed that leg-spinner Mair, a blue-singlet worker from Balmain who was unused to high society protocol, refused to eat off the crockery 'saying he could not enjoy a meal off gold utensils' and proclaimed 'it would put him off his food'.[16] According to Mike Coward, 'Not all members of the Australian team enjoyed the intense social activity'.[17] He noted that Mair 'was constantly irritated at the need to dress for dinner and, among others, was bemused by the often exotic offerings listed on menus'. Mair's reaction to the social demands of the Raj may not fully represent the team's sentiments, however his response demonstrates a defiant rejection of conventions of etiquette exercised by the elite in India.

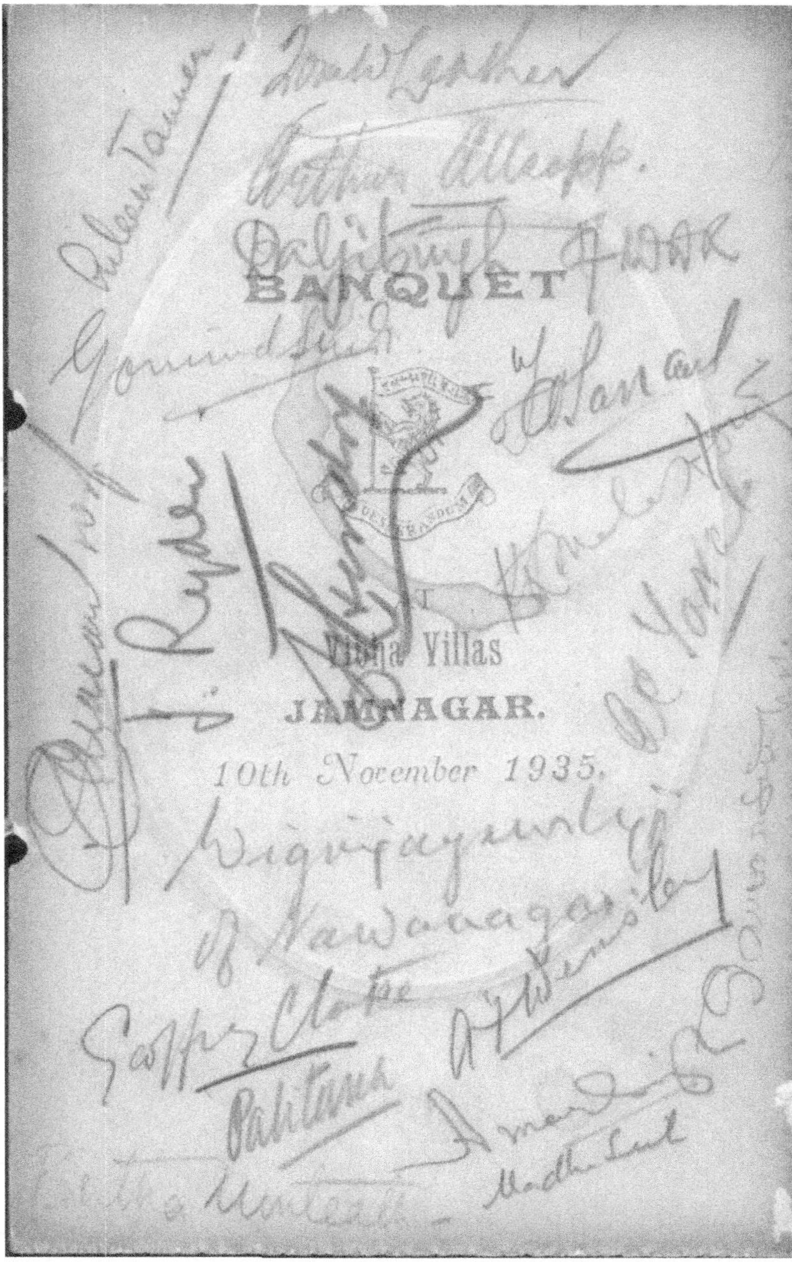

Banquet at Jamnagar. November 1935. Leather archive

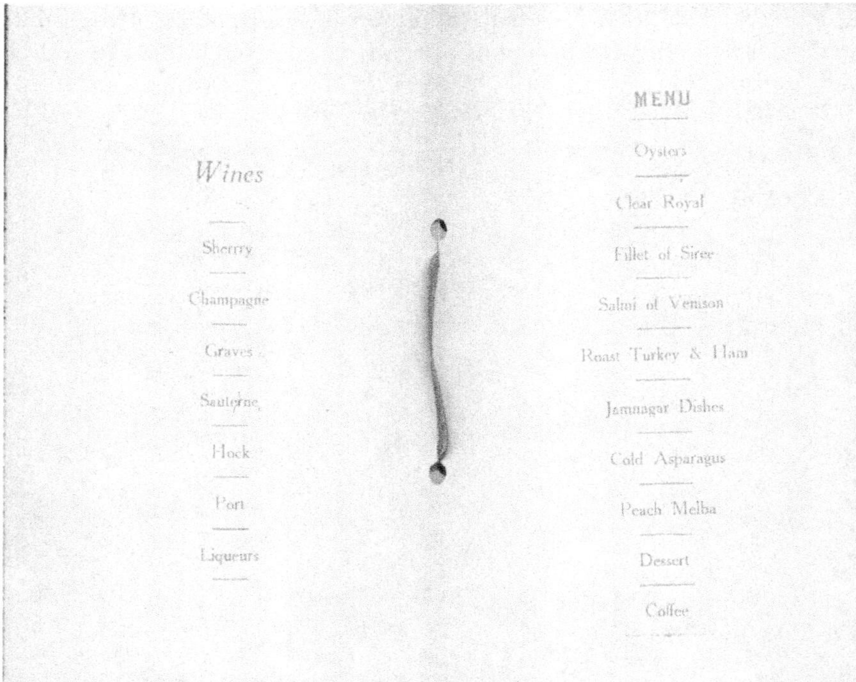

Banquet at Jamnagar. November 1935. Leather archive

Tarrant's scrapbook provides additional information regarding the gold-plate narrative as the same utensils were used during the Gilligan tour of 1926/27. It was unofficial tour protocol for a visiting team to pilfer objects as trophies to commemorate and validate their experience and Tarrant recalled an incident when this protocol was sedulously implemented: 'I had seen players in their excitement putting plates up their white dinner shirts, and knives and forks in pockets'. Possibly the team was unaware that, according to Tarrant, 'they [the English cricketers] had cleaned the table of about £5000 worth of solid gold'. Tarrant went on to relate that Ranji was unsure how he should proceed as 'his watchers, of course, had watched the players taking the plates and had marked down every item'; his concern was 'how … to get the stuff back without making trouble?'. Tarrant, in his customary position as a conduit between the locals and the visitors, entered the negotiation and implored the English cricketers to give back the gold items, falsely proclaiming that they did not belong to Ranji but rather to the state. This wasn't entirely correct, but Tarrant felt it might encourage the cricketers to return the items. Tarrant wrote: 'There followed one of the most remarkable scenes witnessed on any railway platform anywhere, I would say, as the players went into a carriage and disgorged that valuable gold plate. Everything was returned'. Tarrant stated that, ironically as a reward for their latter honesty, Ranji gifted members of the team a personal valuable gift.

Tarrant, applauding the 1935/36 Australian team's honesty and highlighting how different they were to the previous British touring party, proudly wrote, 'To the credit of the Australian team, the members moved among treasures of fabulous value and never once did the idea of [stealing] souvenirs enter the minds of any'.

The Referee appraised the tour to date in an article titled 'Who Wouldn't be a Cricketer' and utilising orientalist rhetoric observed that 'Frank Tarrant's Australian team in India are experiencing the thrills of juveniles reading "The Arabian Nights" for the first time. They are finding high-grade Indians perfect hosts. Hospitality is being showered upon the men. The sights and experiences are like a rare panorama of rich coloring (sic), in which they are actors, and through which they are passing'.[18]

The visiting cricketers were genuinely impressed by the Jam Sahib and thoroughly enjoyed their stay in Jamnagar. The Jam Sahib urged that the cricketers should treat his residence like their own homes and an invitation was extended for them to re-visit. Tarrant said that he would try his hardest to orchestrate a return visit to Jamnagar following the completion of the playing schedule. Oxenham was keen on the suggestion and concluded his article with: 'And would the boys like to go back?….. Lead us not into temptation'.

---

[1] *The West Australian* December 5, 1935.
[2] *The Telegraph* November 18, 1935.
[3] T*he Telegraph* November 25, 1935.
[4] *Newcastle Morning Herald and Miners' Advocate* December 5, 1935.
[5] *The Telegraph* November 5, 1935.
[6] *The Sydney Mail* December 18, 1935.
[7] T*he West Australian* November 6, 1935.
[8] Hunter Hendry manuscript, nd.
[9] *The Sydney Mail* December 18, 1935.
[10] *The Telegraph* November 25, 1935.
[11] *The Referee* December 26, 1935.
[12] *The Sydney Mail* December 18, 1935.
[13] *Newcastle Morning Herald and Miners' Advocate* December 7, 1935.
[14] Dougan 2012.
[15] James 1989, 44.
[16] Tarrant scrapbook.
[17] *Cricket Beyond the Bazaar* 1990, 105.
[18] December 5, 1935

10 REALITY AND POLITICS

Only seconds after the locomotive pulled into the station at Ahmedabad, the cricketers were startled from their slumber by hundreds of enthusiastic cricket fans brandishing autograph books. Wiping sleep from their eyes, and trying to make themselves decent, they were forced out of their bunks as the locals stampeded the train. It was only 6am and the cricket fans were desperate to meet the famous visiting sportsmen. Bill described the awakening as a 'tremendous scare' and he admitted: 'I must confess that the sight of an excited brown-skinned crowd around one's carriage door when awaking from sleep was rather terrifying at first'.[1]

In an article subtitled *Discomforts of Ahmedabad*, Oxenham described the cricketer's arrival at the Grand Hotel which he estimated was 'on a par with very much out-of-date country pubs in Queensland'.[2] If the cricketers knew what they would encounter next, they may have decided to accept the Jam Sahib's kind offer to extend their stay in Jamnagar. Oxenham acknowledged that following the luxury of Jamnagar it was inevitable that any accommodation at Ahmedabad would be judged harshly. The team unanimously agreed that the hotel's name was a misnomer! However, it was the only European guest house in town and alternate plans couldn't be made so they had no choice but to put up with the 'primitive' conditions.[3] The team vehemently complained to Tarrant who was getting rather annoyed with the players' preciousness and the grumbles that accompanied anything they considered below par. Possibly he regretted introducing them to the luxury of Jamnagar and the Taj Mahal hotel so early. India was a country of incredible contrasts and Tarrant felt that an accurate introduction to the country required a balance of luxury and austerity. On arrival at the hotel, Hammy Love assessed that the happiest time in Ahmedabad would be spent on the cricket pitch, as he didn't envisage much fun would be had in the unappealing town. From all accounts he wasn't far wrong.

That evening, Tarrant convinced the disheartened team to attend an exhibition of local dancing. It was an annual event and a cultural highlight of the region. They reluctantly complied as Tarrant promised that they would be back at the hotel in under an hour. Hendry described the 'nightmare drive':

> The drive to the spot was through the narrowest and dirtiest alleys imaginable. How the drivers managed to manoeuvre the big cars round the corners and miss cows, dogs, goats, and straying pedestrians will always remain a mystery. Of course, cows are sacred throughout the country. They roam the streets at leisure and when feeling in need of a tasty snack just stroll into a shop and pick up a

> cabbage or other appetising delicacy. Such an act is regarded as a great honor (sic) by the occupier.

To be fair, the cricketers were impressed by the exquisite costumes and the grace of the dancers, combined with their stamina and their rhythm but after the first few acts, they found the show repetitious as the promised hour dragged on to being close to three. They were the only Europeans in the crowd of 600 and were crammed into a space that they claimed was no larger than a garage. Mosquitos and other insects, almost the size of rats, buzzed around them. It was unbearably humid, and the lack of ventilation suffocated the players. The repetitious hand clapping and stick-rapping was headache inducing and the players felt uncomfortable and exceedingly annoyed that they had been persuaded to attend. The encore seemed endless! They were happy when the performance was finally over, and they returned back to the Grand.

However, the Grand provided little relief. The cricketers barely slept as a dozen dogs in the hotel grounds yapped all night long. Hendry first tried to use his pillows to stifle the high-pitched baying, yet they failed to provide any relief and he tossed and turned for sleepless hours. Around 3am he'd had enough and ventured downstairs to see what could be done. There he met Bryant, Leather and Allsopp who also couldn't sleep through the racket. Armed with shoes, bottles and even cricket bats the players ventured out into the dark night to silence the canines. Fortunately, the dogs moved on but unfortunately their barking didn't stop. The cricketers did however manage to wake and startle a few hotel staff. The Australians were shocked to discover that at night the workers slept in the open air, sheltering under the Banyan trees. The cricketers hoped their missiles hadn't caused injury to the poor employees.

Combined teams at Ahmedabad. November 1935. Leather archive

Captain Jack Ryder in Ahmedabad. November 1935. Ryder archive

During their stay at Ahmedabad Oxenham received an offer to return to India to take up a coaching position with an annual renumeration of £500. 'But', he said, 'I fancy the figure would have to be in the vicinity of £5,000 before I would sit up and take any notice'.[4]

The Australians easily won their fourth match of the tour, this time playing Gujerat, in an unofficial game, with a no-star line-up. It must have been disheartening for the smaller local sides to face off against the Australians or maybe the opposition just appreciated having the opportunity to play against a touring team with a few big names who had competed on the international circuit. Despite their almost inevitable defeat, fifteen thousand spectators turned out to watch the match. Ryder observed that the enthusiasm of the crowd reflected 'that cricket in India is on the crest of a wave of advancement'.[5] The captain excelled with both the bat and the ball. He recorded his first century on tour making 139 and had figures of 6-2-14-4 in the first innings. Mair and Leather were the mainstay of the bowlers and managed four wickets each in the second innings. Seemingly, Leather was enjoying his success on tour and becoming accustomed to fame and a crowd of ever-present cricket devotees. A photograph from his archive portrays him in the dressing room at lunchtime. Tom is caught casually reading a newspaper wearing dark sunglasses and a neckerchief is tied jauntily around his neck. Looking more like a movie star, he casually reclines on a wicker chair in the middle of the room and seems oblivious to the dozen or so cricket fans holding autograph books, eager to meet their idols. Employees of the cricket club also do not attract his attention. His relaxed body language suggests he is becoming blasé about his success and all the attention the team received.

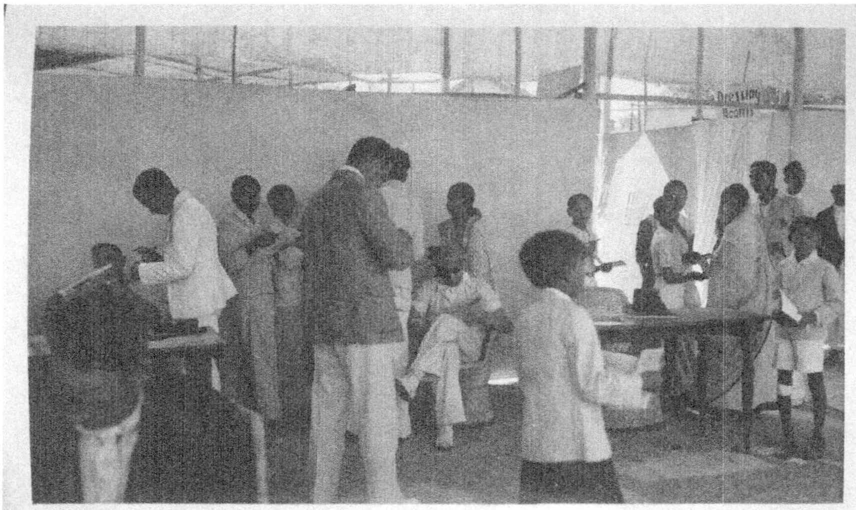

Tom Leather during the match at Ahmedabad. November 1935. Leather archive

Crowd outside the cricket ground in Ahmedabad. November 1935. Ryder archive

Ryder and Love at Ahmedabad. November 1935. Ryder archive

A few days later the players attended an 'at home' tea party hosted by Sir Chinubhai Madhavlal, a young local businessman, in his spacious compound, Shanti-Kunj. Following the premature death of his father in 1916, the highly principled son took over the family textile business and became increasingly involved in the push for inter and intra-communal harmony. One of his major reforms was to open the doors of his temple to the Dalits. Their host was part of a growing cohort of free-thinking progressive Indian intelligentsia and was active, as a social reformer, in the Independence movement.

The team was unsure if they should take the term tea party seriously and Hendry was relieved to see whiskey bottles on the bar as the previous few functions had been dry affairs. Alcohol could help the team to cope with the discomforts of Ahmedabad and the party. This is interesting commentary considering that Gujarat is now a dry state and permits are required to purchase or consume alcohol.

Conversation about the current state of Indian politics was interspersed between chitchat about the cricket match and routine Empire gossip. The players were interested to learn about the increasing inevitably of self-rule and the locals appreciated their enquiries. At the time, Mohandas Karamchand Gandhi lived in a Satyagraha ashram in Ahmedabad and an invitation to meet the Mahatma was extended. Despite the players' interest in the changing political dynamic, it didn't extend to a desire to meet the man described by Winston Churchill as a 'seditious middle temple lawyer now posing as a half-naked fakir'. Oxenham rebuffed the invitation on the grounds that, 'none of the boys could spare the time to pay him a courtesy call'.[6] It's hard to imagine this was a legitimate excuse, as the team seemed to have more spare time in Ahmedabad than elsewhere on tour. The term 'courtesy' is also ambiguous as it is unsure who was extending the courtesy. Hendry also expressed disinterest in meeting the famous Indian and observed that no-one 'hears his name mentioned now a days, and he is definitely a thing of the past'. Seemingly the cricketers wished to distance themselves from Gandhi and his politics and ideologies. A short article in the Australian press detailing the non-meeting titled 'No time for Ghandi (sic)' spells the Mahatma's name incorrectly, which reveals the Australian media's ignorance of global affairs in India or rather political activity that challenged colonisation. The newspaper editorialised that the cricketers had made the correct decision as 'Ghandi (sic) is seldom in the news these days'. The article predicted that Gandhi would fail in any endeavour to overrule British colonisation.

Hendry's manuscript, written decades after the tour, observes his interest in local politics and it also alludes to his ameliorating attitude to culture and race. It is highly likely that his perspective morphed over the years following the tour and it may not have reflected his feelings at the time. Despite containing 1930s sensibilities about race, Hendry's writing simultaneously suggests an alternate progressive worldview. Hendry observed that later in the tour he met an Indian gentleman who 'used to fill me in regarding all the politics of India'. Hendry was evidently interested in the political dynamic and wrote, 'He invited me to go with him to several committee meetings of his party. Presumably bush telegraph had even got through to Madras that I was interested in the welfare of India'.

There is compelling evidence documenting the Australian team's awareness of, and liberal attitudes towards, cultural and racial incompatibility. For example, the Australian team refused honorary membership of any club where indigenous Indians were not granted a similar entitlement. An article with the subtitle 'Color (sic) Line Barred' applauded the Australian team on their decision to refuse membership of two Karachi Clubs and compared their acceptance of racial diversity with the racial disharmony evident in South African cricket. The article contrasted the prevailing racial attitudes of South Africa and India which more directly compared the two Australian tours taking place simultaneously in 1935/36. The article concluded that India and Australia shared a common bond, and a positive cricket relationship was likely to ensue.

An article in Tarrant's scrapbook elaborates on further racial and social unrest in Karachi as the visiting XI objected to the inequitable implementation of rules based on class and race prevalent in colonial society.

The Australian team received a gratis invitation to a reception where the local team was treated 'rather shabbily' and was charged seven rupees for the same function. Tarrant observed: 'This injustice went very much against the grain of our team, who maintained that they had come to "play the Indians", and not to demonstrate in any way white superiority, which, under the circumstances would be poor cricket'. Tarrant revealed that after 'a heart-to-heart tussle with the authorities' the local team was not charged and 'the Indian and Australian players spent a happy evening together'. Such commentary is revealing of the visiting team's attitude to social and racial egalitarianism and their commitment to rectify injustices. Likewise, two decades earlier, Patel in his prominent text *Stray Thoughts on Indian Cricket* wrote with an enlightened perspective, about racial conflict: 'How ardently I wish that in this age of new inventions someone could invent a chemical preparation, or some such thing, which would convert a black face into a fair one, and cut the Gordian knot for all time'.[7]

The *Herald* observed that 'Frank Tarrant, as the Australian Board of Control discovered', was refining his role as 'a real diplomat'. 'After a minor match in India, Frank spoke at a dinner attended by both teams. The home side's performance had not been particularly impressive, but in ringing tones Tarrant declared: "From what I've seen of your cricket in this match. I consider that you should have at least three representatives in the All India team, and …" Wild cheering drowned the rest of his sentence'.[8]

The players' narratives, and many of the weekly newspaper columns in Australia, added to the growing ambivalence towards the role of the British Raj as colonists. Hendry's account is laden with rhetoric about India's (lack of) modernisation and cultural backwardness commonly espoused in historical narrative. However, aberrations manifest as Hendry categorised the bearers detrimentally as 'servants' yet applauded their unanticipated honesty. His criticism of imperialism is unambiguous—he admonished the British administrators for mismanagement: 'I state with great emphasis that my experiences in India convinced me that Britishers there, by their arrogance and ruthlessness, were responsible for the loss of prestige and power there. Our trip took place when Indians were acting as deputies to the Englishmen in all public services. Looking back, I realise how privileged we were to be there before the change took place'. Given Australia's position in the British Empire in 1935 it is unlikely that Hendry would have criticised the British so vociferously had this passage been written at that time. However, his observation that they were 'privileged to be there before the change took place' contains mixed messages as Hendry, despite demonstrating interest in the welfare of India, also suggests he revered colonial rule and viewed it nostalgically.

In his senior years Hendry was vehemently critical of 'a decline in standards of sportsmanship and behaviour on the field'.[9] Conservatism is equally evident in his writing on the 1935/36 tour yet it is encumbered with ambiguity; throughout his narration there is evidence (at times unconvincing) that he complied with the demands of contemporary political correctness. He ostensibly tempered elements of his prose to conform to what was, at the time, acceptable and retold the events of 1935/36 in a nuanced fashion. Hendry was cognisant of social hierarchy and his, and the team's, own position in it. He identified fundamental differences between the cricketers and their hosts in an anecdote regarding the 'Maharawat of Partabgarh (sic)': 'Although we talked a lot together like man to man, I always addressed him as His Highness. He was very Western in his ideas, immaculately dressed in our style although always wearing his turban. He confided in me that he had been compelled to take a second wife in order to link up another state – I did not pursue this'. This text demonstrates Hendry's propensity to, at times, perpetuate conventional Western rhetoric by observing that the Maharawat conceded to dressing according to Western style. Hendry revealed that the royal confided to him that he was 'compelled to take a second wife' to expedite political and economic relations. The use of the word 'confided' suggests that the Indian was embarrassed by the admission. The accuracy of this anecdote (written at least forty years later) is questionable as it is unlikely that the Indian royal would be so dismissive of polygamy as it was routine and culturally accepted in Eastern culture. If Hendry's prose is credible it reveals the extent of the absorption of Western culture by Indian royalty.

Despite the Maharaja's autocratic control of the tour, Hendry's criticism was also directed at the financier of the tour when he alluded to the Maharaja's frequent dalliances; 'the Maharajah of Patiala, our sponsor, was the exact opposite. Ostentatious arrogant and ruthless – the British Government had to rescue a woman he had commandeered whilst in his territory'. However, again we have to view this commentary with knowledge that it was written around forty years later when the Maharaja was long dead, and the full extent of his sexual exploits were exposed and open to critique and censure.

No one was sad to bid farewell to the uninspiring city yet, in the tour narrative, Ahmedabad would prove to represent a watershed moment as it reflected an ideological change in the cricketers' attitude to race and politics. With an enlightened perspective, they once again boarded the train—the next stop was Ajmer.

---

[1] *The Sydney Mail* December 18, 1935.

[2] *The Telegraph* December 3. 1935.

[3] *The Newcastle Sun* December 10, 1935.

[4] *The Telegraph* December 3, 1935.

[5] *Newcastle Morning Herald and Miners' Advocate* November 14, 1935.
[6] *The Telegraph* January 6, 1936.
[7] 1905, 12.
[8] March 13, 1936.
[9] Richardson 1996, 238.

11 THE UPS AND DOWNS OF AJMER

Leaving Ahmedabad didn't immediately raise the cricketers' spirits. Oxenham was especially tetchy as he grumbled about being woken at an ungodly hour and being 'dragged' to the train station to catch the 5am to Ajmer in Rajasthan. He described the journey as an 'unpleasant memory' and complained about the incessant heat and the primitive conditions.

The cricketers were appalled to see the open-air convenience stops, at the stations along the way, which were constructed for the third-class passengers. They were however intrigued to learn that the facilities for the Muslims were kept separate from the Hindus as they couldn't use the same amenities, even sharing a basin to wash was forbidden. Placards identified where the different communal groups could line up and clean and relieve themselves. The poor souls were exposed to the elements and prying eyes. Oxenham noted the absence of towels and toothbrushes—seemingly fingers had to suffice. The bowler was appalled that after washing the Indians shook themselves dry and placed shoes and shirts over wet skin.

He described the 300-mile journey as monotonous and slow, exacerbated by having to travel along a slow meter-gauge track. The train passed through an unremarkable landscape. The cricketers were becoming immune to the poverty and squalor that spread out before them. The farming and agrarian facilities were primitive and even the animals looked unhappy. The novelty of train travel was diminishing. Nothing could please the team that day and they weren't much happier when the train pulled into Ajmer at 10pm after a seventeen-hour journey. No one had slept a wink.

The team was greeted by another large throng and an overpowering scent of henna. Representatives from the cricket club somehow managed to disentangle the cricketers from the enthusiastic crowd and whisked them off to a private club where around 1000 Europeans and local dignitaries, including the royal family, congregated to meet the famous Australians. Despite exhaustion, Oxenham slightly cheered up on arrival at the function. Possibly his ego encouraged him to be a little more enthusiastic and grateful, as his good bowling to date made him the centre of attention and the recipient of many autograph requests and congratulatory drinks. Everyone seemed to be getting into party mode and the discomforts of the day were slowly forgotten. The atmosphere at the party then moved up another notch when one of the prince's guardians slid onto the piano stool and cranked up the baby grand. Soon all the guests were on their feet and didn't stop dancing for hours. Of course, such physical exertion required many refreshing beverages! On creeping into bed hours later, the cricketers realised they'd been awake for over an entire day.

The team was happy with their accommodation and Oxenham claimed that he fell on his feet, as he was billeted to stay with a 'delightful Irish doctor'. He wrote:

> I could not have fallen into better hands. He and his wife made me feel as one of their own. They placed at my disposal a wonderful room, with every convenience. I thought I was in heaven again after that hotel at Ahmedabad. We have had some ups and downs since the tour commenced, but, in my case, I think the "ups" have compensated a hundred-fold for the "downs." For the first time in India I slept without the fans going. The weather was beautifully cool, much on a par with our climate in early September. It amused me, therefore, to find my hosts with a big fire blazing in the drawing room, and to hear their suggestion that I should have a hot water bottle in my bed. Cold? Why, it was simply glorious.[1]

The match in Ajmer was played at the magnificent Mayo College cricket ground which the cricketers described as the prettiest stadium they had encountered. It was a picturesque and well-maintained cricket ground with a near perfect outfield, but the cricketers couldn't believe that again the wicket was coir matting. Mayo College was an elite private school fashioned on Eton in England. A mountain behind the cricket ground provided a picturesque backdrop and Macartney described it just like the Newlands Cricket Ground which lay at the foot of Table Mountain in Cape Town, South Africa. This commentary encouraged further comparisons to be drawn between the tour in India and the Test taking place in South Africa. Many photographs in the players' archives document the beautiful cricket pavilion at Mayo where hundreds of cane chairs were placed on the lawn to accommodate the privileged residents of the educational facility and the many royals who lived in the vicinity. The crowd was full of colourful silks and bejewelled turbans.

Despite their lack of sleep, the Australians put on a reasonable display throughout the first-class game. Both teams found scoring difficult and the conditions best suited the bowlers. Ron Oxenham recovered fully from his grievances the previous day and was in his element. Seemingly he wanted to live up to his reputation and was almost solely responsible for the visitors' victory as he took seven wickets in both innings including one exceptional spell over five overs capturing five for none. None of the Indian batsmen faced him with confidence. At the completion of the game, he boasted outstanding figures of 14-44, including 7-13 in the second innings. One headline proclaimed: 'Oxenham the Destroyer' and another gloated 'Oxenham Deadly on Matting'. Morrisby was the best of the batting order and scored 72 in the first innings. The visitors' first innings total of only 149 was their lowest score to date, yet they won by seven wickets.

Leather incorrectly labelled this Indore. It is in fact Mayo College, Ajmer. November 1935. Leather archive

Mayo college, Ajmer. November 1935. Alexander archive

Mayo college, Ajmer. November 1935. Alexander archive

Ellis, Hendry, Tarrant and Bryant enjoy post-match refreshments in Ajmer. November 1935. Alexander archive

The match however was memorable for another reason as primary material suggests that the results were subtly engineered. No evidence can be located to suggest that any of the matches was fixed during the tour however when the Australian team played in Ajmer, due to the weakness of the opposition, Tarrant was persuaded to allow the local team to make 150 to ensure that the game wasn't over too quickly. Tarrant was warned that when the British toured a few years before, 'the whole side [the local team] was out for 30 and the match was over in a day and a half' which impacted dramatically on gate takings and club revenue and club pride.[2] Tarrant however objected when he felt his good nature had been taken advantage of. He had allowed the opposition to make 131, yet when the Australians came out to bat a few seemingly unfair lbw decisions were given by the umpires. Tarrant was angered when he noticed the opposition 'club secretary cheering and clapping as another of our players was given out lbw'.[3] In light of the goodwill nature of the tour and Tarrant's acquiescence, he objected to the lack of mutual respect demonstrated by the Ajmer authorities.

Despite attempts by cricket authorities to clean up the game, incidents such as this highlight the fact that cricket for the most part still operated according to a model of gamesmanship or, in this case, doctoring the results to achieve a better outcome. Throughout the 1920s there was a plethora of questionable tactics used in cricket, from sledging to ball tampering. During the 20/21 English tour of Australia, both teams admitted to ball tampering. Arthur Mailey confessed to 'lifting the seam' with resin during a candid conversation with Johnny Douglas. Douglas decided against reporting Mailey to the umpire after the Australian asked to inspect the Englishman's thumbnail which showed the irrefutable signs of ball tampering. Both men decided against taking their discoveries any further.

The spirit of cricket was the rather fanciful imagination of Neville Cardus, Plum Warner and the likes who yearned for the 'great days before the War when everything was pristine'. The great days before the War were also, in fact, full of skulduggery, bickering for money, bad sportsmanship and match fixing. WG Grace was possibly the greatest exponent.

Despite the visiting Australians seemingly being interlopers to orthodox cricket, or possibly because they were, Tarrant tried to promote the tour as observing the rules and sentiments that defined the spirit of the game. However, in reality, cricket was a competitive business, where winning was paramount whether for financial gain or reputation, and whatever tactics were required to achieve the ultimate goal were generally put into action.

---

[1] *The Telegraph* December 3, 1935.

[2] Tarrant Scrapbook1918–51.

[3] The leg before wicket rule was constantly being revised resulting in public condemnation and player uncertainty.

12 THE FIRST BIG TEST

The team arrived back in grand old Bombay by train at 5.30am on November 30, following another much-lambasted night trip from Poona. Ellis, Hendry, Nagel and Alexander bunked together and stayed up late playing cards—they didn't get much sleep at all. They were abruptly woken by a bearer bellowing: 'Bombay Sahib, get up Sahib'. The cricketers threw on some clothes or rather, as Hendry described, they 'half-dressed' and hailed taxis to transport them to the Taj where they managed to squeeze in a few hours of rest before arriving at the Gymkhana ground to commence play at 11.00am against the Bombay Presidency. This match served as a trial for the 'Test' a few days later.

The cricketers had driven past the Gymkhana ground when they were previously in Bombay yet when they arrived for the match it was unrecognisable as stands and facilities had been quickly constructed. Much to the cricketers' surprise each communal group had their own temporary facilities at the cricket ground where they could socialise and observe their communal customs. Wall-hung electric fans were situated around the stadium, possibly in response to the cricketers' earlier complaints about the heat.

Without a doubt, the highlight of the day was meeting the Maharaja of Patiala for the first time. The potentate travelled 1200 miles to attend the match and was introduced to the players in the changing room before play commenced. The cricketers were rather embarrassed to meet the financier while they were in a state of half-undress, some being bandaged and smelling of liniment. The Maharaja thanked the team for their hard work to date and, according to script, promptly invited them to a cocktail party that evening. Hendry was immediately impressed by the Maharaja and described him as a striking personality, a great sportsman and a marvellous host. The Maharaja extended an invitation for the team to stay with him in Patiala for a few weeks following the busy cricket schedule before returning to Australia. It all sounded rather tempting to the cricketers especially when big game hunts were promised.

In their first innings, Bryant and Bill scored centuries for the visitors and were startled when exuberant spectators ran onto the ground and flung garlands around their necks. However, it was nothing compared to the reception when the local captain Laxmidas Purshottamdas 'LP' Jai scored a hundred later in the match. It was the first century scored by a local team on the tour and the crowd was overjoyed. Over a hundred spectators swarmed the arena: running around in excitement and shrieking with joy. They threw missiles into the air in celebration and the sky was full of fruit, balls, kites and multi-coloured streamers. It was the most chaotic scene of sporting joy that the visitors had ever experienced. A team of ground staff were sent out to collect the detritus from the arena to prevent any injury to the cricketers. Around twenty minutes later the crowd returned to their seats and play continued. The next ball bowled by Ryder caused confusion as when Jai went to strike it his bat became tangled in a kite that had been earlier released in celebration and had escaped capture. The ball passed straight through to the stumps and the bails fell to the ground. The Indian was adjudicated out by the umpire, yet Ryder tried to influence the decision being reversed. However, everyone knew that the umpire's decision was binding so in the spirit of sportsmanship, Ryder insisted that Mair bowl the next ball whilst holding the kite much to the amusement of the already animated crowd.

Morrisby batting v Bombay Presidency. Leather archive

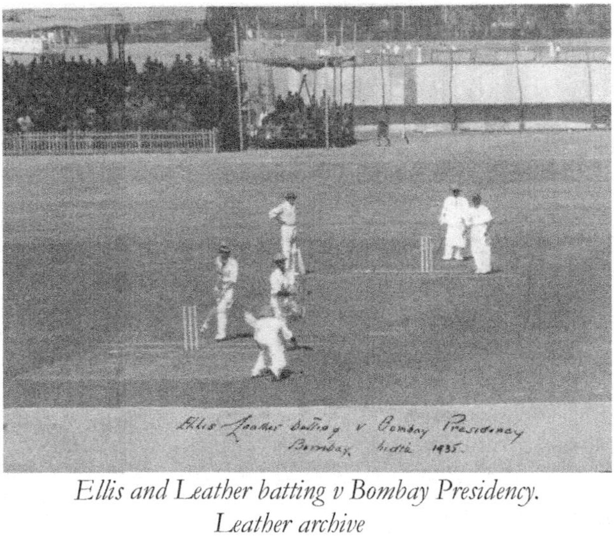

Ellis and Leather batting v Bombay Presidency.
Leather archive

Again, Bombay treated the players to luxury and experiences they were unaccustomed to. An 'at home' with Sir Nowroji Saklatwala, a member of the Tata dynasty and the third chairman of the Tata group was a highpoint. Oxenham was especially impressed on learning that he owned the Taj hotel and that he was cricket obsessed. He made his first-class debut when he played cricket for the Parsi team in the Bombay competition in 1904 and reluctantly retired when his business commitments got in the way or maybe he acknowledged that he really wasn't a good enough sportsman. Following his playing career, he became involved as an administrator and a financier and the development of the game in India is indebted to him just like it is indebted to the Maharaja. His party planners had set up multi-coloured lights that illuminated the grounds and cast psychedelic shadows across the exotically landscaped garden. A temporary dance floor was constructed on the lawn and a full European orchestra kept the cricketers on their feet. Even after playing cricket all day there was no rest! Various acts performed at intervals throughout the long evening which enabled the guests to catch their breath. Waiters in white starched uniforms navigated their way through the ebullient throng without losing a cocktail or a canapé. Supper was served late in the evening, yet the players described it as a sumptuous banquet, and they were impressed by the quantity, variety and quality of the food. They were however unused to eating so late.

The first 'Test' commenced on December 5 and Hendry noted that during the lead up, the players were encouraged to rest up for the match and take 'things quietly'. However, taking 'things quietly' was open to interpretation as the players' manuscripts and letters reveal a busy schedule and a plethora of invitations. One evening they attended a dinner dance hosted by the Automobile Club alongside a raucous crowd of around 400 guests. It was a fun night, yet Hendry did comment that just when 'everyone was getting into their stride', Frank Tarrant quietly tapped them on their shoulders and said, 'off to bed, boys'.[1]

Tarrant was understandably anxious about the 'Test' as it was the first time the visitors would be playing against a collective of Indian big names and it was also the first time the eyes of the cricket world be firmly fixed on the game. It was the first time that the team would encounter local superstar C.K. Nayudu who had captained the Indians against the British in 1932 on their inaugural Test encounter. As a commoner his meritocratic selection as Test captain was a shock as it was customary that a royal would occupy the position. Patiala did not tour in 1932 so the side was initially led by the Maharaja of Porbandar and his deputy was the Maharaja of Limbdi. Porbandar managed scores of 0, 2, 0, 2, 2 and Limbdi helpfully got injured and so Nayudu as the third choice occupied the role of de facto captain. Nayudu himself had been an officer in the army of the Maharaja of Holkar, employed more because of his cricketing prowess.

The game was initially billed as India versus Australia yet at the Australian Board of Control's insistence it was promoted as the 'Yuvraj of Patiala's XI v Maharaja of Patiala's Australian XI' as they didn't want any confusion with the national teams. The Yuvraj captained the local team and on winning the toss, he elected to bat. Much to the crowd's disappointment, opening bats, Wazir Ali and Janardan Navle didn't shine and the situation looked rather dire for the local team as they were two for two. Wicketkeeper Navle had experience as an opener as he received the first ball ever bowled in Indian English Test cricket in 1932. Yet his selection as opener on both occasions was really just an erroneous tactical ploy which can be interpreted as a sign of desperation. Macartney, out injured, wrote for the local press and noted that not all was lost for the locals as Lala Amarnath and Nayudu, batting at three and four, promised 'big things'. Luckily, they managed to stabilise the situation and added enough to give some respectability to the score. However, it was noted that the pair didn't play entirely to their potential.[2] Amarnath lacked the usual 'fireworks' in his innings and was dismissed for thirty-three runs. The Yuvraj was next to bat.

A fellow I know collects cricket footage, it's a half-job, half-hobby. I don't know him well but on a few occasions our paths have crossed. About a decade back I rang him to enquire if he knew of any tour footage. After fossicking through some vaults, he told me I was in luck as a snippet of Movietone film has survived documenting the first 'Test' in Bombay. The newsreel commences with chirpy music—reinforcing that sport was entertainment. Despite the strong political orientation of the 1935/36 tour, the Australian players were primarily in India to entertain the masses. The footage is captioned 'Australians meet brilliant Indians in Bombay "Test"'.

A posh English voice provides the voiceover for the footage and brags about the talent of the local team. The batting of the captain, the Yuvraj, who scored 'forty in half an hour, mostly in sixes' is especially noted. The crowd enthusiastically applaud the royal's impressive innings and especially his opening scoring shot—a six! Oxenham and Mair bowled to the Yuvraj and it has subsequently been speculated that the Maharaja may have arranged for them to deliver a few gift balls. If so, you'd imagine that the Maharaja rewarded the visiting bowlers for accommodating his requests. The Yuvraj seemingly floats down the wicket without needing to exert much effort. Maybe it was a royal trait, I speculate. The Yuvraj looks like he hasn't broken into a sweat in years. A turban elongates his already very tall frame, and he moves majestically as he navigates the wicket.

Macartney in his column for *The Hindu* was impressed by the Yuvraj's technique yet critical of his aggression and noted that the 'over-eagerness to continue with sixes brought about his downfall'. The Australian vice-captain realised he couldn't be too critical of the financier's son so added: 'It was nevertheless a great innings and an excellent display'. This analysis could apply to the whole team who approached the match with gusto and enthusiasm—like we now see in the shorter form of the game. The *Herald* observed that 'Bats were flashed at fast rising balls, and with complete disregard of slow bowlers' spin. Hitting with a cross bat was much in evidence. It should be a lesson to them that sixes and boundaries cannot be obtained off every ball'.[3] A local journalist who also contributed to *The Hindu* was also aware that he couldn't be harsh and observed; 'The Yuvraj, I thought handled his team very satisfactorily. His knowledge of the game was impressive. Naturally he is short of real experience, but I am convinced that the Indian leader has the makings of a really first-class cricketer. Confidence and courage are essential to a batsman-captain and the Yuvraj possesses both, and with the aid of experience and study he must progress rapidly'.

The footage voiceover informs that, 'The crowd walks around at tiffin time'. The mise-en-scene depicts a densely populated crowd promenading around the pavilion during the break. The match was certainly popular with the locals as evidenced by the substantial crowd. The clunky editing of the black-and-white film adds to its charm and there are attempts at passé humour, fuelled by racial profiling. As Amar Singh smashes a ball for a six, the film cuts to footage of a sandal and loin-cloth-wearing local scaling the three-storey high pavilion to locate the missile. The orator reveals that, 'they had to search the grandstand roof for the ball'.

I'm lucky that the footage has survived—not entirely unscathed. Age has taken its toll and the highlights of the film are completely blown out. For example, the bleached sky contains no detail at all. The footage abruptly ends halfway through Ryder taking a run. I imagine the whole reel would have portrayed the Australians in a more positive light as India fell away and the Aussies took control and won the match convincingly. Its brevity heightens its charm and I view the footage now as a treasure that provides a fascinating layer of additional meaning. A persuasive argument in visual theory maintains that moving footage provides greater insight compared to the limitations of still imagery. The presence of the Movietone film certainly enhances my understanding of the tour and illustrates the captivating atmosphere of the time and place.

Following the Indian first innings of 163, the Australians batted. The visitors started in a similar fashion to the local team with the opening batsmen being dismissed easily and only making a combined score of six. Morrisby and Ryder resurrected the visiting team and enjoyed a successful partnership with the Tasmanian making 67, the captain top-scoring with 137. Macartney, in deference to his captain, described Ryder as displaying a perfect 'test match temperament'.

The umpiring was described by Tarrant as 'most unsatisfactory' as numerous rulings were simply false. Love and Bryant were both unjustly given 'out', and Amarsingh survived when he really shouldn't have. The

Yuvraj over-ruled Love's dismissal and the batsman returned to the crease, yet the umpire refused to allow him to continue his innings and the Australian dejectedly walked back to the club house, cursing Indian umpires.

It was the first time on tour that the team encountered local boy Mohammed Nissar who looked more like a pugilist than a cricketer. He was the star fast bowler of the 1930s and was later described by Hendry in his manuscript as a 'big powerful chap who could bowl bumpers at you, like [Dennis] Lillee, particularly fiery on matting wickets. He was extremely dangerous'. During this first 'Test' he didn't disappoint and bowled with intimidation, pace and precision, taking six wickets.

Nissar and Mrs Tarrant. Date and location unknown. Nisar archive

Tarrant, emphasising the popularity of international cricket, described the Australian unofficial Test victory for the Herald and wrote that 'there was not a vacant seat' at the Bombay Gymkhana and 'special trains were run from all over India and all hotels were packed to capacity'. Ryder, in an article for the same publication, estimated that the crowd on Day One of the unofficial 'Test' was 30,000.

The comprehensive Australian victory by eight wickets was described as a 'shock' to the Indians as they had selected their best players and 'they thought it would be easier to work off the Australians'.[4] The big loss urged them to acknowledge their sporting fallibilities and realise that they would have to work harder to prepare for the Test tour to England the following year. The magnitude of the Australians' role in educating the Indians at cricket was fully realised following this first 'Test' in Bombay.

Australian 'Test' team shot, Bombay. December 7, 1935. Ryder archive

Locating the footage encouraged me to search for more. I contacted various film houses in Australia, but nothing could be found. I had a friend who worked for the Cricket Club of India in Mumbai and asked for his assistance. He promised me he'd do some investigation. To my surprise, the starting date of archival film in India is 1947. I was told that nothing exists in official government repositories prior to Indian independence. This encouraged me to think about the pedagogical historical narrative being taught. I imagine that following Independence, film from the colonial period was either pilfered or destroyed or sent back to Britain. Subsequent research in Britain has not managed to locate further film stock.

---

[1] *The Newcastle Sun* December 28, 1935.
[2] *The Hindu* December 6, 1935.
[3] *The Herald* December 27, 1935.
[4] Tarrant scrapbook 1918-51.

13 CELEBRATIONS AT THE CINEMA

Following the victory, the Australian team celebrated at the Super Cinema, a popular film house in suburban Bombay. The management of the Wadia Movietone and Super Talkies hosted a special matinee followed by refreshments. It was another formal occasion and gold medals were presented to the best batsman and bowler. Ryder and Mair were the recipients of the awards.

Cinema and cricket followed a similar trajectory in the early twentieth century—both were growing industries that were embraced by the Indian population and adapted as their own. Later in the twentieth century, the cinema industry in Bombay became known as Bollywood. Further north in what is now Pakistan, the centre of production was Lahore, and the film industry became known as Lollywood. An exceedingly charming photograph of the team's visit to the Super cinema is located in the Leather archive.

The 'Australian' team celebrating their first 'Test' victory, Bombay. December 1935. Leather archive

I can't determine what film they watched at the Super Cinema. It may have been *Bride of Frankenstein* or maybe, if they needed a little light relief, it could have been the Marx Brothers in *A Night at the Opera*. Both were big hits in 1935 and would have provided escapist entertainment if the cricketer's daily routine was becoming too arduous. I do know that a few months later in Calcutta, some of the cricketers were thrilled to see Ginger Rogers and Fred Astaire in *Top Hat*. As sportsmen, I'm sure the tourists would have been impressed by the physical mastery of the dancing duo.

The photograph of the group at the Super Cinema signifies a change in the Indian cultural landscape and the country's growing independence from Britain as a Hindi film poster reveals that the cinema played local movies, not just British or (the increasingly popular) American imports. These productions appealed to the growing nationalistic middle-class of India who embraced the new recreational obsession. The film poster, visible in the top right-hand corner of Tom's photograph, advertised *Hind Kesari*, the popular 1935 action-adventure directed by the Parsi filmmaker Homi Wadia (a luminary in Indian cinema from 1935–78). Wadia's wife, Australian born Mary Ann Evans (performing under the *nom de plume* Fearless Nadia) was frequently cast as the leading lady. Fearless and possessing remarkable athletic talents, she performed her own terrifying stunts. Despite being a buxom blue-eyed blonde who only spoke rudimentary Hindi she was frequently cast in the role as the Indian Warrior in anti-British allegories. The marriage of the director and the film star was another example of Indian-Australian collaboration. The presence of the poster suggests that 1930s India was experiencing a period of immense transformation and that the Australian cricketers were witness to the brewing ideological restructure. What an exciting time to be in India, I've always thought.

The players are photographed holding bouquets of flowers and garlands hang around their necks—an uneasy fusion of a Hawaiian greeting and a wedding ceremony. Macartney explained that: 'Garlands are used in India for farewells, receptions, and the paying of compliments. Members of the team have been garlanded and even banquetted (sic) on several occasions on their arrival and departure. The flowers used for these garlands are local, with little smell, but plenty of stain, as some of the team know to their cost. Several good collars have already been ruined'.[1] I'm sure Ron Morrisby didn't want his clothing to be soiled as the photograph reveals that he wore his favourite (if not only) suit. Macartney's language, describing the flowers, indicates that he was unimpressed with the local floral offerings. Typically, Tarrant was less critical in his appraisal and called it a 'very charming and graceful custom'.[2] He did not object to the 'sweet-smelling ropes of flowers' being placed around the players' necks. This highlights the difference between Tarrant, who perpetually defended India, and the less emotionally involved Macartney who as an established star may have felt a sense of personal, and Western, superiority.

Eva Tarrant stands centrally in the image, exemplifying her role in the team and reflecting the wider dialogue of gender in late-colonial India. She is the sole female amongst a crowd of men, which is not unusual in the team imagery or in the team narrative. However, she does not occupy a position of subordination, nor is she portrayed within the marginalised feminine sphere of domesticity, but rather she is central to the construction of the male world. Many historians have argued that women were active participants in colonisation and played a strategic role in the colonial enterprise despite noting that they were notoriously absent from historical records of the Empire. Eva's presence on tour and her guiding influence over Tarrant and by association the team of Australians is evident, in a demonstrable manner, unlike the experience of most women on sporting tours at the time.

Eva wears a long dress with a delicate floral print. She holds a massive bouquet of flowers that obscures half her body. Possibly she is protecting herself from the intrusive objectification of the camera and she simply just doesn't like being overweight. Or the most likely interpretation is that the biggest bouquet was gifted to the sole female in the party. Eva's central position encourages her to be viewed as a racial divider as she splits the image into two spheres. To Mrs Tarrant's right stands the Australian team, her husband and stepson stand immediately behind the matriarch and to her left is an assortment of non-white unidentified gentlemen. Visually and psychologically, Eva forms a border much like earlier British Raj women in India who 'were seminal in the policing of sex and race borders'.[3] The visual reiteration of Eva amongst the Indian population indicates her comfort in a mixed culture environment influenced by her position as an ethnic (remembering her German heritage) and gender outsider in partial isolation from the team members. Scholars have critiqued the position of Australian women in the Empire and argue that they are viewed as insiders because of their whiteness but simultaneously outsiders from the British Raj due to their colonial origins. Seemingly, Eva conformed to this hybrid position as she is immediately visible as an outsider, stipulated by her gender, yet her position in eliding the cultural dynamics, and the composition, of the image is evident. Eva's position in the image is representative of the evolving racial and gender dynamic in late-colonial hierarchy.

A local gentleman wearing all white, with a white hat, holds a bouquet indicating that he is pivotal to the ritualised welcome of the Australian team but is unidentifiable in the tour narrative. His conspicuous presence reveals the evolving democratisation of cricket and cinema in pre-independence India and the Australian tourists' compliance with the process. The assorted dress of the Indian males reflects communal diversity and a seemingly sanctioned acceptance of cultural difference. Most of the males depicted wear western suits akin to the garments worn by the Australian team yet others wear traditional costume denoting cultural affiliation.

A programme, located in the Bill archive at Cricket New South Wales, reveals the significance of cinema to Indian social life. It outlines a full schedule of social and sporting activities from November 21–24 (a three-day cricket match at the Karachi Gymkhana Ground had to fit in amongst the exhaustive social agenda). The programme proclaimed that 'Free entry has been arranged for the members of the Australian Team at the Plaza and Capital Cinemas' revealing the prestigious reputation of cinema. The Australian cricketers possibly used cinema as a means of escapism when they were tiring of the tour which reminds me of the Indian historian Ramachandra Guha's observation that, following partition, refugee camps set up to accommodate displaced peoples used the projecting of films as a 'two hour break from reality'.[4]

Following the function at the cinema, the cricketers visited Arthur Allsopp and Lisle Nagel at St Georges hospital. The healthy ensemble was shocked, as the sickly duo were seriously ill. Allsopp had contracted enteric fever and Nagel had a severe dose of dysentery. It was last time the team would be united as they were to depart for Allahabad the following morning and both cricketers were too sick to make the journey. In his manuscript, Hendry noted that in retrospect he thought they were lucky that all the team wasn't more seriously stricken with the diseases as they all shared dormitories and bathroom facilities. Due to the severity of the pair's condition, a doctor at the hospital immediately administered inoculations against various ailments on the spot. Mike Coward maintains that Mair, always recalcitrant, avoided having the immunisations because of a morbid fear of needles. Yet thankfully the others complied.

---

[1] *Newcastle Morning Herald and Miners' Advocate* December 14, 1935.

[2] Tarrant scrapbook 1918-51.

[3] as quoted in *Memsahibs and the "Sunny East": Representations of British India by Millicent Douglas Pilkington and Beryl White*, Dohmen 2012, 164.

[4] as described by a social worker in *India after Gandhi: The History of the World's Largest Democracy* 2007, 98.

14 'A MOTLEY LOOKING CREW'

Winning their first big 'Test' was intensely gratifying yet following the victory team temperament started to deteriorate. The cricketers grew tired of travel, the conditions of the commute irritated them and constantly having to relocate was beginning to take its toll. Niggles and grumbles amongst the team personnel intensified. It wasn't just tour malaise as the team was afflicted by serious injuries and more serious illnesses. The twenty-four-hour, 900-mile, train journey from Bombay to Allahabad was particularly unpleasant due to the side effects of the recently administered inoculations. The team was keen to see the culturally significant city that was built on the site where the Ganges met the Jamuna, yet as the journey progressed, they feared that they wouldn't be healthy enough to enjoy.

The team took to their bunks the moment the whistle blew, signalling the train's departure from Victoria terminus, and most players didn't manage to rise from them for the duration of the journey. Only a few cricketers made it to the dining car for meals as the majority had lost any appetite. Oxenham described the stricken cricketers as 'cot cases', couldn't believe 'that such a healthy lot of chaps the day before could look so sick the next day' and he described his travelling companions as 'a motley looking crew'.[1] The doctor had scheduled repeat immunisations a few days later, yet Oxenham imagined that many players would refuse as the first dose had made them so thoroughly sick and they believed that they'd 'suffered enough'.

The following evening, the cricketers arrived at Allahabad. As usual, they were greeted at the train station by an enthusiastic crowd including the host families who lined up to meet their lodgers. In the larger cities, the players were accommodated in European-style hotels however in smaller regional centres that did not contain suitable commercial lodgings they were housed privately.

Amongst the throng, Oxenham immediately noticed a few army men, dressed resplendently in red jackets with gold buttons and gleaming white pants, manoeuvring their way towards him. He was rather surprised when one of the livery men grabbed him by the elbow and said; 'You, Bill and Ironmonger, are to stay at the British soldiers' mess'. The others were billeted out to private homes. Oxenham, with Dickensian detail, acknowledged, in his newspaper column, that for

> once I drew a dud. The officers and .the mess sergeant in particular were very nice and decent to us, but the quarters after the Taj Mahal Hotel—well, it was

> like jumping from the sublime to the ridiculous. Guess they had not been used for ages. Smelly, cold cement walls, without furniture and just a bare stretcher. We had to use our train bedding. There were birds on the roof and rats running around the floor. To make matters worse I had two sick chaps with me. One, Bert Ironmonger, who was that bad that I decided I could not possibly look after him under such conditions so I made arrangements for him to be taken to the hospital. The other Bill, I was able to care for with the assistance of the mess sergeant.

Unsurprisingly, Ryder's accommodation was superior as he was billeted with Sir Harry Haig at Government House in Allahabad. In a letter to his wife, written on Government House letterhead and dated December 12, he declared that despite the luxury of some of the private residences he sometimes wished he could stay in a more relaxed environment (with the company of his teammates) 'as these places tend to be a bit stiff'. Comments such as these illustrate Ryder's antipathy toward the imposed hierarchal stipulations and his frustration that the Australian team was expected to conform to the anticipated role of privileged white cricketers. Charlie Macartney lodged with Mr Justice Allsopp, while Jack Ellis and Hunter Hendry stayed with Mr Rutherford, the superintendent of the railways. Mr Rutherford was preoccupied with his day job, so he left the hosting of the cricketers to his wife. It was an especially busy time for him as he was responsible for orchestrating the railway logistics for the start of the Kumbh Mela festival. The city was anticipating the arrival of around 4 million Hindus to participate in the ritual dip in the spot where the Ganges merges with the Jamuna. The hordes were scheduled to arrive by train over the following few weeks and set up their camping spots on the riverbed. Mrs Rutherford was the daughter of a politician from West Australia, so much talk about home took place during their time in Allahabad. Mrs Rutherford was delighted to point out the eucalyptus trees which surrounded the cricket ground—their smell immediately made the cricketers, and also the superintendent's wife (despite her having resided in India for forty years), homesick.

Hendry feared he was next in line to succumb to the dreaded enteric fever and his manuscript recalls a terrifying incident that highlighted his distrust of Eastern medical practice and equally his suspicion of the Foreign Other that appeared to be encapsulated in Western perceptions at the time. However, his prolonged immersion with the Other encouraged him to challenge his preconceived notions of irrevocable cultural differences: 'I went to bed immediately and fell asleep to be awakened about 8 p.m. by an Indian doctor who made me swallow some black tar-looking potion. I imagined I had caught the dreaded disease but to my complete astonishment, I woke in the morning feeling 100%'. Hendry, due to his instant and miraculous recovery from illness, was able to enjoy his stay in Allahabad.

In the morning of the match against United Provinces, the healthy personnel were counted, and Ryder realised that they were six down. The team would have to manage without Macartney, Allsopp, Bill, Nagel and Ironmonger who were all suffering from enteric or the side effect of the immunisations and Ellis was out with a leg injury. In light of the depleted stock, Frank Tarrant made up the numbers and Ryder courteously handed him the captaincy. Joe Davis, an eighteen-year-old lad from Sydney who was described by the *Hindu* newspaper as the team's 'general factotum' was also called upon to play. Davis, who paid his own way and accompanied the team on their journey around India, hadn't expected to have to pull on the whites.

During the night before the match commenced, unseasonal rain fell for the first time on the tour. Luckily it stopped in the early hours of the morning and the game, a two-day non first-class encounter with the home team playing with 12 men, was only delayed by an hour and a half. The locals batted first and made 137. They were captained by the Maharajakumar of Vizianagram, a name now well-known to cricket fans as he notoriously captained the Indian team when they toured England later in 1936. According to newspaper reportage Vizzy, despite being described by Macartney as being on the 'stout side', anticipated making some serious runs. Yet he was stumped off the first ball he received.[2] Mair was the bowler and Vizzy was standing well out of his crease when Love, the wicketkeeper, knocked the bails of the stumps. Mair was thrilled with his success yet immediately apologised to Vizzy. Tarrant, standing at first slip, cautioned him to silence as he knew what would transpire. The umpire adjudicated it not out and the prince went on to top-score with 40. It was becoming apparent that the umpires were routinely lenient when they encountered politically influential and important cricketers.

The Australians managed to make a paltry 89 (their lowest score on tour). However, on a positive note, Frank Tarrant celebrated his fifty-fifth birthday by reliving his glory days. He batted well and was the second-highest scorer with 22. Oxenham observed that it was 'really a marvellous knock for a veteran'. Despite insisting that he was fine to compete after his health scare the previous night, Hendry only managed a duck and Oxenham (utilising his distinctive parlance) joked in the Australian press that, 'Hendry has completed the hat trick—three blobs in a row. He says he is starting a poultry farm, but is rather concerned as he puts it, that "Mrs. H." might think the heat has driven him to the bottle. In the next breath he says "That is what a man gets for looking after himself."'

Like Bhupinder, Vizzy was a significant contributor to the growth of cricket in India. Both men wished to be celebrated as the forefather of the modern game in the land. Bryant, in a newspaper column, noted the competitiveness between Vizzy and the Maharaja of Patiala who both owned teams that participated in the Moin-ud-Dowlah Cup—it was always a feisty affair. In 1934, the antagonism was so intense fuelled by growing instability in the Indian cricket world and increasing acrimony between the royals. The

Maharaja enlisted the service of some of the Indian Test team to represent Patiala in his team called the Retrievers. Vizzy responded by trying to recruit English big names including Hammond and Larwood to join the Freelooters. Despite the promise of substantial recompense, the Englishmen declined the offer at the last moment. Fearing defeat, Vizzy then pleaded with 'the fast bowler and demon slogger' the highly respected and fearsome West Indian Learie Constantine to participate.[3] Constantine travelled 12,000 miles to compete in the match. According to Mihir Bose, as the game progressed, the acrimony between the financiers, and their desire to win, intensified and midway through the final Vizzy sent Constantine a telegram promising him extra financial incentives for each run and wicket.[4] The monetary inducements assisted Constantine's bank balance but couldn't get the Freelooters over the line. The Retrievers won the match by three wickets. Bryant thought the antagonism of the competition was rather ridiculous as he surmised it was really only a match between two villages.

Throughout the tour, the Australian press reported the health of the travelling personnel in a fashion which seemed to reinforce the backwardness of the host nation. Evocative headlines such as 'Illnesses hamper Tarrant's team' (*Sporting Globe* December 18, 1935); 'Players have Enteric (*Sporting Globe* November 13, 1935); 'Australians in India meet Trouble' (*Sporting Globe* January 22, 1936) and 'Touring India is no picnic for Veteran Australians' (*Referee* February 13, 1936) understandably concerned the players' families and roused wider public xenophobia 'back home'.

The cricketers themselves were conscious of the potential health ramifications of travelling to India as it was common knowledge that enteric fever, despite it being on the decline, was still responsible for numerous casualties. Hendry's manuscript contradicts other reports as he insists that they 'were all advised to be inoculated for typhoid and smallpox before leaving Australia. Hugh Trumble (Australian cricket royalty and secretary of the Melbourne Cricket Club), despite never touring India, advised, "be done for everything Hunter. Tell the Health Medical Officer in Sydney Dr. Morris, I would like him to do this for you". What a wise precaution it turned out to be'.

The touring Australians had no idea how the tour was being reported back home and, I guess, nor did they really care—they would learn this at a later date. However, their knowledge of locally acquired disease was consolidating and was now based on a combination of alarmist racial assumptions, empirical evidence and bitter experience.

The motley crew looked rather more motley on departure from Allahabad yet at least no one was left behind.

---

[1] *The Telegraph* December 30, 1935.
[2] *Newcastle Morning Herald and Miners' Advocate* December 31, 1935.
[3] *Mirror* March 7, 1936.
[4] *The History of Indian Cricket* 1990, 93.

15 THE BIG GAME

The very name of India conjured up so many thoughts of glamour, big-game and the different styles of life that I was delighted to accept Frank Tarrant's invitation to join his team.[1]

One match would be played each week, giving the party plenty of time for relaxation, including big game shooting.[2]

Prior to their arrival in India, the players were tremendously excited by Tarrant's promise of exclusive and extravagant functions and activities, especially the prospect of big game hunting. They were possibly counting their cull before reaching Bombay harbour. The Daily News outlined the importance of big game to colonial culture and to the tour itinerary: 'No Test matches were to be played in India, but the fixtures included several important games against various provinces. During free days, cricketers would indulge in big game hunting'.[3] However, despite all the promises and much to their dismay, the Australian cricketers only attended a few shooting parties where they got to aim at ducks and deer. The opportunity to be involved in a serious Shikar didn't eventuate and taking aim at tigers would only transpire in their dreams.

The Maharaja of Patiala was a trigger-happy fellow, and one has to question which sport he loved more as it was reported that during the English Test tour to India in 1933/34, he rescheduled the hours of cricket, deciding instead to shoot through most of the day during the visitors' match against Patiala. He simply felt that the weather was too good to waste on cricket and estimated that it would be better suited to shooting. Newspaper articles revealed that other royals were also hunting obsessed. Earlier, Ranji was so enamoured by the sport that he designed a 'moveable shooting-box' for use in the Indian jungles.[4] The camouflaged box was meticulously constructed so it could be disassembled, transported by train and then placed on a trolley, where it would be pulled to the desired location either by elephant or oxen. The box would remain in situ until the prey grew accustomed to it and then the recreational shooter would take up position in the box. As was customary with all the prince's toys, the aesthetics and design were paramount and the article reveals that the box was decorated in a Queen Anne style and included sofas that could be converted into beds, writing bureaus, bridge tables, and comfortable occasional chairs, while the floor was parquet and covered with Persian rugs. Ranji's obsession with recreational shooting persisted and during the Great war years he lost the sight in one eye whilst on a partridge shoot in Yorkshire.

English cricket captain (Bombay born) Douglas Jardine (1900 – 1958) was also an enthusiastic shooter. During the 1933/34 tour of India, he missed the highly coveted Christmas party hosted by the mayor of Calcutta, S. K. Basu, choosing instead to venture out into the wild, determined to gun down 'the pride of the Indian forest', the tiger.[5] Unfortunately, he was unsuccessful in shooting the Gwalior tiger and was humiliated on hearing that his cricketing colleague C. S. Marriott had triumphed. Not unlike cricket, shooting formed its own hierarchy and resulted in jealously and competitiveness between citizens of the Empire.

Games that comprised an element of danger, where victory was viewed as a manifestation of personal glory, led to the popularity of the hunting and massacre of animals as a privileged pastime. By the end of the nineteenth century, hunting had become enormously popular and was (ironically) viewed 'as a sport with proper rules of practice, or hunting codes, to which ideas of fairness were central'.[6] Despite the royals using shooting to facilitate relations with the British Raj it was also a cause of fierce competition as the colonists perceived the killing of animals as representing hegemony over opposing regimes 'who dared to get in the way of Britain's imperial conquest'.[7] The massacre of animals and the associated ceremonial activity adhered to a strictly constructed hierarchy and was a highly popular pastime.

The hunting and massacre of animals has been critiqued in academic scholarship as a hegemonic demonstration to reinforce man's superiority over the untamed beast. Hussain describes it simply as a profound 'struggle for control over nature'.[8] The inherent risks in opposing a wild and untamed animal, whether it be for sportsmanship or for survival, resulted in the victor being attributed with superlative traits of unheralded courage, bravery and heroism which, within the context of the Empire, acquired a profoundly romantic sensibility.

Big-game hunting was an exclusively privileged pastime during the nineteenth and twentieth centuries. However, it wasn't just sportsmanship and pleasure as the highly hierarchal cultural activity enabled an avenue of interaction between the Raj and the local elite. Shikars were frequently tactically planned to facilitate an atmosphere that stimulated political, economic and commercial debate.

A photograph of the Australians on their lunch break during a shooting expedition is found in the Alexander archive. Like all activities devised by the Indian royalty, the scene is finitely orchestrated and constructed. The shooting party casually recline on the ground, which eradicates any hierarchical structure and suggests that the individuals were all equal and psychologically aligned to the land. A tablecloth, placed on the ground, is covered with snacks and beverages. Props cushion the shooters and provide some comfort. Numerous Indian retinues supply the shooting party with food and beverages.

Indian royalty and the British elite (surprisingly one unidentified European woman is present) attend the luncheon and the image captures them ensnared in intense conversation that potentially involved negotiating business deals or plotting political ventures. The casual atmosphere of social intercourse could conversely facilitate dialogue of strategic political and economic magnitude. No primary evidence confirms what was being discussed on this occasion, however the intensity of the body language suggests that the participants were deeply enthralled by the dialogue. Despite visually adhering to the *mise-en-scène* the Australian cricketers' contribution to the presumed politicking would have been negligible. Tarrant is the only Australian present who potentially could have assisted any business negotiations. The Australians portrayed are superfluous to the interaction and, more broadly, to dialogues reverberating around in late-colonial India. Possibly their ambivalence to the colonial enterprise was being slowly unveiled.

Lunch following the Duck Shoot, Patiala. 1936. Alexander archive

Lunch following the Duck Shoot at Patiala. January 1936. Alexander archive

Akin to other cultural practices in colonial India, additional primary evidence reveals that, despite their initial enthusiasm, when the Australian cricketers encountered shooting, they tired of observing fealty to the custom. Despite Hendry nominating big-game hunting as one of the reasons he joined the tour, he soon found aspects of the elitist cultural practice tiresome, fraudulent and outmoded within the context of an increasingly nationalistic climate.

In an article subtitled 'Shoot to Kill!' Oxenham described a duck shoot on the Ana Sagar lake in Ajmer that took place when a cricket match finished prematurely. Oxenham observed that 'shooting in these parts is great sport, but talk of tiger hunts in the Jungle later on leaves me quite cold. They say there's nothing to worry about, all you have to do is to shoot to kill, and that's all there is to it'.[9] Oxenham's lacklustre opinion by the prospect of shooting big-game does not conform to colonial expectations. Seemingly, the longer the cricketers were in India, their attitudes towards colonisation, and various

British-introduced cultural activities, were challenged. By the 1930s, some of the Indian royalty were also tiring of the practice (and other pastimes introduced by the British colonisers).

Al-Haj Nawab Sir Hafiz Muhammad Hamidullah Khan Bahadur, otherwise known as Hamidullah Khan and president of the Indian Board of Control, was one such gentleman who was a key player in the tour narrative. In all the Australian literature he is referred to as the Nawab of Bhopal. A few months into the tour, the team spent a few days at his estate in Bhopal which functioned as tour respite and also possibly solidified their attitude to the ethics of Shikars.

The team first met the Nawab at the welcome to India ceremony in Bombay and midway through the trip a luncheon at his palace was scheduled. Frank Tarrant was absent, as he had remained in Bombay to receive a shipment of goods for the Maharaja of Patiala, yet images reveal that Eva was present. The cricketers seemingly enjoyed having the luxury of some time away from the tour manager. They arrived in automobiles fully stocked with whiskey and cigarettes. Oxenham noted that it was a welcome change from the 'beastly train'. The road trip was a pleasant journey made all the more wonderful when they rounded the driveway bend and saw the fairy-tale palace nestled amongst the manicured gardens.

Bhopal. Ryder archive

Australian team at Bhopal with Eva. Leather archive

The Nawab of Bhopal's palace. Leather archive

Following a convivial lunch, the players were to be dropped off at the railway station to continue on their journey to Nagpur yet the Nawab spontaneously extended an invitation for them to stay a night or two. The team unanimously agreed. Oxenham was especially happy and he noted that the break would be handy:

> I have no hesitation in saying that these few days did more for our side than it is possible to imagine, I don't mind telling you-that when we reached Indore things were getting somewhat desperate. With so many players unfit, and others nervy/jaded and ill-tempered. I was a bit afraid that the happy relationship that had existed was coming, to a "sticky" end.[10]

The change in schedule certainly lifted the cricketers' spirits. The Nawab's palace was a sportsman's paradise and included many recreational facilities. The cricketers quickly changed into their sporting attire; some played golf while others played tennis—made all the more enjoyable as the Nawab had a number of ball boys on staff. A few rode the Nawab's priceless polo ponies and racehorses. At the day's end, they all languished in the sunken marble pool which was reported to have healing properties. The next morning, they adjourned to the Nawab's summer house which was twenty-six miles from the palace and housed his famous shooting range. The cricketers were armed with rifles, as they were warned that tigers and panthers roamed the jungle. They didn't see any and were unsure if they should be relieved or saddened. They did however engage in some shooting practice on the man-made lake. Missing all their targets, the players were happy that they hadn't encountered a wild animal. They were however successful in finally disposing of the large wooden kangaroo emblazoned with the words 'WELCOME - WE'RE HERE' which they used for target practice. They were rather happy to finally be rid of the kitsch knick-knack that was gifted to them earlier on the trip and, from all accounts, it still sits on the bottom of the lake at Bhopal.

The players couldn't believe the tranquillity of the countryside. Macartney noted that apart from the absence of snow-capped mountains they could have been in Switzerland. Bill described the magnificent setting: 'Here, with dense jungle on three sides and the beautiful lake on the other, we had tea on gold plates and champagne from gold goblets, so an idea of the luxurious conditions can be imagined.'[11]

A vibrant sunset provided a spectacular backdrop as the team motored back to the palace. That evening they dined with the Nawab and following pudding they adjourned to his private cinema to watch some home movies. First up was the Test match at Headingley in 1930 when Bradman made 334 and annihilated the Englishmen. It was team-building footage. Providing commentary, the Nawab applauded the Australian players, and their nation, on their cricketing prowess. He noted that Charlie Macartney and Victor Trumper were the only cricketers, other than the Don, to have scored a century before lunch on the first day of a Test match. Charlie felt rather chuffed and grew in stature in the darkened home theatre.

Seeing the footage of Bradman reminded Morrisby of his offer made a few months earlier, in Adelaide. He'd really have to give it some serious thought and discuss it with his parents on his return.

The cricket footage was followed by films of wild animals in Bhopal shot by the Nawab.

Hendry's manuscript, and an earlier *Truth* article he penned, identifies changing ethical attitudes to the recreational massacre of animals as during the twentieth century a new public consciousness challenged the sport of shooting. Hendry noted that the Nawab of Bhopal had 'shot so many tigers that the thrill had gone out of it so he now photographed them in the jungle and showed us films within 50 yards of huge beasts'. This is revealing commentary on the Indian ruler's changing priorities and ethical perspective: tiring of recreational shooting, he employed new technologies to collaborate with the wild animals rather than orchestrating their demise. Electing to cinematically, rather than literally, shoot the animal indicates a new perspective to affluence, sportsmanship, hegemony and massacre. The royal embraced cinema as a symbol of prestige and had the available finances to facilitate the hobby. Hendry praised the inherent danger of filming the animal in such close proximity and applauded the bravery of the Nawab in a similar fashion to the way in which the killers of these animals were previously revered. Such ideas were surely challenging the cricketers previously ingrained ideologies. That the act of photographing wild animals, rather than killing them, was not embraced by all the royal families as primary material reveals that many royals, including the Patiala family, remained seduced by the shooting of animals with its inherent psychological symbolism and correlation with the racial and social hierarchy of colonial India.

Earlier in 1901, the Viceroy Lord Curzon declined an invitation extended by the Nawab of Junagadh to shoot lions in Gir (since 1965 known as Gir National Park). A few months later in an address to the Burma Game Preservation Association, Lord Curzon spoke of his refusal to partake in shooting at Gir and noted a changing philosophy to the recreational shooting of animals. This inspired the Maharajas to rally for a lion census to be conducted and on seeing the results they closed Gir to hunters as they realised that Asiatic lions required protection. Despite the Nawab of Bhopal and Lord Curzon's changing attitudes to shooting animals, it took many decades for the practice to become officially illegal.

Another image from the Leather archive documents Alexander, Mair, Bryant, Bert Tarrant and the Australian-born professional cricketer Frank Warne photographed with a tiger skin.[12] The photograph is not dated, and the location is unknown. The image is devoid of women—not particularly unusual in tour imagery—and the men are demonstratively masculine as signified by their clothing and physicality. Prankster, Bert Bryant lies parallel below the wild animal with the beast's face positioned immediately above his. He mugs for the camera. The cricketers' expressions suggest they are greatly amused by the shenanigans taking place. They perform for the camera, consciously contriving a narrative and orchestrating how the tour would subsequently be memorialised and remembered. They have autonomous control and determine their role as active participants. Sramek describes the 'curious late Victorian and Edwardian spectacle' of being photographed next to a deceased carcass as a symbol of the 'successful conquest of Indian nature'.[13] The cricketers ridicule the imperial tradition of a photograph being taken of a deceased animal as an act of triumphant nationalistic rhetoric or as a demonstration of masculine self-identity. Yet this mockery isn't the only example of the cricketers deriding customs in colonial India.

Warne, Alexander, Bert Tarrant, Mair and Bryant with an animal skin. Date and location unknown. Leather archive

Ironically, despite the apparent jesting and the cynicism of the participants towards the imperial practice, Hendry revealed that the players were eager to attend a shoot and, when they couldn't they still wished to acquire trophy heads and skins. 'His Highness the Maharaja of Pratapgarh arranged a panther shoot for a couple of us in his State during the Indore match, but Tarrant refused to let us off. Considering he had four panthers, practically leg-ironed and collared, all ready to be knocked over by us. It was a cruel blow'.[14] In light of not being able to attend the shoot the cricketers requested skins from the generous and obliging Maharaja of Pratapgarh. Hendry's manuscript observed: 'Half a dozen of our team had asked and received tiger skins from His Highness – they cost eighty pounds each – and were asked for as though requesting a cigarette from a pal'. The prestige of returning home with a trophy skin was embedded in tourism culture and colonial hierarchy, however the kudos usually correlated with the capture of the animal.

Interviewing the descendants of the Australian players, a common theme emerges. They all recall (exaggerated or imagined) glamorous and swashbuckling stories of Shikars and the very presence of animal skins in their descendants' archives suggests that shooting game, or rather the promise of it, dominated their India experience. However, there is also enough evidence to suggest that attitudinal changes increasingly prevailed which challenged the legitimacy and appeal of shooting game as a recreational pastime.

---

[1] Hendry manuscript.
[2] *Warwick Daily News* February 27, 1935.
[3] October 14, 1935.
[4] *Evening News* January 9, 1908.
[5] Guha 2002, 215–16.
[6] Hussain 2012, 1223.
[7] Sramek 2006, 661.
[8] 2012, 1212.
[9] *The Telegraph* December 3, 1935.
[10] *The Telegraph* January 6, 1936.
[11] *Sydney Mail* January 15, 1936.
[12] Frank Warne (1906–94) played first-class cricket in four continents. Travelling as a professional he spent two cricket seasons in India while he coached a local side (Bill January 15, 1936). Due to the illness and injury to the Australian team he played for them in the match against Southern Punjab (January 5–7, 1936).
[13] 2006, 659.
[14] *Truth* April 12, 1936.

16 CHRISTMAS IN CALCUTTA

London was the most important city to Australian colonies in the twentieth century, Calcutta was surely the second most important.[1]

By the time the players reached Calcutta they had been away from home for almost three months. The twenty-four-hour train journey from Nagpur was another excruciating exercise, yet the team brightened up on arrival at Howrah Station as Calcutta held the reputation as the party town. For centuries, visitors from faraway places had been lavishly entertained there. The players had especially heard glowing reports about the cosmopolitan city during the Christmas festive season. Macartney noted in his regular newspaper column that, 'Everybody was anxious to reach the capital city of Bengal, and once the capital of India, as it held a greater historic interest than any other place we have yet seen'.[2] Macartney's observation was based on the large British population and the predominance of Pommy culture and customs. The colonisers hadn't skimped, and the city was a symbol of British triumph.

Arriving by train in the early morning of Christmas eve, the cricketers were eager to get amongst people like themselves. Somehow, they thought that they'd be singing carols under the mistletoe and eating plum pudding and mince pies with the European elite. Surmising that after weeks of being largely in the company of Indians, they would feel more at home with the colonisers, yet they soon realised that despite deeming that they were British, they were dismissively viewed as convict stock—not vastly superior to the locals.

Driving from Howrah train station to the hotel in the early hours, they anticipated that the first glimmer of light would unveil a magical metropolis. Instead, Hendry critiqued: 'The streets were filthy, and the taxis, rickshaws, gherries, motorbuses and electric trams would scarcely find a place on our junk heaps. If Melbourne is ashamed of her approach from Port Melbourne to the city, then Calcutta should never show her face'. Macartney was equally unimpressed: 'We arrived at 7 a.m., and the motor run from the railway station to the hotel was, for the most part, through the worst slums and dirtiest neighbourhood I have ever seen. Filth and squalor abounded in plenty, and I was well pleased when we emerged from that locality into more respectable looking surroundings, and to our hotel'.

On arrival at the Grand Hotel, on Chowringhee Road, the player's moods lifted. They feared that it may be another Grand Hotel just like the one in Ahmedabad, yet their first impressions were favourable. They would be in residence at the hotel for ten days, which would be the longest time the team would be stationary in any one spot, and the cricketers hoped that it would provide them with respite from the harsh realities of India.

A diligent, yet overly eager, representative from the cricket club confronted Tarrant as the team alighted from the cars. Despite demonstrating convivial diplomacy, the unknown gentleman was abrupt and determined. Possibly he'd been given a directive from the Maharaja and, as the cricketers knew, the potentate's demands had to be obeyed. The hotel was simultaneously receiving many new guests and a sea of attendants tried to manoeuvre the players through the circular doors. The cricketers seemed reluctant to comply. Ron Morrisby wandered off to a vendor at the front of the hotel; obviously something had attracted his attention. Cricket enthusiasts shadowed the players—some held autograph books and others just wanted to chat about the state of the imperial game. Porters and the bearers were desperate to keep an eye on the various items of luggage. The number of trunks that the cricketers carried had almost doubled as they'd made numerous impulsive purchases items along the way. They had also been the recipients of many gifts. Oriental carpets, silverware and animal skins bulged from the luggage and the leather straps were straining. The players continually justified their acquisitions by not wanting to miss out on a bargain.

Touring cricketers with their luggage. 1935_36. Alexander archive

The club representative continued to bark commands at Frank as they entered the swanky hotel.

The hotel foyer's high-quality carpet felt soft and spongy. Tarrant gestured to the cricketers to sit on the Chesterfields and the two gentlemen continued their heated discussion. Paperwork detailing the social schedule for the next ten days was being thrust at Frank. Over 15,000 Europeans lived in Calcutta and seemingly almost all had extended invitations to the playing personnel. Even the boundlessly energetic Frank couldn't believe the number of social functions they were expected to attend. Somehow, three cricket matches were to be squeezed in as well.

The team just had time to quickly dress for the Garden Party at Viceroy House. It was one of three highlights of the Calcutta social season and the team had managed to score invitations to them all—the Viceroy's Garden Party, the Viceroy's Cup and the Viceroy's Ball. Tarrant was thrilled and couldn't believe his luck or rather his connections. It was all rather a rush to get ready in time and, luckily, they had their bearers to assist. The younger players grumbled and complained. Oxenham hurriedly tried to tidy and re-part his hair and buff his shoes with spittle.

Taxis picked up the team, and Hendry was mortified by the dilapidated car that was assigned to collect him. Despite his middle-class background (or maybe because of it), he wanted to make a good impression. He was adamant that such a bomb would be taken off the road at home. It certainly looked out of place amongst the Bentleys and Rolls that lined the road, so nearing Viceroy House he insisted that the driver drop him and Jack Ellis off a few blocks earlier. They trudged along the dusty road to the four colossal gates emblazoned with the Britannic Arms. Hendry introduced themselves as the touring Australian cricketers. The guard must have been surprised that they were on foot yet knew not to query any European guests.

The Garden Party was a long-winded affair with its own convoluted set of customs and rituals. After what seemed like an interminable wait, a trumpeter signalled the start of the function and a grand procession of the A-list commenced. The invitees had to wait until they were officially welcomed before they were seated. It was only then that they were offered refreshments and the party could start. The guests of honour paraded around, and the 4000 guests patiently waited in turn to meet them. It was a sea of top hats and turbans. Men bowed and the women curtsied. Snippets of the same conversation could be heard as the top brass moved from group to group. However, when the official party reached the touring cricketers they were treated to a dramatically different welcome as Lady Willingdon gushed that she had a special connection to Australia. Her father, Lord Brassey, had been Governor of Victoria and she treated the group like long-lost friends. They hadn't been the recipient of such female kindness for quite some time, with Eva being the exception. The cricketers could see the jealous side glances of the British, and the royals, who couldn't believe that the Australian cricketers were being received so affectionately. At one point an attendant informed Lady Willingdon that an influential Maharaja wanted to speak to her. She dismissed the request and said, 'He'll have to wait. I'm loving hearing news from home'.

The cricketers rated Lady Willingdon the highlight of the afternoon. They loved her buoyant personality, her sense of humour and her genuine kindness. Lord Willingdon described his wife as a human dynamo, a most apt description the cricketers thought.

During the tour planning stages, Frank Tarrant had invited the counsel of Lord Willingdon. The Viceroy requested; 'Bring back a nice team of Australians' and Tarrant cheekily and audaciously replied that 'there would be no Jardine cricket if he did bring a team back' revealing the extent of damage Bodyline had done to the global reputation of cricket.[3] Willingdon was the right man to give advice as he had serious cricket experience having played 18 first-class matches for Sussex and 20 for Cambridge University. In 1915 and 1918, he captained an England side against India in two star-studded matches. Tarrant actually played in the first one and captured 16 wickets, Patiala was his opposing captain in both.

Bad blood existed between the Viceroy, Patiala and Jardine following an incident at Simla, two years before the tour, when the Maharaja (with a reputation as an eternal letch) made advances towards the young daughter of Willingdon. Folklore suggests that the Maharaja was heavily intoxicated at the time. Following the incident, Jardine invoked the wrath of an apoplectic Willingdon when the English captain invited Patiala (as an MCC member) to play for the visiting side against the Viceroy's XI. Including the Maharaja in his side was a diplomatic bomb… however, when Willingdon told Jardine that he would not like it, the England captain just pulled on his pipe and remained silent. Who was Willingdon to tell him who to include in his side? Lady Willingdon even took Jardine for a long walk in the palace gardens to convince him, but he remained unmoved. Ultimately Jardine did not include Patiala in his side against the Viceroy's team. But played him in another match against Delhi Club and Ground. Against the Viceroy, the English captain let loose Nichols and Verity and defeated the star-studded side by an innings. Jardine had been insulted and he showed no mercy.

Back at the Viceroy's Garden Party, the scene was picture-postcard perfect. The seemingly innocuous sun was fierce, and the guests were thankful that canopies and umbrellas protected them from its' savage bite. Afternoon Tea was served on the terraced lawn by a retinue of liveried staff who almost outnumbered the guests. The exotically landscaped garden functioned as a historical timeline and featured a dragon shaped canon, a pair of colossal sculptural rampant lions, marbled arches, Mughal tiles and ornate water features which celebrated the various influences of India.

Later, some of the guests were invited inside for a few more aperitifs. The steps and corridors that led to the interior lounge room were lined with magnificently dressed lancers who formed a guard of honour. They wore a military uniform of black pants with red trim, matching double-breasted jackets with big brass buttons and they all carried gleaming gold swords held upright. The cricketers were delighted to meet a particularly charming Aide de Camp, who took an interest in Australian issues, and they chatted over a number of beverages.

Hendry enjoyed the exchange so much that he was one of the last to leave the Garden Party. He foolishly hadn't thought about how he'd return to the hotel when he curtly dismissed the earlier taxi driver. He imagined that he'd be able to hail another one yet as he stumbled across the garden, he wasn't too sure. Most of the guests had already left and there were only two limousines remaining. Luckily a gentleman magically appeared who realised the cricketer was caught without transportation and offered him a lift.

The car wound its way around ritzy, well-appointed houses with their fertile gardens and English trappings. Hendry got to see how the locals lived (or rather how the affluent colonials lived). In his memoire written roughly forty years later, Hendry noted that despite their impressive facades hints of financial insecurity were evident. Subtle signs of disrepair—rotting window frames, that a coat of paint couldn't quite disguise, and overgrown gardens were evident. A number of 'To Let' signs were placed on entrance gates to comfortable bungalows. Possibly here, Hendry was confusing the historical timeline and creatively reimaging history as despite his suggestion that the end of colonisation was imminent and evident, the concept of independence was still quite far away from British minds. In 1917, the War Cabinet had predicted independence after 500 years. In 1943, Viceroy Lord Linlithgow predicted 50 years … even then with several thousand British to handhold the country as it stepped into self-rule.

Hendry chatted to his 'driver' and when they arrived back at the Grand the cricketer profusely thanked him and spontaneously decided to repay his kindness by shouting him a few rounds of drinks in the bar. Most transactions and gratuities in India seemingly involved alcohol.

Dinner that night at the Grand Hotel consisted of quail, Australian lamb, Scottish salmon, caviar, tortoise soup, a curious array of vegetables compiled in an exotic fashion and a plethora of desserts. Despite, the extravagance of the menu, the cricketers grumbled, as they really just wanted some simple fare. Bill stated that he'd always taken food for granted and had never really thought that much about what he ate and how he disposed of it until arriving in India. Pre-dinner drinks were served around 8pm, dinner a few hours later and dessert wine wasn't poured until well after midnight and was followed by dancing. It was 2am when the players finally went to bed. It was the end of another long day. Undressing, Leather suddenly realised that it was Christmas day—the first one he'd spent away from his family. It both thrilled and slightly unnerved him.

Ron Oxenham, in the room next door, was also tired but he was keen to read a few Christmas greetings from home. During dinner a butler in a starched white jacket and carrying a silver tray had whispered to him that a few letters had arrived, and they'd been placed on his writing bureau in his room. Ron was anxious to read them. A letter-drop always caused great excitement. The first letter he opened was from Reg Stephens, the secretary of the Queensland Cricket Association. Reg wished Ron a Merry Christmas and congratulated him on his excellent performances with the ball. Ron felt enormous pride when Reg revealed that the bowler's fine performances were being comprehensively reported by the Australian press. Ron hoped his family had collected all the clippings, as he had requested.

Likewise, Jack Ryder sat in his bedroom reading Christmas greetings. As captain, his pile of letters was by far the biggest. The postage stamps revealed that Jack received correspondence from the far reaches of the Empire. Jack devoured the letters from his family in Melbourne first. It took quite some time to read the ten-page letter from his son Tam who filled him in on all the news from home. Tam's writing was small, and it was sometimes difficult to decipher words, yet Jack persisted. He read the letter slowly not wanting to overlook any details. The room was silent bar the crinkling of the pages as he digested their content. Tam told Jack about the state of the suburban cricket competition and his own impressive involvement in a few games. Jack felt immensely proud as Tam showed promise. Jack was interested to learn how his club Collingwood was faring in his absence. Club politics were always bubbling away, and cautious Jack was a stabilising influence. He hoped the club would survive in his absence.

Jack received fan mail from India inviting the team to attend social events, which he knew they wouldn't have time to attend, and requesting autographs with enclosed stamped self-addressed envelopes and he made a mental note that he'd get back to these. He skimmed numerous Christmas cards from folk he'd met in India. He devoted far less time to these, however the card from the Maharaja of Patiala attracted his attention as it was unlike all the other ones. It didn't include conventional Yuletide iconography. It was a Christmas card with a picture of three Sikh warriors on the front. The semi-naked figures held spears and looked rather menacing. Jack wondered why the Maharaja had produced a card that paid no homage to Christmas conventions. Maybe it reflected the potentate's unorthodox and rebellious personality combined with his rather eccentric sense of humour, thought Jack. The card rather unnerved Jack and he went to sleep dreaming of the menacing 'warrior class'.

Christmas card from the Maharaja of Patiala. December 1935. Ryder archive

WITH EVERY GOOD WISH
FOR A
HAPPY CHRISTMAS
AND A
PROSPEROUS NEW YEAR

FROM
MAHARAJADHIRAJ OF PATIALA.

Hendry mulled over the activities of the day. He was quite annoyed on learning that a few of the younger boys had played truant and missed the prestigious garden party. As one of the senior fellows in the team he felt responsible for keeping the younger chaps in line. Earlier in the morning when the cricketers were leaving for the Garden Party, the boys redirected the taxi and instructed the driver to drop them off at the cinema. Apparently, they were more excited by the prospect of seeing Ginger Rogers and Fred Astaire in *Top Hat*.

The Christmas day schedule was no different to any other day in Calcutta—it was a tight schedule of social activities largely revolving around alcohol consumption, some formal procedures and a fair amount of tedious small talk. Despite Christmas day being part of the Sheffield Shield fixture (provided it didn't fall on a Sunday) the cricketers were usually surrounded by family in a familiar setting. Yet December 25, 1935 was quite different. The day did however start in a typical fashion with attendance at St Paul's cathedral. The cricketers woke early and selected their cleanest clothes. Tom Leather brushed off yesterday's dust that covered his dress shoes and asked Walgi if he could give them a polish. Ron Oxenham had to wear a dirty shirt; he hadn't been organised enough to have one laundered. He knew he wouldn't be removing his jacket so he hoped the oversight wouldn't be noticed.

Despite it being only a few blocks from the Grand Hotel, the attendees caught taxis to church. Maybe it was unnecessary, but the cricketers enjoyed being able to indulge in such luxuries. Ron Oxenham and Frank Bryant shared a ride but quickly realised something was wrong. The driver either hadn't understood the destination or rather, as Oxenham surmised, he just wanted to leverage some extra money from the cricketers and the duo found themselves in the backblocks of Calcutta. Despite their fervent demands that they were going in the wrong direction, the driver was oblivious to their protests. Oxenham didn't believe that it was an innocent mistake and chastised the driver. It was all rather pointless, as seemingly the driver couldn't understand what they were saying. They eventually arrived at the bluestone church, to the deafening chimes of the pealing bells. The driver indicated the price. Oxenham in his customary earthy fashion told the driver, in no uncertain terms, that he would only receive half what was being demanded. Slamming the door, the cricketers hurriedly threw coins at the driver and ran to the church doors.

Christmas lunch followed at Eden Gardens. The players were genuinely excited to see the renowned cricket ground. Comparisons were frequently made with the Melbourne Cricket Ground or Lord's. The previous year, Eden Gardens had hosted the Test encounter against the English and the Australians would be playing there in a few days' time. The Australians were keen to check out the wicket and they were relieved to see predicable turf following the predominance of coir matting in India.

It was another long afternoon with too much food and drink. Despite their earnest attempts, the caterers didn't quite get the Christmas Day fare right and the cricketers grumbled. Following lunch, the cricketers attended a polo championship. Teams, captained by royalty from different Indian states, competed and Jaipur, the pre-eminent team, won easily. The Jaipur team had recently returned from a tour of Europe where they had won every contest in a clean sweep. Bill was amazed by the extravagance of the sport and tallied the cost of transporting at least eighty horses across India and internationally. In attendance was Curtis Skene, an Australian polo player, who patiently explained the rules to Tom Leather who knew little about the sport. Curtis was in a similar situation to the professional cricketers as he was in India employed by the royal families and was being paid handsomely.

Despite the busy schedule in Calcutta, Ryder found time to dash off two letters to his wife, written on Grand Hotel letterhead. As captain of the team and representing Australia, in a quasi-geopolitical role, he was reluctant to be too publicly damning in his criticism of Indian politics and Indian culture. However, the letters express Jack's candid attitudes. Jack informs Fan that, 'this spot is meant to be the bright spot of India at Xmas but I still have not found it out'. Ryder describes a function where his attendance with the Calcutta Cricket Association was mandatory. He is brutally critical of the British Raj and the event and observed, 'These shows are inclined to be boring at times', yet he reluctantly acknowledged that, as captain of the 'Australian' team, 'It has to be done'.

---

1 Alexander E. Davis 2013, 82.

2 *Newcastle Morning Herald and Miners' Advocate* January 15, 1936.

3 *The Mail* March 2, 1935.

17 HORSE-RACING, GIRL CHASING, TURNING ON THE 'FIZZ', THE BLACK HOLE AND ANOTHER 'TEST'

On Boxing Day, the team split up. A match against the Maharaja of Cooch Behar's XI was taking place at Woodlands, his 100-acre private residence. The team expected something special as the guardsmen unlatched the iron gates emblazoned with the Cooch Behar crest and the cars wound their way up the seemingly endless, tree-lined, crunchy gravel drive. The residence, a large white stucco building constructed by the British in the classical East India Company style, sat on elevated land. The welcoming committee mingled with the team on the deep verandas that buffered the house. They overlooked the well-maintained cricket ground, which sat adjacent to a substantial garden bursting with the scent of jasmine, frangipani, roses and poinsettia. Two tennis courts, stables for about thirty horses, and a garage that accommodated over twenty cars nestled into the landscape.

From all accounts the one-day game, described as 'bright and enjoyable from beginning to end', was an informal affair where enjoyment was the primary objective. Only half the regular Australian players participated, and a few ring-ins joined in. Bill's article in the *Sydney Mail* details the match and relates that despite being greatly taken with the 'attractive ground' the wicket was one of the worst they'd encountered. 'On taking strike to a medium fast-medium bowler', Bill 'received a rude shock when the first ball just grazed his chin, the next knocked his topee clean off his head, and then, much to' Bill's relief, 'the umpire declared that the wicket was not fit for play and that a mat would have to be procured. The match was adjourned pending the arrival of the mat' which arrived an hour and a half later. Bill described the game as a queer, but pleasant, practice match.

The Maharaja of Cooch Behar was permitted to shine— he took two catches, bowled out Charlie Macartney and scored 18 not out. The Australians scored at nearly five and a half runs per over. The match ended in an inevitable draw considering the hours lost locating the mat. For almost a quarter of a century, Frank Tarrant had periodically been on the Cooch Behar payroll in a coaching and cricket promotion capacity so it's hardly surprising that sportsmanship was the theme of the day. At the day's end, the visiting cricketers were the recipients of golden gifts.

The Australians not playing cricket attended the Viceroy Cup which was one of the biggest horse races in the Empire, if not the biggest in the world. It was known as the 'Ascot of British India' and Ryder described it as 'a sight unrivalled in racing history'.[1] Tarrant had warned the cricketers to keep track of their highly prized member's enclosure passes as they were worth their weight in gold.

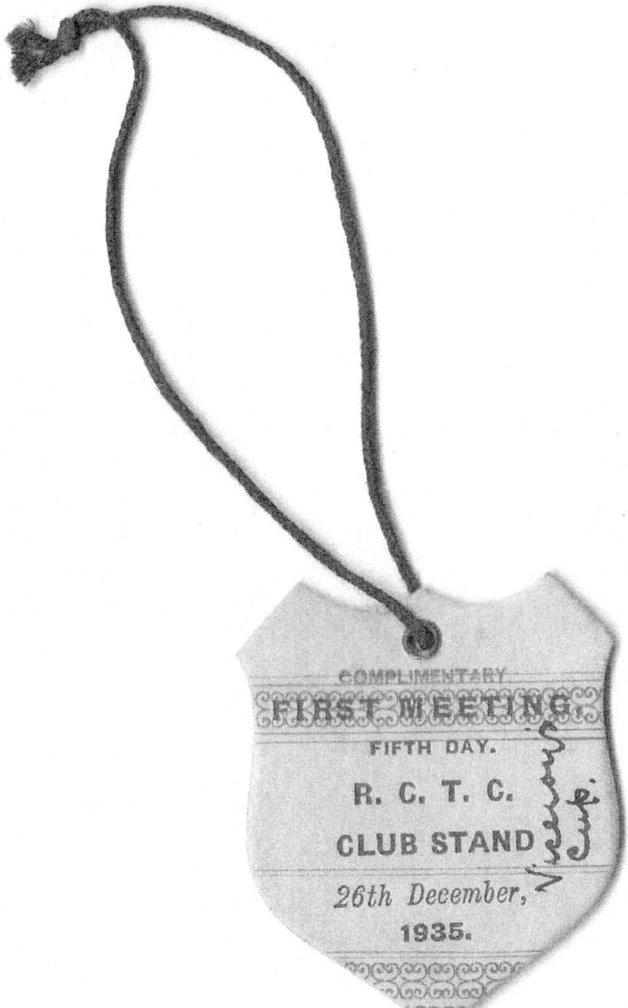

Ryder's pass to the Viceroy Cup, Calcutta. December 1935. Ryder archive

Dozens of lancers on horses, dressed in military uniforms with gold trim, regiment hats and equestrienne boots carried flags which flapped wildly in the wind. Bassoons and trumpets playing patriotic tunes signalled the arrival of the Viceroy royals and the crowd of almost 100,000 lustily applauded as Lord and Lady Willingdon entered the arena. 'God Save our Gracious King' bellowed out over a crackly loudspeaker. Four military guards wearing pith helmets with vibrant purple plumes escorted the Viceroy in a golden horse-drawn carriage. The couple waved for over fifteen minutes to the sea of adoring British people as their carriage circled the track. Lady Willingdon wore a feather fascinator firmly attached to her brown kiss curls, as the wind would have blown any other headwear away. Likewise, Lord Willingdon attached his paisley handkerchief firmly to his jacket lapel. They were well-prepared for the noisy and blustery affair. They had obviously done this before.

Viceroy Cup, Calcutta. December 1935. Leather archive

The cricketers were happy when the formalities were over, and the racing commenced. French-bred horse *Mas d'Antibes* easily won the Viceroy Cup with press reportage revealing that the horse 'romped home'. *Mas d'Antibes*, a muscular bay colt, was a prized possession and had been purchased by the Nawab of Bhopal from the Aga Khan. The exorbitant expense was worth it.

Earlier, in Bhopal, the Nawab suggested that they should place a wager on the horse. During the chaos of the race day in Calcutta, some of the cricketers remembered this tip yet, with all that had happened over their time in India, some of them forgot. Additionally, a few were encouraged to bet on the Nawab's horse when they realised that Australian local-boy, Ray Wilson, was the jockey. Some in the team had encountered Wilson in Melbourne. What they didn't immediately realise was that the entire field was ridden by Australian jockeys. They hadn't previously comprehended the level of exchange between India and Australia on the racing and equine circuit.

Like Tarrant, Wilson's sporting story was a rags-to-riches tale. A working-class youngster, Wilson sold newspapers from a stand on Melbourne's Collins St. He was enthusiastic and amiable, and in his capacity of salesman, he befriended businessmen who advised him to invest any spare pennies in stocks and shares. Over time his small nest-egg grew. One busy evening, whilst selling newspapers, a car mowed him down. Mr Ben Chaffey, a well-known identity in financial and racing circles, was behind the wheel of the Bentley and was devastated by the near fatality. A guilt-ridden Chaffey promised to provide for the injured paperboy.

This led to an unlikely friendship and Wilson was introduced to the world of thoroughbred racing. Chaffey gifted Wilson a pony for Christmas and the newspaper boy proved to possess natural equestrian aptitude. When the Depression intervened, Wilson, like most of his regulars, watched his hard-earned savings go up in smoke. The racing industry seemed to thrive in the depression years when other more orthodox industries collapsed so Wilson pursued riding professionally. He acquired an apprenticeship as a jockey and within his first six months of racing he won sixty races including five in one day at Ascot. Wilson was invited to ride in India. Details are sketchy yet I guess he was employed by the Nawab of Bhopal and was offered significant recompense. Unlike Tarrant, Wilson didn't warm to India and following the season he returned home—significantly richer. Newspaper articles hint at Wilson's illicit tendencies, which I guess wasn't unusual in the racing industry at the time, but maybe the Australian press was just sceptical of anyone who chose to ply his trade in the East.

Following the excitement of the day at the races and the day spent at Woodlands, a few of the boys, with surplus funds, and golden trinkets at their disposal, decided they would go out in the town to celebrate. They were growing in confidence and getting rather weary of the finitely orchestrated schedule and the claustrophobia of the sanctioned activities. Fuelled by a bit of daring, they decided to venture further afield after declining a few invitations to attend routine 'at home' functions.

Adventure beckoned and a few of the boys set off in a taxi, yet soon they were in unfamiliar territory as the car steered away from the privileged greenbelt. Colonial charm and manicured bungalows rapidly turned into a parade of indigence. Out of their comfort zone where the locals lived in conditions that the Australians hadn't previously encountered and couldn't believe. Large families were crammed into makeshift huts without water, power or sanitation. Malnourished children and rabid dogs inhabited the landscape. This was an India that the cricketers had been mostly shielded from. They knew the Maharaja would be upset if he discovered that they had gone out unsupervised. Hendry as the senior statesman instructed the driver to take them back to the hotel. The cricketers desperately hoped that he understood the command.

Seemingly the driver did understand as he reversed into a narrow lane and retraced his steps. However, he took a sharp turn, and the players encountered another side of Calcutta that they hadn't imagined existed. This was the red-light district of Calcutta and just as the players had been horrified about the living conditions of the underprivileged, they were aghast at the demonstrative subjugation of the local women. I imagine the cricketers had found their way to Sonagachhi, the largest red-light district in Asia, however the location cannot be confirmed. In the background a pimp could be heard cajoling the girls into action.

Frequently European gentlemen in imported cars roamed the streets seeking reprieve from the missionary position. Journeying into this part of town was like frequenting the risqué dance halls on the Left Bank in Paris without the glamour and the safety. Women, scantily clad with lacquered red lips and hennaed hands, beckoned the players, wriggling their hips to the jingle jangle of anklet charms and the promise of Eastern pleasure. The Australians wound up their windows and in no uncertain terms instructed the driver that they wanted to return to the hotel immediately; horrified that the driver had mistaken their requests for fun as prurient intentions. The scene shocked the cricketers as evidenced by Hendry when he recalled the incident in his memoire written close to fifty years later: 'It was pathetic and inhuman to pass down the 'Red Light' street where the women were in cages like wild animals, priced according to attire!'

By contrast, the following evening the team was back at Government House for the Viceroy ball. In tuxedos they sipped cocktails, engaged in genteel conversation and, when they needed to expend some energy, made their way to the dance floor and swivelled to music under cantilevered ceilings studded with immense crystal chandeliers. Butlers in white jackets navigated their way through the compact crowd carrying endless silver trays of drinks and hors d'oeuvres. The players let their guard down and ate lustily untroubled by the fear of dysentery. It was far removed from the previous night's entertainment.

The cricketers were keen to visit the Black Hole of Calcutta as it played a significant role in the colonial narrative. Commentators and the tourists alike wrote about their impressions of the monument and observed its historic significance. Bill noted that as a youngster he was drilled with the pedagogy of the Black Hole. Macartney revealed that he also was familiar with the story: 'Every schoolboy has been told of the "Black hole of Calcutta" so the name of this city was on all tongues'.[2]

In the 1930s, the Black Hole of Calcutta was an imperially significant monument as it commemorated the death of 123 British prisoners after Nawab Siraj-ud-Dowlah locked them in an underground gaol. The monument celebrated the revenge of the British following their recapture of Calcutta and their victory at the Battle of Plassey in 1757. Memorials were commonly constructed by the British to commemorate their role and to justify their colonial presence by mythologising their contribution to the success of the Empire and to simultaneously emphasise the barbarisms of Indian rulers. These monuments embodied the battle between East and West with implicit messages of racial superiority.

Ryder wrote about the experience for the *Herald* in a predictable manner. He observed that 'The notorious Black Hole of Calcutta sent cold shivers down our spines. That hideous dungeon, a grim relic of the Indian mutiny (sic), is still preserved, enclosed with an iron railing. A tablet tells part of the terrible story'.[3] Yet in a letter to his wife, he observed that he was unimpressed with the memorial and noted that, 'there was very little to see'. His private lacklustre response to the monument can be interpreted as his lack of investment in the colonial narrative yet publicly he had to support the enterprise. The British used stories such as that of the Black Hole to validate colonisation and any challenge to the authenticity of the event was deemed anti-imperial.

Another match was squeezed into the itinerary with the Australian team coming up against Bengal & Assam. The calibre of the local team was impressive as future Test bowler SN Banerjee captured five wickets with pace and accuracy alongside stalwarts like AL Hosie, Kamal Bhattacharya and captain (Cambridge Blue) TC Longfield. Despite the potential of the local team, the Australians won easily by nine wickets. Macartney (in his first serious game since injury), Morrisby and Bryant starred with the bat whilst Leather was the pick of the bowlers.

Partying was central to the sojourn in Calcutta yet somehow three cricket matches had to be squeezed in. Despite winning, Frank Tarrant was a little disappointed by his team's performance in the first two matches and attributed it to the excessive socialising and alcohol abuse that had become commonplace. Frank was particularly critical of the standard of fielding.

During a team meeting he chastised the players and imposed a curfew to try to limit the excessive drinking. He demanded a better performance in the upcoming 'Test'. I'm sure Bert Ironmonger hadn't been on the receiving end of such parental vitriol for almost fifty years. It also seemed a little contradictory, as Frank was always one of the last to retire at night and in the wee hours of the morning was encouraging 'just one more for the road'. Even when the players were inflicted with serious illness, Tarrant had encouraged 'alcohol for the fever'. Surely, he was partially responsible for the beast he had created.

Irrespective of Tarrant's demands, the players were also tiring of the exhaustive social pressures. Attendance at an 'at home' organised by the Bengal and Assam cricket club was compulsory and Tarrant was peeved when he counted heads—only the hardcore imbibers; Harry Alexander, Lisle Nagel and Bert Tarrant were in attendance. Hendry had resolved to give some of the official functions 'a wide berth' and he commented that, 'the pace was altogether too hot'.[4] Even the customarily disciplined captain, Jack Ryder, decided to give himself a night off.

During his post dinner speech Tarrant apologised and attributed the players' absence to the strenuous nature of the tour. Always prone to embellishment, he creatively suggested that it may have had something to do with the weather. Truancy seemingly was his theme for the evening as Tarrant audaciously criticised the British in India and their non-attendance at the cricket matches: further highlighting imperial instability. The relationship between Australia and India was solidifying at the expense of both countries' kinship with Britain. Caustically Tarrant reminded the crowd at the reception that, 'cricket was an English game, but the Englishmen did not come to see them'. He continued with a further snipe at the English: 'Everybody knew how the Australians played cricket, and that, when they wanted to get a man out, they would not hit him on the body to do so'.[5]

Little is known about how the players saw in the new year. The only reference to it is found in Hendry's column in the Sun where he alludes to alcohol consumption. He wrote, 'I always thought that New Year's Eve was a Scotsman's night. Evidently, the European population of Calcutta contains many Scotsmen. To most of us it will be a memorable night, and though we broke resolutions that we had just previously made, we managed to give a good account of ourselves next day on the field, and so the second unofficial Test was another hallow victory'. Hendy's lack of enthusiasm about the match reflected team sentiment.

The 'Test' match commenced on New Year's Eve day on a wet wicket, which was most uncommon during winter in Calcutta. The officials had difficulty locating a tarpaulin and eventually had to compromise with an old piece of shabby cloth that almost covered the wicket but not quite. Macartney described the 'piebald pitch' as 'absolutely the worst wicket to play on with any degree of certainty'.[6]

The visitors won the second 'Test' easily. Put in to bat on the wet wicket, India's performance was dismal as they scored a measly 48, with six of their batsmen out for ducks. Macartney, asked to operate with his by now seldom-used left-arm spin, made splendid use of the sticky wicket and picked up five. The disharmony within the Indian team and their lack of experience in managing the weather conditions, and handling the attention of the cricket world, was glaringly evident. Their Test star Amar Singh sat in the stands and watched the damp dismal game. The all-rounder maintained that he was too sick to play yet the medical staff assured the public that he was indeed healthy enough. Some suggestions have been made that his relationship with the captain C. K. Nayudu was so divisive that they couldn't play together. This game saw the last instance of Nayudu in the role of captain and it was becoming evident that intra-region, personal and communal issues would have to be resolved if the Test tour to England later in the year was to be a success.

Australian cricketers at Eden Gardens, Calcutta. Leather archive

The Australians were no closer to understanding the machinations of Indian cricket, yet they were satisfied that they had easily won their first two 'Tests'. Hendry wrote that 'Tarrant almost danced with joy at our success, for it proved conclusively there could be no-longer any doubt about the strength of his side. He let his head go and turned on "fizz". Some of the teetotal members of the side indulged and let out quite a few secrets as a result'.[7]

To wrap up their visit to Calcutta, the Bengal and Assam Cricket Club arranged a dinner for the team on January 2, the evening before the last day of play. Very little information can be located about the event bar an autographed menu located in the Leather archive. In attendance was a suite of esteemed diners, including the Maharaja of Porbandar. The menu includes the signature of English cricketers Herbert Sutcliffe and J. B. Hobbs who, beyond their signature on the menu, are not mentioned in any literature pertaining to the tour. Considering Hobbs was possibly the most famous English professional cricketer of the period and Sutcliffe was also very highly regarded, it is puzzling that they are not referenced elsewhere. Both Hobbs and Sutcliffe had previously travelled to India, where they assisted the cricket industry and received generous remuneration. They had played for the Maharajakumar of Vizianagaram's team in India and also turned out for them in Ceylon. The purpose of their presence at the function is unknown as was the certainty of their appearance. It is feasible that the signatures on the menu may be one of the Australian players playing a prank although they appear to be authentic. It was also possible that the signatures could have been procured during the 1930/31 season when Hobbs and Sutcliffe had been in India however it looks like the same pencil has been used. The Leather archive also includes an autographed portrait of Hobbs, an indecipherable inscription on the back of the image could say 'at Trent Bridge' however this is not clearly legible. Although the provenance of the image is impossible to establish, its presence amongst the other objects suggests it fell into Tom's hands in India. It is possible that Tom and Jack Hobbs may have encountered each other on another occasion or possibly the autographed image in Tom's collection was simply evidence of a young man's admiration for a cricketing great.

Surprisingly, the menu doesn't include many signatures of the travelling personnel which suggests that, despite Tarrant's earlier demands, the team may have played truant. Another explanation could be that only the eminent guests were required to sign the menu, as Ryder and Tarrant are definitely there. Inexplicably Tom Leather's signature is clearly legible however it is written in ballpoint pen whilst all the others are pencil inscriptions. The pen was not commonly used until after the Second World War which suggests that Tom signed the menu at a later date to verify his presence at the event. Seemingly over time his presence in India became more important to him as the profile of India and Indian cricket magnified.

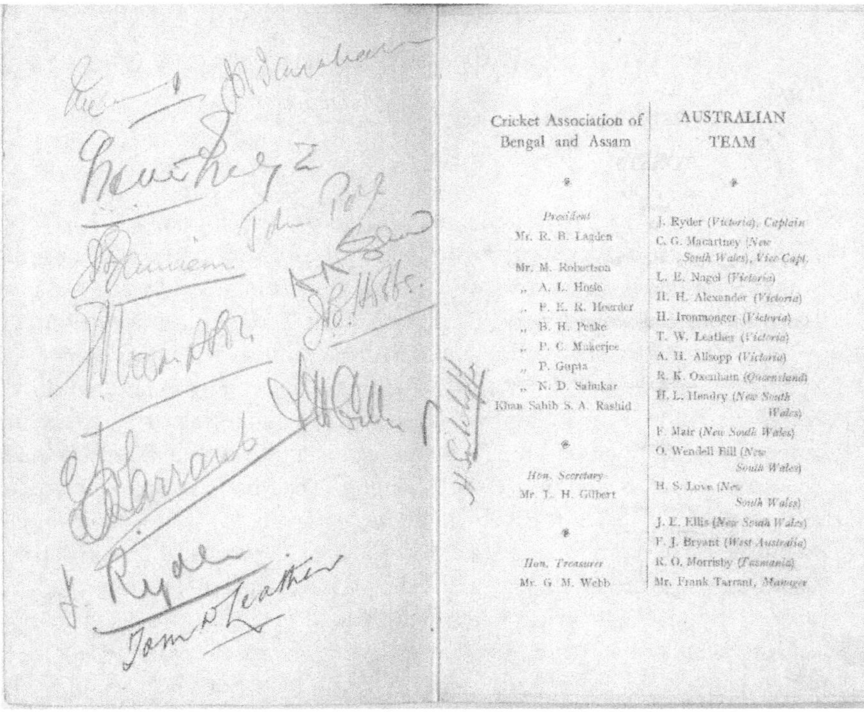

Cricket Association of Bengal and Assam

President
Mr. R. B. Lagden

Mr. M. Robertson
„ A. L. Hosie
„ F. E. R. Hoarder
„ B. H. Peake
„ P. C. Mukerjee
„ P. Gupta
„ N. D. Saimkar
Khan Sahib S. A. Rashid

Hon. Secretary
Mr. L. H. Gilbert

Hon. Treasurer
Mr. G. M. Webb

AUSTRALIAN TEAM

J. Ryder (*Victoria*), *Captain*
C. G. Macartney (*New South Wales*), *Vice Capt.*
L. E. Nagel (*Victoria*)
H. H. Alexander (*Victoria*)
H. Ironmonger (*Victoria*)
T. W. Leather (*Victoria*)
A. H. Allsopp (*Victoria*)
R. K. Oxenham (*Queensland*)
H. L. Hendry (*New South Wales*)
F. Mair (*New South Wales*)
O. Wendell Bill (*New South Wales*)
H. S. Love (*New South Wales*)
J. E. Ellis (*New South Wales*)
F. J. Bryant (*West Australia*)
R. O. Morrisby (*Tasmania*)
Mr. Frank Tarrant, *Manager*

Signed Bengal & Assam menu. January 1936. Leather archive

---

[1] *Sporting Globe* February 26, 1938.

[2] *Newcastle Morning Herald and Miners' Advocate* January 15, 1936.

[3] March 12, 1936. Ryder is actually incorrect here as the Black Hole is a remnant from an incident that took place 100 years before the Indian mutiny.

[4] The *Sun* January 23, 1936.

[5] *The Sydney Morning Herald*, January 1, 1936.

[6] *The Hindu* January 1, 1936.

[7] The *Sun* January 23, 1936.

18 THE ATMOSPHERE VIBRATED WITH TRIUMPHANT JOY

Research tends to progress in fits and starts and in early 2015 it took a fortuitous turn. It was a sticky summer night in Melbourne. I'm unsure if it was the sound of the cicadas or the heat that woke me. However, for some reason I did wake up. It wasn't a night for sleep. Maybe some computer time may assist, I wondered. I knew it wasn't recommended by sleep specialists, yet I decided to check my emails. Amongst University generated junk was one from an unknown recipient, it attracted my attention as it was identified by the *gov.au* domain and the intriguing subject: 'Greetings from Islamabad'.

Marzio introduced himself as a senior Australia Federal Police member and following some formalities he invited me to visit Pakistan. From memory, he was the Senior Liaison Officer of Serious and Organised Crime or something intriguing like that. He had been given my old work email address by ex-Pakistan cricket captain Majid Khan and it had taken some time to track me down through my new staff presence online. I'd been in touch with Majid a few years earlier telling him about my research. When I told my non-cricket friends about our contact, I explained ... 'he's the cousin of Imran' which made females swoon and the general public take notice. I replied to Marzio immediately saying that I was interested but could we schedule a phone meeting?

By this time, I'd already travelled to India multiple times. Despite my affection for the country, I had been frustrated by the lack of interest in the 1935/36 Australian tour. Research in India had seemingly come to a halt as I'd retraced the steps of the cricketers almost eighty years earlier numerous times and each time I came home with less. How many times does one need to visit the Cricket Club of India library, I wondered? I'd contemplated research in Pakistan on a few occasions as the tour took place prior to partition and the team played a match in Karachi and an unofficial 'Test' in Lahore. I realised that an Indian-only interpretation of the tour was a little unbalanced, yet I'd given up dreams of visiting Pakistan as my PhD scholarship was running out and I needed to submit. Yet to be honest it was fear that rejected the idea. My research phase was over, and I was confident that I wouldn't find anything there anyway.

How wrong I was.

A few phone calls between Islamabad and Melbourne convinced me that I should visit Pakistan: the part of the subcontinent that Westerners no longer visit. I did my due diligence and checked up on who these people were. There was a tenuous connection between Marzio and his cohorts and Cricket

Australia, which, of course, I verified. I even managed to track down Geoff Lawson who, despite being sacked from the position of Pakistan cricket coach in 2008, enthused about the country. He gave positive feedback about Pakistan, its people and cricket. Booking tickets was difficult and expensive. Flight Centre didn't deal with Pakistan International Airlines, so I had to book my flight from Lahore to Delhi directly through the airline. I estimated it the most expensive 400 kms I would ever travel. It was either that or travel on buses and cross the Wagah border on foot. I wasn't keen on the latter option as a bomb had recently been detonated there.

Essentially, I was being invited by the Australian Federal Police and the Australian High Commission as a goodwill gesture between the countries. I knew I wasn't their first choice, but I was rather chuffed that I was somewhere on their list. The AFP was fundraising for the families of Pakistani policemen who had died in action and would hold an event during my visit to generate some income for the Fayyaz Sumbal Foundation. We decided to coincide my visit with the start of the Cricket World Cup in Australia and New Zealand. In the end I decided that I'd stay for a week. If it was too horrid, I could just spend the time holed up in my hotel room and watch the World Cup.

Prior to departure, I worried about Pakistan. It wasn't just the bombs, the terrorists and the white slave trade, it was my wardrobe. Worrying about whether I should cover my face, my neck, my legs, my forearms and my feet occupied me. My new contacts at the AFP suggested I speak to an Australian woman who was married to a local and was living in Lahore. She told me that she wore 'skinny jeans, T shirts and heels' and after meeting her in person I realised, in certain circles, these items were *de rigueur*. Certainly, at a function I attended I was one of the few women not dripping in diamonds, vertigo-inducing Jimmy Choo heels and strapless sequins. However, I was still sceptical, people were telling me to conceal, cover and hide my body parts. I worried more.

My trusty Noel and I spent a few nights in Bangkok en route to Islamabad. I enjoyed the comparative security and stability of Thailand. However, possibly, this was just a façade as a political coup had taken place the previous year and Smartraveller recommended a high degree of caution. My sense of ease in Bangkok reminded me of how the cricketers must have felt during the last few days on the SS *Chitral* before their arrival in Bombay. I was still incredibly anxious about Pakistan having read too many blogs about the safety (or lack thereof) of Westerners traveling there. Getting Pakistani rupees was impossible in Melbourne. Each obstacle made me realise that no one visits. It was certainly not on the tourist trail and possibly the only visitors were daredevil thrill-seekers and Australian Pakistanis returning for family reunions or weddings.

Islamabad was a modern city, constructed in 1960, so my cricketers didn't experience it, yet it was our entry point. Our arrival was unremarkable. The plane was late. The airport seemed to function, unaffected by the obvious absence of any luxurious trimmings. I had been told to avoid eye contact, ignore any offers by touts to carry my luggage and head straight to the diplomatic line. On entering the public space, I braced myself, expecting the worst and it didn't happen. The most notable feature of my arrival in Islamabad was the number of Singapore shoppers with their distinct red, blue and white weave on the luggage conveyer belt, far outnumbering the taped boxes and scuffed suitcases sans wheels. My Samsonite stood out as, I'm afraid, I did.

Marzio and his wife lived in a comfortable five-bedroom, heavily armed, house in the diplomatic enclave of Islamabad. In fact, the whole city seemed to be a diplomatic enclave. They were generous, kind people who had done a number of stints in Pakistan. I was surprised that they kept on putting their hands up to return to the posting. Marzio was retiring soon and he seemed to want to get as much out of Pakistan as possible. We were woken at 6am the following morning by the omnipresent call to prayer. It was a magical way to be stirred.

On day One, we attended our first cricket match at the Islamabad gymkhana: a goodwill event between an Australian diplomatic XI and the PCB chairman's XI. Australian High Commissioner, Peter Heyward captained the Australian team and played alongside British High Commissioner, Phillip Barton and Pakistani cricketers Adnan Akmal and Rana Mansoor. The sprightly, eternally youthful Intikhab Alam, who played cricket at the highest level from 1959-77, captained the PCB team, which also featured Umar Amin. This game shared some similarities with the goodwill exercise of 1935/36 when the Australian team ranged in age from 20 to 53 with varying degrees of experience and talent.

It was a sunny day in Islamabad—winter seemed to be coming to an end. The previous night was cold, yet the day was gorgeous. The Serena Hotel sponsored wide-brimmed white hats were dispersed amongst the small crowd and they came in handy. Security, as always at these kinds of events in Pakistan, outweighed the crowd. The scene conformed to an orientalist cliché and I felt like I could have been in an Arabian desert or Hollywood's version of it: oriental rugs covered the dry grass presumably to protect our shoes, willowy bright orange and stark white seat jackets concealed vinyl chairs and the arid hills and minaret formed a backdrop and constantly reminded me of where I was. A large marquee was erected to accommodate the lunch rush. The food was tasty and plentiful, however I didn't have much time to eat as over the lunchtime break I was seemingly introduced to everyone, business cards were thrust at me and hands were shaken. I forgot my previous concern as to whether it was appropriate to shake hands or not, I just did. We stood and ate. I was constantly being introduced to people and found the juggle of hand shaking and holding my plate in one hand and a drink in the other quite difficult. I met an Indian employed to administer visas to Pakistan. He said he loved Islamabad and after Russia it was his favourite posting. During the lunch break I was interviewed for a sports slot on PakTV. An erudite journalist with Hollywood good looks conducted the interview. He confessed that he found the pronunciation of my name incredibly difficult, as I did his. It was my first television interview ever and I was relieved that no one I knew would see it. I was asked about my research, my cricket linage, my thoughts on the state of contemporary cricket and most pertinently who would win the World Cup. I answered all questions with the utmost diplomacy.

Following lunch, I was invited to join the commentary team in the media box for an interview that was broadcast over the stadium loudspeaker. I hoped they realised that I wasn't a cricket expert and wouldn't ask me to commentate on the day's play, as I was a history student with a very narrow area of expertise. Again, I felt terribly out of my depth.

That evening, the Serena Hotel hosted a function to celebrate the start of the Cricket World Cup in Australia and New Zealand. Security was tight and we had to queue up for some time before we passed through a vigorous scanning procedure. I chatted to someone who whispered that he was from ASIO. I'm still unsure if he really was. A few people in the line grumbled about the length of the queue and the slowness of the guards. I was rather happy that they were doing their job.

The scene that evening defied all my expectations about Pakistani culture. It was one of the glitziest events I have attended. The invitees were a mix of diplomats, moneyed locals and high-end civic officials. The locals were the cream of Pakistani society: the most glamorous and well-heeled group of people who were not embarrassed to flaunt their success. Middle-aged men, who went to the gym, wore mirrored sunglasses perched on their dyed hair and gloated about their latest acquisitions—conversations about the purchasing of cars and the booking of holidays could be overheard. The party was raucous and the chinking of glasses, the hubbub of conversation and the easy-listening cocktail band that played sets throughout the evening reverberated into the wee hours. Butlers in white jackets circulated with silver trays. Trophy wives with plunging necklines and towering heels stridently laughed at jokes. Bleached teeth, coiffured hair, plunging necklines, cosmetic enhancement and diamonds were seemingly mandatory. Maybe these women were a contemporary version of the ones that the team encountered in 1935/36.

Just like cricketers in 1935/36, I was conscious of the excessive amount of liquor consumed that night and the drinking culture that seemed routine amongst the privileged classes. I'd imagined Pakistan would be dry and before I left Australia, I decided that I would abstain while I was there. However, during the evening and due to the insistence of the waiting staff, the ever-present French champagne and the enthusiasm of the other guests I changed my mind. Despite the consumption of alcohol being encouraged and flaunted by the invitees, I was interested to see a local cricketer who was on the periphery of selection. He had narrowly missed out on being in the squad that had recently flown to Australia and New Zealand and I spied him discreetly skull a few quick whisky shots. He waited until the members of the Pakistan Cricket Board left the room.

Seemingly my Pakistan experience was not too dissimilar to that of the 1935/36 cricketers.

The team arrived in Lahore at 9.00pm and the players were delighted to see a familiar face. Loris Tarrant was awaiting their arrival at the train station. He spied them first and almost knocked over other travellers as he rushed towards them, vigorously shaking his father's hand and hugging his stepmother. Frank was thrilled to see his eldest son as it was almost a year since their previous encounter. The three Tarrant males and Eva would be spending the following week together in Lahore and the euphoria of the family reunion couldn't be stifled.

The organising committee acknowledged that the travelling schedule was taking its toll and dates were pushed around to allow a few extra leisure days. This pleased everyone greatly, especially the Tarrant family, and they now had forty-eight hours before they even had to think about cricket. Despite them all needing some rest, the cricketers didn't want to miss out on seeing the highly acclaimed tourist sites of Lahore. The Lahore fort, Jahangir's tomb at Shahdara built in the 17th century for the Mughal emperor, the Shalimar gardens and the museum where Lockwood Kipling (the father of Rudyard) had been a senior curator in the late nineteenth century were priorities.

Rudyard Kipling held the reputation of a literary Goliath and was widely read in the early twentieth century. The Nobel prize winning author became known as the voice of the Empire and was largely responsible for the team's understanding of India prior to arrival. He was an incurable imperialist and all his books, without exception, underline the racial superiority of the English. Despite only living in Lahore for five years, the city was at the heart of Kipling's India and the setting of some of his best-selling stories. A number of the players paid homage to him by noting their motivation to visit the Zam-Zammah (Urdu for lion's roar) gun referred to in Kipling's immensely popular novel Kim written in 1901. I'm sure they recalled the famous Kipling phrase: 'He who holds Kim's gun holds the Punjab'.

I wonder if the cricketers had read Kipling's classic account of the old walled city of Lahore in the short story *The City of Dreadful Night*, written in the late nineteenth century. Kipling's protagonist, in a manner that is typical of the author, describes the historic city as a terrifying, unfathomable, torrid place—stifling hot and smelling foul and concludes that it's the most dreadful city of the night. The cricketers most likely avoided the walled city at night as it was not generally frequented by tourists. Possibly they caught a glimpse of it when visiting the fort during daylight hours. It was a designated space that post-colonial parlance would now refer to as the 'Other'.

Despite Kipling's portrayal of Lahore by the 1930s it was a modern, upbeat, prosperous, progressive city marked by a cosmopolitan flow of goods and ideas and the movement of people either in the course of education, business, migration, tourism, sport or organised political militancy. From all accounts, it seems as though there was little for the cricketers to grumble about in Lahore, so their vitriol turned to the bitterly cold weather following the warmer climes of the south (which they equally objected to). In most photographs they wear overcoats and Oxenham even suggested that Lahore was as cold as the North Pole. As usual, he was prone to exaggeration.

I'm rather surprised by how dapper the team look in the holiday snaps around Lahore. Maybe the few days of rest improved their spirits as they are captured in a relaxed mode. Tom's double-breasted fawn Mackintosh is belted tightly around his waist, a camera bag is slung rakishly over his right shoulder, a newspaper is tucked under his shoulder and he carries a small briefcase in his left arm. I knew Tom as an old man who rather lived in the sporting shadow of my grandfather and I really enjoy these glimpses of him celebrating his own cricket journey. I'm unsure when the man in the photos became the man I knew. Likewise, it would have been nice for Tom to have known that I would spend well over a decade researching the forgotten and overlooked 1935/36 inaugural Australian tour of India, yet he didn't.

Bishop of Lahore, Mr Gray, Ryder, Leather and unidentified gentleman, Lahore. January 1936. Leather archive

The team met Bishop George Barne, an Anglican clergyman, and a mutual admiration was immediately evident. Barne became their unofficial tour guide—driving them around in his car, which was a nice touch as most British insisted on using a driver. Many long evenings were spent being entertained at his private residence. The cricketers responded to the Bishop's easy-going nature—he was by far the friendliest Brit they encountered. The Bishop had played county cricket for Somerset. Despite only playing in one first-class game where he batted at number eleven and did not bowl—it seemed like he was just making up the numbers. Notwithstanding, his unimpressive record, he did have an invested interest in the success of the game in India. Morrisby's twenty-first birthday fell on the third day of the 'Test' and the team celebrated at a dinner with the Bishop. Morrisby claimed it was the highlight of Lahore and even possibly the entire tour. He was now old enough to vote and was considered an adult. Seemingly, he'd matured through experiences on the tour and he no longer resembled that anxious boy onboard the Mongolia.

Alexander observed that the Bishop was the most broadminded clergyman he had ever met. He certainly was a well-loved character within a city of progressive thinkers. An earlier English-language Indian newspaper article suggested that Barne was a heretic and exhibited philosophies closer to Muslim than Christian. This commentary may have been infused with Western bias but does suggest that Barne was an unorthodox character who did not entirely espouse the philosophies of the British colonists. The cricketers were possibly drawn to his alternative ideologies and his nonconformist perspective.

Through Bishop Barne, Macartney caught up with Rev. H Noble, a long-forgotten old school friend. It was an unexpected, yet pleasant, coincidence as the reverend had just arrived in Lahore to fill the vacancy of one of Barne's chaplains who had unexpectedly died. Despite not having seen each other for thirty-three years, the two relived tales of schoolboy high jinks.

The cricketers were greatly taken by the Shalimar garden which was evocatively known as the 'Gardens of Pleasure'. Alexander claimed the gardens emulated the design of Versailles in France. Maybe such an observation spoke more about Alexander's attempts at sophistication, as many in the team had the tendency to do. Late in the afternoon, a party was held in the gardens to celebrate the tour. Bill recalled the lyrics of the famous 1902 song *Pale hands I loved beside the Shalimar*. The song, based on a Laurence Hope poem, about the nostalgic unfolding of an intimate affair that took place in the gardens was an immensely popular, yet ultimately misunderstood, tale about lust in the exotic east.

For a change of tempo, the team watched *She married her Boss* at the cinema on the first night of the 'Test'. It was a lightweight romantic comedy and for close to 100 minutes the cricketers were consumed by the complexities of modern-day gender dynamics in the office. No primary material reveals what the cricketers thought of the movie yet I'm sure they were just happy to spend some time in a fictitious Western void not having to think about anything but the unfolding screwball comedy.

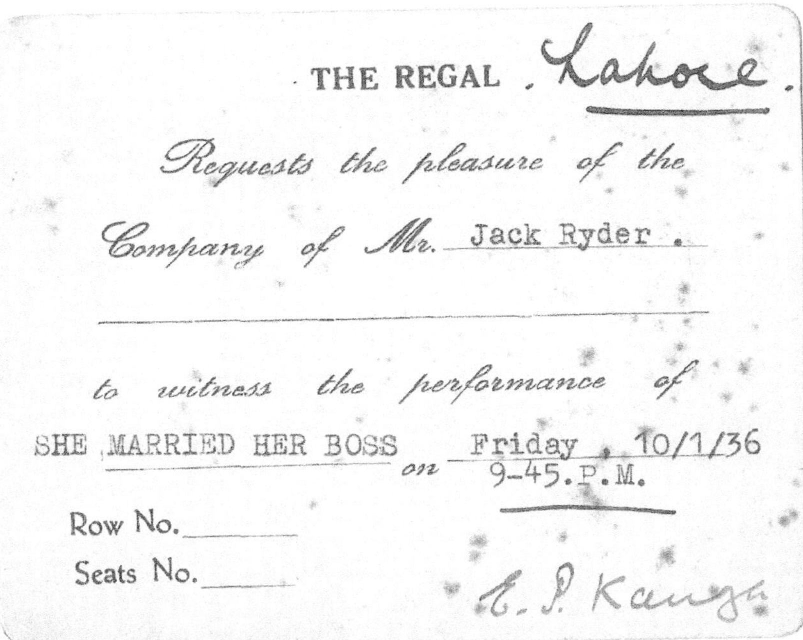
THE REGAL . Lahore .

Requests the pleasure of the

Company of Mr. Jack Ryder .

to witness the performance of

SHE MARRIED HER BOSS on Friday , 10/1/36
9-45.P.M.

Row No.

Seats No.

E. P. Kanga

Invitation ticket to the Cinema, Lahore. January 1936. Ryder archive

If I were to nominate my favourite image from the tour it would have to be one, I unearthed early on my research journey, from the Alexander archive. I was delighted when Harry's daughter, Kim, suggested that I borrow her photographs so I could scan them and have my own digital copies. It's been my screensaver for years and in my opinion the signature image from the tour. I located the same photograph at the Lahore Gymkhana Museum in 2015. It is distinctively different from the other team portraits, as it possesses a compelling combination of staid formality (routine for team portraits) combined with a surge of overpowering spontaneous *joie de vivre.* It's the only image that I have located from archives in both the subcontinent and in Australia and it appears that the image, and what it represented, was treasured by East and West alike.

The image depicts the scene at Lawrence Gardens in Lahore following the first Indian 'Test' victory on the tour and the first Indian win against a touring XI since the late nineteenth century when the locals won against GF Vernon's side and Lord Hawke's XI. The players do not congregate in a formalised rigid team composition as cricketers, administrators from both teams and a few lucky fans squeeze into the frame of the photograph. All are desperate to be part of this victory. Seemingly any hierarchal stipulations that controlled and determined Indian cultural life and racial division could not be contained by the exuberance of sporting *joie de vivre.* The Australians appear equally thrilled by their opposition's success and, in this case, the joy of sport and the thrill of victory were universal.

Combined Team Shot, Lahore. January 1936. Alexander archive

A copy of *Indian Cricket* located in the Leather archive describes the sentiments of the match, which are reinforced by the photograph: 'Ryder, in an interview, said that Wazir Ali's team fully deserved their victory. It had been a great game, full of interest from the very start, and it had been a pleasure to have participated in it. The Australians were not disappointed because this victory would do a lot of good to Indian cricket, especially in view of the nearness of their team going to England and it will give them more confidence in themselves'. Likewise, an Indian historian writing on the tour compellingly described the definitive emotion of the victorious occasion: 'The atmosphere vibrated with triumphant joy'.

The image exudes a sense of celebration, not just of sporting victory but it also pays homage to a rejection of communal, religious, social and racial segregation. Communal tensions ran high in Lahore and in the 1930s the city was known by its epithet 'the Ulster of India'. Yet this photograph challenges the reputation. Research has revealed that cricket in Lahore was a culturally progressive activity. The official competition across the country was mostly organised on communal lines like in Bombay and Karachi, yet Lahore cricket was organised on geographic lines. The Northern India Cricket Club (with its home base in Lahore) featured in the national Ranji Trophy competition intermittently throughout the 1930s and 40s. Unlike opposition teams the squad comprised a communal mix.

Victory for the local team was apparently unexpected. The January 13, 1936 issue of the *Argus* revealed that the Indian team was substandard due to the fact that some players, fearing failure, made themselves unavailable:

> The Australian cricketers appear to be frightening India's leading players. For the third match against All India, which began at Lahore yesterday, the Indian team was weakened by the refusal or inability of good players to take part. C K Nayudu said that he needed a rest, Pataudi is reported to be ill, Armanath (sic) is on the injured list, Nazir Ali is reported to have been bitten by a mad dog, Jai finds himself unable to obtain leave and Lall Singh gives no reason for his absence. The result is that Wazir Ali is leading practically a second team.

The article is peppered with racism and cliché; the Indian players are portrayed as cowardly with the journalist suggesting that they fabricated reasons to avoid being part of what they anticipated being a losing team. Attributing the absence of Syed Nazir Ali to being bitten by a 'mad dog' portrays India, and Indian culture, in a clichéd manner as hazardous, uncivilised and barbaric. Syed Nazir Ali was the brother of the Lahore 'Test' captain Wazir Ali and it is questionable whether under the circumstances Nazir would create excuses not to play. The journalist identifies Pataudi as one of the many Indians who declined to play but as Pataudi did not play in any match during the series, including him in this discussion, to highlight the fears of the cricketers and by association the failings of a nation, is prejudicial and inaccurate. Tour reportage attributes the omission of C.K. Nayudu to his refusal to play under the captaincy of Wazir Ali, which is a further reminder that Indian cricket selection appeared to be driven by communal politics rather than merit. In light of the many absentees, *The Advocate* reported on the team's composition and observed that if the objective of 'the present tour' is to namely 'help the Indian selectors to choose a side to visit England in the summer, is not likely to be attained'.[1]

However, the Australians had to acknowledge their defeat for what it was. It wasn't just luck or *kismet* and the visitors were to be held accountable. Their fielding was the worst 'of the tour. Five easy catches were missed; Bill, Mair, Morrisby, and Alexander were principally at fault'.[2] Again, the game witnessed injuries to some of the key personnel. Oxenham, the mainstay of the Australian bowling, pulled a muscle in his leg and Bryant was struck above the right ear by a fiery Nissar delivery. Nissar was the fastest bowler of the era and Oxenham noted that his bowling 'created some ill-feeling among the tourists'.[3]

The image depicts the crowd and the players of both teams physically entwined reflecting the camaraderie shared amongst the combined playing group. Morrisby places his right arm reassuringly, yet tentatively, on the shoulder of Masood Salahuddin which demonstrates his culturally ameliorating perspective. This surprises me as earlier in the tour the young Australian cricketer displayed categorical reservations about Eastern culture and people. Mian Mohammad Saeed places his arms on the broad shoulders of Mohammad Nissar who bowled well and took four wickets. Even the royal Yuvraj of Patiala is not conscious of personal space and his knees make contact with Ryder and Oxenham. Bryant opened the batting and leans into the frame, and bulk, of Nissar despite the West Australian being struck and injured by the Indian's fast delivery. Wazir Ali, appointed the role of Indian captain on this occasion, jauntily crosses his legs and looks exceedingly proud of his own match-winning performance—he top-scored with 77 in the first innings and 92 in the second—and the team's victory. Both Frank and Bert Tarrant appear strangely unmoved by the event considering their investment in it. Possibly they were preoccupied with the emotion of the family reunion that had taken place. On this occasion they are outfitted in seemingly incongruous matching overcoats, ties and fedoras. Bert indulges in a celebratory cigarette, as does Bryant.

A large crowd of men and children congregate behind the players, clamouring to be part of this momentous and historic occasion. The photograph confirms Tarrant's expectations for the tour: 'The Australians had come to India to play cricket. They meant to enjoy their cricket here, and it was their intention to try to make their hosts enjoy their cricket as well'.[4] Bill described the Indian victory and the subsequent celebration: 'The great crowd literally mobbed the ground and pavilion, the last-named structure, a rather frail one, being in great danger of being pulled down in the general scramble and excitement. All the Indian players were garlanded with beautiful flowers and carried shoulder-high to the pavilion'.[5] Bill was evidently wrong about the fragility of the stand as the quaint 1880's pavilion remains intact over eight decades later.

Following the Indian 'Test' victory, Bill observed the players' exuberance which is evident in the image: 'The players themselves were so excited that they kissed each other, an example followed by many of their followers. Many caps, hats and even shirts were lost in this melee, the most enthusiastic I have ever seen'. Bill concluded by perpetuating what has become the most enduring Indian cultural stereotype noting, 'Perhaps it can be understood when it is realised that the Indian people are absolutely 'cricket mad''. The Indian response is understandable given the victory was the first time the team had won either an unofficial or an official Test match against an international team. They had, after all, not won any of the previous encounters with the Australians and had been defeated in the Test series against England in 1933/34 where they played three matches, losing two and drawing the other.

The picturesque cricket ground still sits in the middle of Lawrence Gardens (now known as Bagh-e-Jinnah) which possesses the quaint charm of London's Kew Gardens on which their design was based. The gardens were a botanical sanctuary and provided a tranquil setting and some refuge from the chaos outside. It's probable that the cricketers visited the famous Lahore Zoo which was a popular attraction and also situated in Lawrence Gardens. The zoo opened in 1872 and is still operational. It is one of the oldest zoos in the world.

The gardens also contained a stately Victorian building that is now the Quaid-e-Azam public library, in 1936 it was the home of the Lahore Gymkhana. Despite the official website gloating about its technical facilities, when I visited in 2015, the library looked old-worldly and charming yet antiquated (and I fear under-appreciated). It still features original wooden display cabinets, teak floors, decorative gilt inlays, brightly coloured stained-glass windows and multiple gigantic chandeliers. During the 1935/36 tour, the players spent much of their spare time at the Lahore Gymkhana Club and indulged in the club's hospitality.

A function was held in Montgomery Hall, the magnificent domed ballroom of the Gymkhana club, to commemorate the Australians' final night in Lahore. Injured Oxenham rose to his feet with difficulty when the Governor of the Punjab, Sir Herbert Emerson, toasted the Australian team and Australian cricket. Everyone in the ballroom stood and celebrated the noble game as the governor observed, 'While Australia's official team is employed defeating South Africa, that such a team as is now touring India should be hitherto unbeaten is proof of the great strength of Australian cricket'. He added that, 'the fact that those whose names were household words years ago were still making centuries and getting wickets—or both—suggested that Australian cricket had learnt the secret of eternal youth'. He professed absolute confidence 'in the visitors, whose clean sport and good fellowship would do a world of good to Indian cricket'.[6]

The cricketers were becoming accustomed to the presence of their bearers. Hendry's manuscript recounts that returning late one night in Lahore, Hendry was alarmed to see Lalla guarding the front of his room. Wearing a light cotton uniform, he sat on a wooden stool in the hotel corridors safeguarding the cricketer's possessions. A chilly wind blew through the passage and ricocheted off the plaster walls and the marble floors. Hendy enquired as to if his bearer was cold. Lalla shook his head, but Hendry wasn't convinced. Hendry made him promise that, if the situation arose again, he could sit in the room by the fire. It made sense to Hendry, as

Lalla had access to the room to stoke, and fuel, the fire so why shouldn't he stay warm. Lalla had evidently earned Hendry's trust as at night he emptied the coins from his pocket onto the side table and never once did a rupee go missing. With the tour coming to an end, Hendry, obviously caught in a compassionate moment, thrust some money at Lalla and insisted he buy some warm undergarments.

Some of the cricketers who represented India (either in the unofficial 'Tests' or the regional games) in 1935/36 would play together in the 1936 and 1946 tours of England. However, post-partition, some individuals, who competed at Lawrence Gardens, would belong to opposing national teams (India and Pakistan) and warring countries that would be philosophically and physically at loggerheads.

Mohammad Saeed did not shine on his international debut when he represented his country in the third unofficial 'Test' of the series. Perhaps he was overawed by the occasion, making a duck in his first innings, yet he improved with a more respectable score of 20 (some records say 28) in the second innings. Despite the inauspicious start to his international career, he would subsequently feature prominently in Pakistan cricket. He was the designated cricket captain of Pakistan in 1947 (before the country acquired Test status in 1952). Age prevented him from playing Test cricket for Pakistan however he played a few international games prior to ICC accreditation. He was subsequently involved as an umpire and in 1954/55 he adjudicated the fifth Test against India. This game did not include any of his 1935/36 teammates, however some Indian players who competed against the Australians in regional games participated in this game of national importance.

Post-1947 interaction between India and Pakistan (and subsequently Bangladesh) in sporting, political, military and civil encounters would be marred by discord and hostility yet conversely the photograph depicts a group of united countrymen and international cricketers celebrating sportsmanship, cultural diversity and cricket victory. It was a significant moment in sporting, cultural and political history, as it would never be replicated. The capacity of the photograph to suspend and memorialise historical transience and to celebrate the developing Indian-Australian goodwill is celebrated through the production of this image.

Seven days in Lahore had been enjoyable and had provided the Australians with some respite yet time was starting to drag, and they were now increasingly keen to keep moving. Despite enjoying the jubilation of the Indian victory, the cricketers were distracted by the fleet of luxury cars which lined the street next to the Lawrence Garden's gates. They were waiting to transport the Aussies to Patiala. The bearers had packed up the players' possessions and everyone in the entourage was ready to depart. The players didn't want to seem disrespectful, and they felt that their hasty departure may be viewed as bad sportsmanship, but the lure of Patiala called.

---

1 January 13, 1936.
2 *The Inverell Times* January 13, 1936.
3 *The Telegraph* February 3, 1936.
4 Tarrant scrapbook 1918–51.
5 *The Sydney Mail* February 26, 1936.
6 *The Advocate* January 13, 1936.

19 PATIALA POMP

The cricketers travelled through the Punjab in style. They hadn't previously experienced commuting in such luxury in India, or indeed anywhere, before. They were transported on the first leg of the journey in a fleet of prestige cars of various types—there were a few 16-cylinder Rolls, at least one Bentley and Macartney travelled in a Cadillac. Bill described the 130-mile journey in 'such powerful and beautiful cars'; a trip that was accomplished in the record speed of under two and a half hours. Impressed with the pace he observed, 'Some going, considering that many large caravans drawn by bullocks barred the centre of the road on numerous occasions'.[1] On reaching the state of Patiala the team was upgraded to two luxurious parlour coaches for the remaining sixty miles. Valued at £7000 each, these vehicles contained every mod-con imaginable. One was designated for dining and the other included a wood-panelled cocktail bar and both according to Hendry's manuscript, 'contained every luxury possible, even a shower and a radiator'. Macartney observed that the only thing missing was a bed.

Oxenham described the luxurious transportation and revealed how unaccustomed they were to it: 'I hope the Queensland boys who ride to and from the Melbourne ground in mere taxis will not be jealous when I mention that, from Lahore to Patiala—a distance of some 200 miles—we travelled deluxe in Rolls-Royce cars and private coaches'.[2] Oxenham's attention then turned to the endless supply of refreshments on the bus and described the players' unbridled consumption of alcohol. Despite being a non-drinker, Oxenham stated that, he was 'quite certain those buses did not have to pay any heavy vehicle tax on the return journey. We emptied them pronto'.[3] Bill was slightly more reserved in his account and although he did reference the consumption of alcohol, he avoided details of the debauchery.

Boarding the Bus to Patiala. January 1936. Ryder archive

Considering the luxury of the transportation, the cricketers were rather disappointed when they arrived at their quarters at the Patiala residence. They anticipated that they would be domiciled in spacious suites in the Moti Bagh palace, just like they had in Jamnagar, yet they were somewhat dismayed when they saw that tents had been constructed on the lawn to accommodate them. Oxenham complained about the arrangement yet soon realised that it was a step-up from the type of camping that he was familiar with. The tents contained a myriad of rooms including a communal lounge area with hand-carved side boards and reading tables. Oriental carpets lined the floor and were warm and soft to touch. Electric heaters were found in every room which was not only a luxury but a necessity, considering Patiala's proximity to the Himalayas. The bathrooms were luxurious too and contained full-sized baths. Meals were served in an adjoining upmarket mess-tent and the cricketers were impressed by the food and the service staff. Ryder commented that the dining facilities were so good that they wouldn't be out of place in a palace.

Hendry at the Moti Bagh palace, Patiala. January 1936. Leather archive

Despite the players already having visited many grand estates around the country, their tour reportage unanimously praised Moti Bagh palace. Special note was made of the games room with its three full-size billiard tables. Over the years, I've visited the palace on a few occasions: the east wing now houses the Indian National Institute of Sports. The games room is slightly different now. The cricketers described the exquisite *objet d'art* and the ornamental interior decoration—the flags, the portraits of monarchs and aristocrats, the drapery, the military medals, the shields and the wallpaper; yet now it is comparatively austere. Hendry was most impressed by the Maharaja's collection of Victoria Crosses on display.

The players knew something special was in store on their first night in

Patiala, so they didn't object on being instructed to get dressed up into their 'glad rags', as Oxenham observed in his February 3 column. The Maharaja was feeling a poorly so after a quick welcome speech, he excused himself and retired to his boudoir. The cricketers were left to enjoy the generosity of their absent host and from all accounts they did. Luckily, the tents were within a stumbling distance.

The evening commenced with a display of local dancers and the cricketers were mesmerised by the beauty of the women, yet somewhat shocked by their exotic moves. Hendry remarked that the Maharaja of Patiala 'gave the team a banquet and stated he had engaged the best dancers in India to provide dancing partners for us. My bearer whispered to me they were women from the bazaar!!'. Utilising the double exclamation mark suggests that despite expressing his horror at dancing with 'women from the bazaar' he was somewhat captivated by the possibility. This prose also suggests that Hendry formed a union with his 'bearer' who confided the identity of the women to him. Seemingly on this occasion, racial and social codes were broken (as well as the unconditional loyalty of the bearer to the Maharaja) which reveals the breakdown of the established hierarchy and the position of the Australians within it.

The highlight of the evening was the post-dinner entertainment where the billiard tables doubled as display cabinets. The Maharaja's jewellery collection was placed on the tables and the cricketers were invited to peruse—yet they were instructed to keep a two-foot distance. However, it wasn't just a diamond necklace here and there, it was gold, silver, bejewelled swords, tiaras and prized stones stacked onto these three massive tables. Tarrant spoke of an emerald the size of a hen's egg and the bedazzling diamond necklace that had previously belonged to Empress Eugenie of France. Morrisby described the tables as resembling pyramids, all piled high with priceless jewels. I guess the Patiala Necklace was somewhere there—unless the Maharani was attending a function. The renowned necklace, designed by the House of Cartier and commissioned by Bhupinder, was created in 1928 from 2,930 diamonds with the centrepiece being a massive De Beers diamond, the seventh largest in the world. Bill noted that one diamond crown on the table was valued at £2,000,000. The cricketers were in awe of the dazzling collection and tallied up the unimaginable wealth it represented. I guess the cricketers shouldn't have been that surprised by the display as Hendry's manuscript observed that the Maharaja 'always wore a pair of emerald and diamond earrings worth thirty thousand pounds and emerald and diamond bracelets worth sixty thousand pounds'. The cricketers nominated the jewellery stash one of the most astonishing sights they encountered in India, which considering my knowledge of what transpired on the tour is noteworthy.

When I visited Patiala in 2007, I felt closer to my cricketers than I previously had. Visiting the various sites throughout India and Pakistan, as I roughly followed the 1935/36 itinerary, nothing really resonated like it did until I reached Patiala—maybe because the Punjabi city remained relatively unchanged. At this point, my research came alive and I really started to see events through the players' eyes and could picture the jewellery stash glistening against the green felt. The presence of the cricketers in the billiard room could be felt.

The following morning, the bearers woke the cricketers well before dawn to attend a 'de-luxe' duck shoot. The team was becoming accustomed to late nights and early mornings. They were driven thirteen miles into the countryside to an artificial lake called *Bhupinder Sagar* which was purpose built by Dick Bowles, the Maharaja's engineer. Here, they were reacquainted with the Yuvraj who looked devastatingly regal in his hunting outfit. The cricketers felt rather ashamed of their appearances and discreetly tried to neaten their hair, remove the sleep for their eyes, and disguise the previous night's indulgences. The Maharaja didn't participate in any activity modestly and Hendry described that 'a hydroplane with an aeroplane engine to disturb the ducks whenever they were on the water' was used to assist the hunt. As was the ceremonial custom, a bugle signified the start of shoot and the Maharaja fired the first shot. The cricketers and other guests of the Maharaja were 'given a shotgun and a dozen cartridges plus a bottle of beer', along with 'two servants' and were sent out to enjoy the day. Despite the extravagance of the exercise and the best intentions of the social schedulers, Hendry observed faults in planning and wrote, 'Shooting started and after a short time a halt was called to receive more cartridges if needed and to partake of the liquid refreshment – but with all the organisation no openers were provided'.

Nagel at Duck Shoot at Patiala. January 1936. Alexander archive

Hendry was successful in shooting a duck but was rather sceptical of the praise the shot received and recalled, 'My two servants were as excited as through I had bagged an elephant with a catapult and congratulated Sahib on a wonderful shot and rushed into the water and retrieved it'. Possibly Hendry was rather more insulted that racial and social hierarchy necessitated that his 'two servants' should behave in such a sycophantic and obsequious manner. The following morning 400 birds, of various varieties, were laid out for display and a photograph was taken of the booty to record the shooting success. Hendry expressed scepticism that all the birds on display were killed the preceding day and proposed that, 'there must have been a number from a previous shoot'. The duck shoot demonstrated orthodox colonial fantasies, yet Hendry identified flaws in the exercise regarding the planning, the overindulgence and even with the manner in which the staff were expected to oblige the visitors.

Duck cull with cricketers. Patiala, January 1936. Leather archive

The photograph of the duck shoot from the Leather archive (versions of it are located in many archives of the Australian cricketers) functions as a reminder that, as previously discussed, shooting played an important role in colonial culture. The photograph functioned as a visual trophy to memorialise the event. I imagine the Maharaja gifted the image to the Australian cricketers and Leather, acknowledging the importance of the photograph (and the event), wrote the names of the players over the image. The black-and-white image is mounted on a cardboard backing and is toned with a sepia pigment which differentiates the image from others in the collection and provides proof that the shoot was viewed as an especially prestigious event. The image depicts the cricketers (dressed in their cricket whites as they commenced a match shortly after the image was taken), along with numerous other important European and local guests, crowding over the dead, and no doubt malodorous, birds. The European women are dressed stylishly, and the landscape is well manicured—the scene is demonstrative of wealth, privilege and the 'success' of modern India in the late colonial period.

Later that morning, January 15, the team arrived early to inspect the cricket ground before play commenced in 'perfect' conditions. Hendry claimed that the pitch and the outfield were equal to the Sydney Cricket Ground. The players frequently complained to Tarrant about having to play on coir matting and were delighted to see the almost perfect grass pitch at Patiala. Bowling was a joy when you were able to control the ball. The Maharaja was guaranteed a big crowd as he had granted the Patiala state servants and public officials leave so the match was well-attended throughout its three-day duration.

For many reasons, the match was quite unlike any other cricket games the Australian cricketers had experienced. The match didn't run to a timetable and the playing of cricket appeared to be of secondary importance and had to fit in amongst a busy schedule of music, theatrics, political propaganda and sexual politics.

Four orchestras and bands performed at intervals throughout the day. A crash of cymbals and a flourish of trumpets rang across the ground. The bands entered the arena with military precision and performed their musical routine—initially they propped in a spot where they could be best viewed by Maharaja, then his wives and then guests in order of descending importance. This continued until everyone at the stadium had an unimpeded view of the musicians. The bagpipe band was especially popular with the crowd. On numerous occasions, the cricketers were paraded out on to the arena and received a round of rousing applause. The Australian's were unsure why exactly they were being cheered and realised that they must somehow contribute to a broader cultural discourse. Seemingly, the day was simultaneously a celebration of the Patiala dynasty and international cricket. It also paid homage to the burgeoning relationship between Australia and India.

The players' captivation with Indian women became increasingly more overt as their journey progressed. The women in Patiala with their come-hither kohl lined almond eyes, petite waistlines and generous curves drove the cricketers crazy. They were undeniably beautiful, graceful and mysterious, echoing Orientalist stereotypes; however the gender dynamic baffled the tourists. The women acted like soubrettes—the plaything of men, yet they possessed an inherent power that simultaneously undermined and challenged the males' sense of authority. The cricketers found their interest in the local women rather unnerving, yet they couldn't avert their gaze or dampen their intrigue. It was a sexual dynamic that they were unfamiliar with and they seemed incapable of controlling their fascination, not only with the women but also with the oriental concepts of polygamy and 'purdah'.

Bagpipe band at Patiala. January 1936. Leather archive

Bagpipe band with Love, Leather, Macartney and Bill, Patiala. January 1936. Leather archive

Patiala pavilion. Leather archive

The Patiala pavilion spread over two levels—purpose-built for functionality and for pleasure. The ground level contained the players' dressing rooms, a library and a well-stocked bar while the top floor was designed to accommodate the wives and concubines of the Maharaja. The entire space was divided into tiers, and spaces, all designed according to an inflexible hierarchy. The wives of the Maharaja had the best view of the play and consorts of lesser importance surrounded them, guarding them like Queen Bee.

Patiala pavilion. Leather archive

Hendry observed that the wives arrived 'at the ground in purdah motorcars. They are hidden from the public gaze by Japanese blinds'. The screens allowed the women to see out, but they remained concealed. Hendry acknowledged his captivation with the 'harem ladies' and in his manuscript confessed that during the game he 'deserted the slips position and fielded in the outfield' telling the slow bowler 'to toss up some full tosses' so he could chase 'and just miss the ball on the way past the tents, anxious to see just who was inside'. In disbelief he stated, 'Believe me …there were women of all nationalities, black, white and yellow!'

However compelling and salacious it would be, sadly no evidence can be located that confirms that the touring team engaged in relations with the local women. However, Ramachandra Guha in his book *A Corner of a Foreign Field: The Indian History of a British Sport* does comment: 'One chronicler tells us that this team had their fill of whiskey on tour; I suspect they had their share of women too (they were, after all, playing under Patiala's colours)'.[4]

To excite the crowd further, the match included a cameo appearance by the Maharaja and Tarrant when they joined the ranks of the Australian team.

Crowd shot, Patiala. January 1936. Leather archive

On this occasion, the Maharaja played with some difficulty. He found it hard to run the twenty-two yards as his thighs chafed, his stomach cramped, and his lungs felt like they were burning as he frantically gulped for air. Maybe the latest Marylebone rules of cricket had added a few yards to the pitch, he jestingly imagined! He hadn't realised that he was quite so match-unfit—maybe carrying a few extra pounds didn't help. He didn't play regular cricket, yet he regularly roamed around his estate shooting wildlife and he had no problem doing that. However, I guess there were always a few lackeys and a palanquin on hand to carry him if necessary. The only consolation was that his cricket buddy, Frank Tarrant, down the other end of the pitch was finding it just as difficult! Frank had a gammy knee and was a decade older so maybe his fatigue was legitimate. The seniors felt beholden to play as the number of available Australian personnel was depleted—Allsopp, Bryant, Ellis, Hendry, Ironmonger, Mair and Oxenham were missing from the regular line-up. Both men realised their obligations and donned their pads in Patiala in the name of duty and sportsmanship.

Frank Tarrant and the Maharaja of Patiala, Patiala. January 1936. Leather archive

The Tarrant family reunion continued as Bert's older brother, the mysterious Loris, again re-joined the team in Patiala and also played for the visitors—making an unbeaten 16. Researching him has been problematic as leads frequently go nowhere. However, in the mid-1930s, he resided in India and was employed by the Maharaja in various capacities. He frequently starred in domestic cricket matches playing under Patiala colours and, like his father, also functioned as umpire. Records in 1934 reveal that Loris umpired a match at Amritsar between the Marylebone Cricket Club and Southern Punjab. Just like his father, over time the Maharaja became increasingly dependent on Loris and by the 1940s he became the first and only non-Sikh to be employed as the potentate's aide-de-camp.

Bhupinder raised his hand and stopped the play, as only he was entitled to do. He was after all financing the whole exercise and paying everyone on the field a small fortune. In a way, they were his marionettes, and he held the strings. The Indian fielders on the ground froze and tensely waited to see what he would do next. The umpire, who was normally the only person who could suspend play, didn't bat an eyelid either. The Maharaja's unpredictability unnerved his loyal subjects. Customarily the cricket pitch was common ground, yet in this situation Bhupinder held absolute authority over all the players and indeed everyone in the stadium. In the pavilion, tail-ender Tom Leather, the next Australian to bat, looked over to Jack Ryder and queried what was going on. Jack placed his calloused forefinger to his lips—gesturing Tom to be silent.

All eyes were on Bhupinder. He beckoned Frank with a gentle summons of his bejewelled index finger. It was a subtle gesture yet Frank, in his role of factotum, knew what was expected. Despite feeling his age combined with exhaustion, sore muscles and his troublesome knee, Frank trotted down the wicket to see what his friend and employer wanted. I imagine the conversation went something like:

The Maharaja: 'Think we've had enough, Frank. You look pretty plum-tuckered-out. Shall we call it quits'?

Frank knew the potentate well enough to know that this was a question that didn't require an answer. Frank was also aware that he was being used as the scapegoat—another common phenomenon. Bhupinder would never acknowledge his own physical fallibilities. They'd spent almost twenty years together and defying social norms they represented a successful and equitable Oriental-Occidental alliance. Despite being Bhupinder's closest confidant and, in many ways, best friend Frank knew his position.

Bhupinder informed the umpire that they could do with a few of the young boys doing the running as Frank's 'arthritic knee' was troubling him. Morrisby and Love were summoned from the pavilion and took their positions as runners for the ageing batsmen. Morrisby had batted earlier at number three and top-scored making 145 in only 142 minutes. It was one of the highest scores on tour. He'd robustly smashed thirteen fours and also managed a six, which for him was a novel and exciting experience as such fast and dynamic scoring was always appreciated. Luckily the youthful Morrisby possessed endless stamina and still had the energy to run for Bhupinder. Love's innings had been less taxing, and he was also primed to be the legs for team manager Frank. The young cricketers were bemused, as they'd never previously witnessed a cricket game where both batsmen required runners yet had been in India long enough to know not to snigger or query.

A few months earlier, Bhupinder had fallen ill whilst in England to celebrate King George's Silver Jubilee. He always loved visiting the mother country and luxuriated in the sartorial splendour of the Empire on these occasions. Despite ailing, Bhupinder and his team of lackeys and carnal playthings crossed the channel on the enticement of some fun on the Continent. On reaching France his medical condition deteriorated dramatically. Luckily for him, Sikh prayer and a team of Parisian Cardiologists facilitated his recovery.

Bhupinder was cognisant that his loyal Sikh subjects were aware of his recent indisposition, so he lifted his bat to assure the crowd that there was nothing to worry about. In response a ripple of applause emanated from his people in an act of fawning sycophancy. Just like a Mexican wave it magnified as it encircled the stadium. Seemingly, he was popular with his people however there is evidence that suggests otherwise. A lot of husbands disappeared or were found dead when the Maharaja took a liking to their wives. As previously mentioned, a few years earlier, the British investigated complaints against him in a report titled the 'Indictment of Patiala'.

His oldest son and heir apparent, the Yuvraj of Patiala, was captaining the opposing team and approached his father to enquire if he really was well enough to continue batting. Only the son of the Maharaja was permitted to take such liberties. They spoke in hushed tones. The Maharaja was delighted that his eldest son had grown into a true gentleman almost a mini version of himself. The Yuvraj was the total package—handsome, elegant and erudite, with impeccable manners, and to top it off he was also a decent cricketer.

The Yuvraj was one of the few people who didn't have to look up to his father. They were both slightly over six foot four and towered over their Indian teammates. The senior royal assured his son that he was fine to proceed. Bhupinder's pearl and diamond drop earrings animatedly jingled as he nodded in an attempt to convince his son. Satisfied his father was fit enough to continue, the Yuvraj took his position in the out-field. A few deliveries later the Maharaja hit the tricky medium-pace of Amir Elahi towards his son and the Yuvraj easily caught it. The crowd lustily celebrated the brilliance of the catch and the sporting spirit of the Maharaja. Bhupinder, exhibiting his customary refined demeanour, and Morrisby, like an obedient footman (keeping a deferential distance) exited the field. The crowd rose to their feet and applauded their ruler's every step. Unbeknown to them they were also applauding a near-unique occurrence as it was a rare occasion when two sets of father and sons played in a first-class match. Ron Morrisby had never previously departed the field to such a reception and realised it was unlikely to happen again. Providing you toed-the-line and obeyed the ruling family, Patiala was a fine place to live.

Engaging in the spirit of the match, the Maharaja also enjoyed bowling for eight overs later in the game. He was responsible for a 'unique turn' in the match as he bowled two overs of lobs. Despite being a legal delivery, underarm bowling, as noted by the press, 'had long been extinct in international or even village green cricket'.[5] The Maharaja managed to take two wickets with this obsolete style of bowling. Possibly he was assisted by the umpires in the name of goodwill and maybe even the opposition batsmen played in a fashion that allowed their financier to shine. All involved put it down to the sporting spirit of the tour and the day.

Fittingly, the match ended in a draw with impressive performances from both sides.

Unluckily Bill was injured during the match when he was hit in the face by a menacing Nissar delivery as he attempted to hook the ball. Following the day's play, the Maharaja insisted that he be x-rayed by a team of highly qualified medicos (the best in the country, the potentate bragged). A fractured jaw was diagnosed. He would play no further role on-field during the tour. The number of available players continued to dwindle. Luckily for Bill, and for myself, he could still use his writing hand and he continued to produce highly informative articles for *The Sydney Mail.*

---

[1] *The Sydney Mail* February 26, 1936.

[2] The Sheffield Shield competition was taking place simultaneously. Queensland played Victoria at the MCG on December 18-21, 1935.

[3] *The Telegraph* February 3, 1936.

[4] 2002, 233.

[5] *Wagga Wagga Express* January 18, 1936.

20 THE KING IS DEAD

The team commenced travelling due south and the next stop was Delhi. The cricketers arrived late in the evening after a day long commute in the Maharaja's luxury coaches. They were full of anticipation as the city had a grand reputation and, if the Swiss Hotel was anything to go by, they imagined that they'd thoroughly enjoy their stay.

The city had undergone a recent period of major transformation. During the Durbar in 1911, Delhi was named the nation's capital having taken the mantle from Calcutta. A name change took place in 1927 with New being added as a preface to Delhi and the new capital was inaugurated in 1931.

Bill was immediately taken by the city and claimed it had no rival in greatness. Oxenham was likewise impressed by New Delhi and observed that 'words cannot describe its charm and loveliness. It is a place of real wonder'.[1] From a geopolitical and cultural perspective, he was impressed and proclaimed that Delhi was to the people of India, 'what Athens is to Greece, Rome to Italy, or London to England'.[2] Yet it wasn't solely its historic legacy as the players also admired the modernity of New Delhi. The players noted the city's sophisticated urban planning with its wide, tree-lined, boulevards, meticulously designed botanic gardens with artificial lakes and fountains and a plethora of state-of-the-art civic buildings. New Delhi immediately reminded the cricketers of the Australian capital city, Canberra.

New Delhi was built and designed by the British and demonstrated a functionality and order which was a point of difference to other Indian cities. Sir Edwin Lutyen's architecture was completed in the late 1920s, which was the grandest of projects and a 'Monument of Folly' according to some.

Over a late-night supper, Tarrant informed the players that the following morning they were to commence a match against the Cricket Club of India. This was met with grumbles and complaints as the team would have liked some rest and relaxation before the commencement of any cricket commitments. I guess having the few extra days in Lahore put pressure on the tour itinerary. And it wasn't just a paucity of sight-seeing opportunities that irritated the players as the mounting number of injuries resulted in some having to play when they felt that they were really due for a rest. Oxenham's leg injury prevented him from playing but he still complained on behalf of the participating cricketers. Much of his February 6 column is devoted to chronicling tour fatigue. 'The players are fed up with cricket', he whined 'and we are glad that the tour is nearing its end'. The players' commitment to the tour was being challenged which caused bickering and niggles between the personnel. They questioned who was really well enough to play and who wasn't. The legitimacy of illness and injury was highly contested.

However, it wasn't just the cricketers' favourable impressions of the city or their irritation at having to play another cricket match, their time in Delhi will be remembered by something else. This was an incident of historic high drama as late in the evening on January 20, 1936 the ruling British monarch King George V passed away at Sandringham Estate in Norfolk, England. His death was announced during the last day of play and the match was immediately suspended. In some way, it was a fortunate turn of events as it saved the Cricket Club of India from an inevitable crushing defeat.

The local team was a mixed bag and comprised a number of first-rate cricketers, a few nobodies and the remainder were enthusiastic royals. The Maharwal of Dungarpur (the ruler of the state who had been knighted the previous year) was named captain.[3] He won the toss and elected to bat. Despite the ideal conditions and the weather being described by the press as 'brilliantly sunny', the Indians only managed 167.[4] The captain possessed some cricket ability, yet he made only a solitary run in the first innings before being bowled by Leather. The batting sensation Lala Amarnath top scored with a half-century, including seven fours, in a faultless fashion, yet he was the only positive in the batting line-up. Amar Singh was another positive for the locals as he bowled over 39 overs with barely a dud ball, ending with 5-91. The Australians scored 268 in their first innings with the runs evenly distributed amongst the batting personnel. Amarnath again batted well in the second innings and looked like putting in a great performance. He reached 35 and was running out of partners when play was disbanded due to the announcement of the death of the king.

Departing the field in Delhi. January 1936. Ryder archive

Following the king's death, citizens of the Empire, as revealed by the *Advocate*, commenced a period of compulsory mourning. A celebratory dinner, which had been scheduled at the day's end, was immediately cancelled and a few days of chaos followed as tour plans were constantly changed. Despite the long-term precarious health of King George V, his advancing years and the fact that he hadn't eaten for days, the tour schedulers didn't have a contingency plan in place for his death. I guess, however, it had been a quarter of a century since the death of his father, Edward VII. No one really seemed to know what to do nor did they know who was in charge. Oxenham noted that the team spent at least four days wandering the streets, 'not knowing where they were to play next, hearing rumours of an impending departure one moment, and finding the plans altered an hour later'.[5] He joked about their uncertainty saying that at the start of a meal plans were scheduled however by the arrival of dessert they'd been changed.

A match in Secunderabad was scheduled next on the itinerary however following the king's death it was cancelled, then rescheduled due to the outrage of the locals who didn't think it fair that they missed out on hosting international cricket. The game was eventually put back a few days which added further pressure to the tour itinerary as they would have to cram the remaining few matches into a condensed time frame.

The Empire was compelled to commence a period of intense mourning for the monarch and cricket was not permitted. Indeed, all hedonistic activities were to be curbed. The cricket community (and the Australian players) were conscious that they had to be seen to be behaving in a respectful manner. Although social functions were cancelled Bill observed that the death did not totally suspend all pleasure as the players managed to locate 'gaieties in the pleasant surroundings of the many fine clubs'.[6] The team also covertly used the mourning period to fit in some extra tourist activities and even managed to squeeze in an unscheduled visit to Agra which included a luncheon at the Cecil Hotel followed by a visit to the renowned Taj Mahal. Seemingly they enjoyed the unanticipated highlight, as the team wrote about being greatly impressed by the architectural structure and Bill noted that he was 'spellbound at the superb and majestic sight'.[7] The cricketers benefitted from a few days off and especially enjoyed playing games of tennis at courts just near their hotel. Luckily, they remained incognito and managed to avoid public censure. From all accounts, the team did not use the period to mourn, as was expected of subjects of the Empire, but rather they utilised the spare time to fulfil personal wishes, which within the highly orchestrated nature of the tour had not previously been possible. This was not the only time that the players would observe hedonism over fealty and prioritise Indian tourism over imperial obligations.

A club In Delhi. January 1936. Leather archive

The Taj Mahal, Agra. January 1936. Leather archive

In Delhi, the team reunited with Ironmonger who had spent the previous six weeks hospitalised in Allahabad. The team was shocked by how he looked as he had lost at least two-stone, had aged significantly and, using colloquial parlance, according to Macartney, he looked 'wasted'.[8] Before his illness, he already looked older than his fifty-three years—possibly a consequence of the harsh Queensland sun. His weather-beaten and lined face always makes him easy to identify in photographs, yet no images can be located of him following his illness, so the players' accounts have to be trusted. Despite being back with the team, there was no chance of him being well enough to participate in any of the remaining matches. Reuniting with Ironmonger reminded the team of their other missing colleague—Arthur Allsopp remained in St Georges hospital in Bombay. They worried that he may not be well enough to join them on the *Strathnaver*, for the return trip to Australia the following month, as from all reports his situation remained precarious.

---

[1] *The Telegraph* February 6, 1936.

[2] *Sydney Mail* March 4, 1936.

[3] The Maharwal of Dungarpur was the father of Raj Singh Dungarpur, the first-class cricketer who turned administrator and virtually ruled Indian cricket throughout the 1980s and 1990s. His 'Mian, captain banoge?' (Monsieur, you want to be the captain?) question to Mohammad Azharuddin is part of the folklore of Indian cricket.

[4] *The Maitland Daily Mercury* January 20, 1936.

[5] *The Telegraph* February 18, 1936

[6] *Sydney Mail* March 18, 1936.

[7] March 11, 1936.

[8] *Newcastle Morning Herald and Miners' Advocate* February 5, 1936.

21 BEER, BANQUETS AND A PATIALA PEG

> Outside cricket, very little is known in India about Australia or her products. It seems to me a position that needs rectifying. India offers a vast market for Australian to exploit. I saw only two Australian products in India, Tasmanian jam at Calcutta and a Melbourne beer at Madras.[1]

Searching through Tom's archive I became increasingly intrigued by the numerous menus. Each one is a beautiful object with its own distinctive design elements including gilt font, graphic layout and charming illustrations. Their production was made possible by rapid technological advancements in printing processes. The almost-indestructible menus have survived well and look like they'll continue to outlive other items in Tom's box, in direct contrast with the rapidly fading black-and-white images.

However, the menus are more than just beautiful objects, as they also reveal the eating habits of the era and speak about the cultural customs of late-colonial India. Food and alcohol in India in the 1930s represent an increasingly unstable cultural dynamic and reveal a consolidating nationalistic sentiment.

Newspaper articles and letters written by the cricketers indicate that they unanimously appraised the exotic Indian food and culinary customs in a critical fashion. The local cuisine became another symbol of India to fear, in a similar vein to the Western tourists' anxiety about illness and hygiene. Due to the predominance of gastric outbreaks on the tour, the Australian players viewed all food and drink suspiciously as revealed when Hendry complained to the press that 'Strange food and water are having an effect on the players'.[2] On the cricketers return home, the *West Australian* noted that it was 'small wonder that their fellows had regarded every dish placed before them and every jug of refreshment brought on to the field with trepidation'.[3]

Indian historian, Ramachandra Guha cites Muhammad Ali Jinnah's (who would become Pakistan's first Governor-General and was regarded as the founder and the 'father' of Pakistan) prescient appraisal in 1940 of the inevitability of partition, which he claimed was due to the incompatibility of the population. Jinnah justified partition by proclaiming that 'Hindus and Muslims belong to two different religious philosophies, social customs and literature' and qualifies this by observing that 'they neither intermarry, nor interdine together, and indeed they belong to two different civilizations which are based mainly on conflicting ideas and conceptions'.[4] Likewise,

Appadurai, an Indian anthropologist, details the divisive nature of eating and proclaims that 'food taboos and prescriptions divide men from women, gods from humans, upper from lower castes, one sect from another'.[5] However Appadurai also identifies food as a unifier: 'Eating together, whether as a family, a caste, or a village, is a carefully conducted exercise in the reproduction of intimacy'.

Despite the number of diners frequently reaching three figures, mealtimes provided a safe haven for the Australian cricketers. Invited guests would congregate in an intimate, private domain: a sanctuary within—as potentially perceived by them—a broader, possibly dangerous environment. A photograph from the Alexander archive illustrates a typical lunchtime tableau during a cricket match, with both teams eating together. The image depicts a harmonious and integrated racial and social space as the Australian players and their Indian counterparts intermingle along the table. It negates the claims made by Jinnah and Appadurai as the divisive nature of food consumption does not apply to the heterogeneous diners depicted and illustrates the liberal and progressive foundation that underpinned the tour to India.

Lunchtime scene during match with both teams. Alexander archive

Despite the safety of mealtimes, the Australians were highly critical of the formalised rituals and protocols they were expected to endure and the foreign cuisine they were required to consume which generally consisted of substantial quantities of a combination of Eastern spices and available produce prepared in accordance with European culinary traditions. The availability of produce was dependent on what could be imported within the confines of the Empire and what could be bred, slaughtered, grown and cultivated by the locals under the direction of the British. Although the majority of dishes were European in origin, most meals would include one course as a tribute to the host country. Despite the general consensus that the construction of a contemporary Indian national cuisine was a postcolonial development, indicators of this fare were already evidenced in the 1935/36 tour. The cricketers exhaustively complained about the Indian food on tour, yet its presence suggests that the tour ethos embraced a progressive ideology that would evolve and flourish in post-colonial India.

During the match against the Western Indians in Rajkot, Fred Mair was fielding and was keen to escape the harsh sun. Slowly, he inched towards the line of shade that fell on the outfield to provide him with some relief from the sun. Seeing that the fielder was out of position, the bowler Tom Leather stopped play to insist that Mair go back to where the captain required him to be. However much to the amusement of the crowd he slowly inched back to the line of shade. To reward Mair for his cheeky insubordination, and because they found it amusing, the enthusiastic crowd fed the fielder a constant supply of fruit throughout the afternoon which resulted in him spending most of the match in the shady portion of the ground being well nourished. Seemingly on this occasion local fruit was used to reward the crowd favourite. So, it seems that local food wasn't always something to fear and avoid.

Guha observes that, 'Places such as the Calcutta Cricket Club and the Madras Cricket Club provided English food and English entertainments'.[6] According to Uma Narayan, an Indian feminist scholar, in an endeavour to protect their colonial rule and defend British culture in India, the nineteenth-century British colonists avoided Eastern symbols, such as locally sourced produce, to distinguish themselves from their colonial subjects. Appadurai concurred and observed that, 'Court cuisines drew on foods and recipes from great distances'.[7]

Yet ironically, back at home in Britain curry was consumed in fashionable houses, chinoiserie was flouted as a status symbol and even Queen Victoria (the Empress of India) felt compelled to learn Hindustani. During Victoria's reign, India represented the ultimate triumph of the Empire and the Queen acknowledged her strategic importance. She orchestrated the design of a durbar room at Osborne House (her summer retreat on the Isle of Wight) and famously employed the devoted and loyal Mohammed Abdul Karim (known as the Munshi) in her domestic service. The next royal generation, likewise, demonstrated a politically and fiscally advantageous interest in India. In 1867, Queen Victoria's son, Prince Alfred (the Duke of Edinburgh) embarked on a world tour of several of Britain's most important colonies. A venture of such a type was interpreted 'as a shrewd attempt by the British government to reward colonial loyalty with a personal encounter with royalty'.[8] Edward VII (the Prince of Wales and the future king) toured India and Ceylon for four months in 1875/76 where he immersed himself in

Eastern culture. Similarly, Prince Albert Victor (Duke of Clarence and Avondale) was so greatly impressed by the Madras Prawn Curry from the Madras Club that he instructed the 'native cooks' to teach his personal chefs how to replicate the dish. Some historians argue that gestures from the West to 'understand' Eastern culture were solely self-serving in an endeavour to 'maximize the surplus value that could be extracted from the subject peoples'.[9] The British interest in India can be cynically viewed as being purely political resulting in economic advantages.

However, by the 1930s, the nationalistic agenda was advancing, and the Indian cricket community encouraged the presence of non-European symbols on the menus and embraced a changing culinary tradition. Despite the Australian team's ambivalence towards Indian food, as revealed by complaints in letters, manuscripts and newspaper articles, most banquets included at least one locally inspired dish. Although it would have been possible to serve Western food exclusively to the Australian team the Indian food appeared as evidence of a nationalistic response to colonisation.

Alcohol was also a significant feature and revealed the cultural dynamic of the tour. The menus found in the players' archives disclose that an extensive list of beverages was available at most functions and the cricketers vehemently complained when events were dry. A list of beverages is generally listed on the opening page of the menu and occupy almost the same spatial dimension as the list of food which suggests food and alcohol were equally important. The author of the history of the Madras Cricket Club (formed in 1846) critiques the significance of alcohol and claims that during its first 100 years it took precedence over food.

Guha cites a document located at the British Library in London quantifying the liquor consumed in a year at Government House Inn in Poona while Lord Harris was at the helm. The document reveals the number of bottles consumed in the year 1890–91 and identifies Harris's predilection for whisky: Champagne - 2,414; Claret - 1,123; Hock – 368; Sherry – 411; Port – 271; Liqueurs -144; Brandy -123 and Whisky -545. Poona Inn was one of the many holiday abodes used by Lord Harris (the Governor of Bombay from 1890–95) and these figures do not reveal the total consumption of his many households.

Alcohol consumption, amongst the various European communities, was customary in colonial India from the early seventeenth century for numerous reasons: boredom was commonly cited, alcohol was readily available, water quality was poor and drinking was pejoratively acknowledged to be a symbol of home. However, research on alcohol in colonial India reveals that 'the very existence of an alcohol problem among the members of the self-styled "ruling race" called into question the legitimising myth of an alleged civilisational superiority that was undergirding the colonial "rule of difference"'.[10]

The Anglo-Indians were responsible for the creation of the alcoholic cocktail punch—made by mixing the local spirit Arrak with sugar, lime-juice, spice and water. The word punch, which is now part of English language common parlance, means five (Hindustani and Bengali, *panch* or the cognate *panji* in Persian), referring to the number of ingredients used to make the drink. However, the history of alcohol predated the British in India and its consumption, and correlation with religious observance in the East has a complex and contradictory history. Some historians argue that wine consumption in India, prior to British colonisation, was a rarity except between the sixteenth and eighteenth centuries when the country was under Mughal rule. However other historians maintain that alcohol consumption in some Indian communities was endemic and Guha remarks that tribal groups known as *adivasi* (meaning original inhabitants) consumed alcohol as 'part of their festivals, their rituals, indeed their daily life'.[11]

Alcohol in India, like all symbols both Western and Eastern, formed an inflexible hierarchy. Imported alcohol was revered however it was unaffordable to all bar the Indian aristocracy and the British elite. The Indian monarchs perceived the consumption of liquor, especially imported liquor, as a coveted status symbol. The Patiala family's close association with alcohol resulted in a measure of liquor being named the *Patiala peg*; this portion of alcohol is approximately 120ml however the measurement is inexact as it is gauged by the height of three (rather large Sikh) fingers. The Maharaja of Patiala, who was familiar with alcohol and the consequences of consuming it, introduced the measure into parlance after a night of tomfoolery where he encouraged the intoxication of a visiting Irish tent-pegging team to facilitate a victory for the locals.

An absence of research into indigenous drinking habits in colonial India is lamentable however contemporary analysis concludes that locally produced country liquor (Desi Sharaab, Daaru, Urrack and Feni) ranges in concentration from forty to seventy per cent pure ethanol. Standardised pouring measures in rural areas are non-existent, which contributes to a high degree of alcoholism. One can assume that drinking habits in the 1930s were even less regulated and therefore many citizens were prone to alcohol abuse. Rural regions throughout India produced various spirits and variants of Arrak: different spirits were produced in the various Indian regions due to the availability of ingredients and the climate. For example, the prevalence of the Palmyra palm (Borassus flabellifer) in the south encouraged the production of palm toddy in the region. In Eastern India, rice and molasses were key ingredients in the manufacture of spirits. Somrasa, a liquor derived from the soma plant, is mentioned in the Vedas and was a part of the religious rituals. It is close to Mead. Similarly, liquor made out of the Mahua plant is famous/infamous through history and antiquity for the associated intoxication.

Local spirits were cheaper, and one has to imagine that they were of a dubious quality. The prevailing consensus among the colonists was that Indian liquor was inferior and could even potentially cause physical and physiological damage.

Alcohol consumption was perceived as a leisure activity of civility however simultaneously it was increasingly viewed by the medical profession and nineteenth-century ethicists as unhealthy and injurious to the moral fabric of society. Historian Fischer-Tiné writes, 'Punch houses were associated with "evils"—or "social diseases" as the late-nineteenth-century parlance had it—that were viewed as being closely related, indeed inseparable from "intemperance", namely gambling and prostitution'.[12] Thus, paradoxically, intoxicants were perceived as an affectation of the upper classes, yet at the same time viewed as an atavistic trait of the socially and economically disenfranchised sectors of society, who continued to rely on their affordable and presumably inferior locally produced alcohol.

Abstaining from alcohol consumption in the twentieth century was partially driven by political policy as the increasingly dominant and popular independence movement urged the Indian population to boycott British goods, including British liquor. The consumption of alcohol was viewed as an 'English vice' and a symbol of exploitation and oppression. Therefore, it is not surprising that a philosophy of prohibition, encouraging complete abstinence, was incorporated into the constitution after India attained independence in 1947.

Hendry's manuscript, a primary-source evidentiary treasure trove, revealed that most members of the Australian team habitually drank alcohol throughout the tour. Hendry attributed his good health on tour to his diligence in maintaining high levels of hygiene and stringent dietary restrictions. He wrote, 'I should state here that I never drank a drop of water or ate any vegetable grown above the ground throughout the entire tour, concentrating on whiskey an (sic) soda, burra and choka (sic) pegs'. Hendry's observation that he never 'ate any vegetable grown above the ground' complies with contemporary Western medical instruction however it can also be evaluated through an Orientalist prism as autochthonic items were avoided. Coward, referring to 'Alexander and Nagel, the enfants terrible of the party' wrote, 'Like all fast bowlers on the subcontinent they sought solace in more than an occasional chota peg and religiously changed from beer to whiskey the moment they changed for dinner'.[13] Coward also comments that, 'whisky for the fever' was a common team cry and Tarrant rewarded the team with ample supplies of spirits under the guise of its consumption providing medical benefit. Coward observes that Alexander and Nagel took delight in commandeering the alcohol rations from the teetotallers on tour. Despite increased medical research into the potential detriment of alcohol to good health and social activism which drove the temperance movement and led to prohibition in the USA, it is interesting, yet not altogether surprising, that Tarrant in the mid-1930s was still encouraging 'whisky for the fever'. Sentiment seemingly didn't change as almost two decades later, when England toured India in 1951/52, George Duckworth's advice to Tom Graveney and the rest of the team was to drink whiskey and eat egg and chips.

Hendry noted the pressure to consume alcohol placed upon his host, Mr Purdy, as a member of the colonial class: 'He was a teetotaller but was always served with ginger ale in a whisky glass. I used to say to the native butler, what about giving our host a drink. He would look at me hautily (sic) replying "my sahib doesn't drink". He must have been exceptional amongst the Britishers not only in Bombay but also throughout the country'. Evidently, alcohol abstinence was to be ridiculed as Hendry humorously taunts the butler that his employer doesn't consume alcohol. The Englishman is cognisant of the pressure to consume alcohol and adheres to cultural expectations by drinking ginger ale in a whisky glass.

At times, the Australian team also tired of alcohol excess. Despite the proliferation of material revealing that the 1935/36 cricketers spent much of the tour over-indulging, evidence of restraint also exists. Oxenham, one of the few non-drinkers, observed that 'one is expected to drink the whole time, and, of course, this does not suit me. "But," they say, this is nothing to what you will get later on; they'll be simply pouring it down your necks as the tour progresses. Fortunately, there are also plenty of cool soft drinks available, Bert and I have, been able to keep our heads above water — a rather apt expression!'[14] Later Oxenham, noted the pressure to imbibe and described the extensive social activities where the players were expected to attend multiple functions. He observed that 'they [the hosts] are very hurt if you do not have a "spot" or two at everyplace'.[15] Hendry also observed that the team felt pressure to drink. He described the final night in Bombay: 'Music, dancing and drinks were on but I could neither eat nor drink and poured my beer surreptitiously into the numerous flowerpots about'. This rejection of alcohol late in the trip may be interpreted as a changing palate, however it can also be symbolically viewed as discarding the conventions of the British Raj in favour of Indian customs.

Hendry observed that in one of the smaller provinces Alexander was billeted to stay with a British bachelor who had a reputation as being 'a heavy drinker and playboy'. Hendry's host expressed sympathy with Harry Alexander. However, Hendry assured his host: 'Don't worry about 'Bull' (his nickname) I told him, he will come out on top. Sure enough, Harry took his car and drove around visiting our other guests after his host had fallen asleep'. Seemingly the Australians were at times prepared to admonish the English traits of alcoholism and excess.

The Indian population, for religious and cultural reasons, largely abstained from intoxicants and therefore the consumption of alcohol was viewed as a distinctively Western trait. However, a close reading of Hendry's manuscript reveals that alcohol was, surreptitiously, consumed by some Indians: 'I mentioned previously that most Indians did not drink intoxicating liquor but I will never forget at a big function in Delhi I was having drinks with three of their test players at a little bar in the banqueting room when all of a sudden they disappeared like magic, only to return in a short time after the Indian Board of Control members drifted out of sight'. Alcohol consumption by the Indian population was motivated by its symbolism of the West and as an act of defiant non-conformist rebellion.

Apparently, some cultural customs haven't changed and in Muslim Pakistan the consumption of alcohol is still not generally condoned and at cricket events throughout the country liquor is discreetly consumed, away from the eyes of administrators and disapproving elders.

A culturally revealing document from the Bill archive is a seating plan for a dinner held at the Poona Club in November 1935. The seating arrangement exposes the rigid hierarchy that informed all aspects of cultural life in colonial India. The invitees and their placement suggest the multifarious objectives of the dinner. According to the rigid social class structure the 112 guests are listed indicative of their rank and importance. Twenty-five invitees sit on the main table, on the stage, including Jack Ryder and Frank Tarrant. The captain and team manager are the only Australians seated on the table, the remainder are predominantly British civil and military dignitaries and four notable locals including cricketer Professor Deodhar, the Maharaja of 'Partapgar (sic)' (according to Hendry, 'the most important guest'), the Chief of Jath and Mr Shete (a name indicating he belonged to the Brahmin caste). Hendry's observation that the 'Maharaja of 'Partapgar (sic)', in the presence of numerous British dignitaries, was 'the most important guest' reveals that the Australian cricketers did not pay homage to conventional and widely accepted British colonial delegations of social authority. Deodhar and the Chief of Jath played for the Maharashtra team against the Australians at Poona. The Poona Club provided a strictly devised and inflexible hierarchical environment and the inclusion of Indians on the principal table is indicative of a relaxation in racial segregation and hierarchy.

Professor Deodhar (1892–1993), seated on the head table at the Poona club, is a somewhat overlooked yet significant contributor to cricket in the early-twentieth century as an aggressive batsman and a courageous captain characterised by his intense nationalistic philosophy. Exhibiting enormous batting ability, yet marginally too old when India played its first Test match in 1932, he missed out on Test participation. Deodhar authored the *March of Indian Cricket*, which is an invaluable primary source and provides a contemporary Indian perspective on colonial cricket and its correlation with bourgeoning nationalist sentiment. The preface to the book optimistically proposed that cricket 'will be rejuvenated in the new era of Indian freedom'.[16] Deodhar was critical of the communal competition, with its inherent and divisive factionalism, and argued that cricket should operate according to a meritocratic and egalitarian model. Cricket and political scholar Ashis Nandy attributes the lack of recognition of Deodhar's contribution to Indian cricket as due to his refusal to pay homage to the aristocratic, upper class and western connections. However, possibly, Nandy's argument has flaws as the domestic limited overs inter-zonal competition is called the Deodhar Trophy and he is also is frequently referred to the Grand Old Man of Indian Cricket. Deodhar was pragmatic in his approach to cricket and despite philosophical objections he realised that he needed to acquiesce to the prevailing power brokers to achieve his objectives. He was an instrumental figure in assisting the transference of cricket, 'a national institution', from the traditional custodians, the British, into the hands of the locals where it facilitated 'social mobility for the lowly and the downtrodden' and became a defiant 'affirmation of democratic principles'.[17] It would be nice to think that dinner conversation in Poona involved Deodhar chatting to Tarrant and Ryder about his hopes for the political future of India and the trajectory of cricket within it. Hopefully, they envisaged that Australia would play a strategic role in the exercise.

Traditionally alcohol is consumed to celebrate a sporting victory and to assist team bonding. A populist view of Australian identity portrays alcohol and sport as entwined entities and sportsmen who decline alcohol are treated with scepticism. Despite his unrivalled talent with the cricket bat, Donald Bradman was considered un-Australian when he elected not to join his colleagues in post-victorious celebratory drinks at the bar. J and S Edelheim observe, 'We were also fascinated by the connection drawn between being Australian and heavy alcohol consumption, and wondered if the opposite, not consuming alcohol or consuming it in a moderate way, would be regarded as 'un-Australian''.[18] Likewise in India alcohol consumption was considered an idiosyncratic trait of the colonial class and individuals who defied the stereotype were treated with suspicion and contempt.

The Australian cricketers on tour would not have questioned whether their alcohol intake or abstinence or their opinion of Indian curries correlated with national identity. However, these attitudes are revealing of the visitors' perspective to their role as cricketers and equally, if not more so, to revealing the extent of their embrace of British colonisation and endorsement of impending Indian sovereignty.

[1] *The Herald* March 5, 1936.
[2] *West Australian* November 11, 1935.
[3] February 26, 1936.
[4] *India after Gandhi: The History of the World's Largest Democracy* 2007, 41.
[5] *How to Make a National Cuisine: Cookbooks in Contemporary India* 1988, 10.
[6] 2002, 6.
[7] 1988, 5.
[8] McCreery 2013, 439.
[9] 2003, xx–xxi.
[10] Fischer-Tiné 2012, 385.
[11] 2007, 127.
[12] 2012, 388.
[13] 1990, 105–06.
[14] November 25, 1935.
[15] December 16, 1935.
[16] 1948, *v*.
[17] Nandy 2000, 83.
[18] 2011, 25.

22 'STALE AS CUCUMBERS'

Next the team headed further south to Secunderabad. The train journey dragged on for an interminable forty hours. The temperature gradually rose as they inched towards the equator and soon the players started fantasising about fans rather than fires. At a stop along the way, the cricketers alighted the train and in defiance, and just because they could, they delayed the train's departure. According to Oxenham, they had 'some fun with the train staff' as they 'refused to leave the refreshment booth on one station' until they had finished their meals.[1] 'The guard anxiously poked his nose in the door on several occasions, only to be told that "It's all right, we won't be a minute."' Following each interruption, the cricketers defiantly continued to eat their meals, and the train obediently waited until they had finished. I doubt they would have behaved in such an arrogant fashion early on the tour and even Oxenham noted, 'Fancy getting away with that in Australia!'

In light of the death of the King, the three-day match in Secunderabad against the Nawab of Moin-ud-Dowlah's XI was put back by a few days and commenced on January 29. The Australians were still without their full personnel and Tarrant pleaded with a few of the cricketers to play despite them not really being fit enough, or having the necessary enthusiasm, to do so. Oxenham was coerced to compete despite his leg still troubling him and he went through the unpleasant process of being shaved and bandaged with sticking plaster in the morning before the game. He described the barber as an unqualified butcher as the shaving process resulted in more injuries. The bandages were attached too tightly and prior to the start of the game, everyone could see he was in pain and in no state to play. He could barely walk let alone run, bat and bowl. Tarrant convinced someone else to take their turn and Oxenham was again rested.

Despite it being called a social game, the Australian's came up against a very talented and determined opposition. The Nawab's team pretty much resembled the Indian XI despite Vizzy, once again, being named captain. The nobleman, never one for being humble, took outright credit for their victory. Speculation was mounting that he would leverage his successes as captain against the Australians and was already scheming his integral role in the Test team touring England tour later in the year. His team at Secunderabad comprised eight Test players and included three exceptionally good pace bowlers, including the fiery Mohammad Nissar, his famed partner Amar Singh and the wily swing bowler Shute Banerjee. Their first innings was outstanding—Amarnath scored 144, in 140 minutes with 24 boundaries. The home team declared at 413 – on what was a tour record aggregate. Vizzy missed out on batting which I'm sure miffed him, yet he acknowledged the state of play and decided on a 'team-first' decision. The overwhelmed

Australians could only manage 144 in reply and then they had to follow on. The visitors were exhausted, and the core-matting wicket resulted in blisters and muscle aches. The Australian's second innings looked more promising, yet it couldn't be sustained in the face of Amar Singh's 6 for 36, and the only joy the match provided was Leather taking his fiftieth wicket and Ryder top scoring with 38 and, more importantly, reaching 1000 runs on tour. Following the match, Ryder was enthusiastically praised by the crowd as it really was an exception achievement. On being urged to respond, he could only summon: 'Thank Heaven there are only three more matches to go'. The Australian's loss by an innings and 115 runs was described as 'the most humiliating' defeat they experienced.[2]

Australian team v Moin-ud-Dowlah XI, Secunderabad. January 1936. Nisar archive

A barrage of complaints followed the match as the Australian players were sore and exhausted and the novelty of the trip was wearing thin. They were annoyed to learn that their opponents were accommodated at the magnificent *Bashir Bagh* palace whilst they were put up in a 'very ordinary hotel'.[3] They also couldn't believe the mosquitos which they claimed were the size of rats and of course perpetual complaints about the 'intense heat' abounded.

All in all, the players just wanted to go home.

Bill's second last column on March 11, 1936 describes a visit to the Moin-ud-Dowlah's private zoo in Secunderabad. The cricketers were impressed by the novelty of a private zoo but were rather shaken when an encounter with big-game went wrong. Bill wrote about the power struggle between man and beast in a typically convoluted fashion. Employing aggrandised prose, Bill noted, 'Here we came face to face with huge panthers and lions, only a few bars separating us from their savage jaws'.[4] The article reveals that the animals were rather too close for comfort: 'One of the team, in an unguarded moment, turned his back too close to one of these cages whereupon his coat was badly ripped by two big paws which came through the bars, and just scratched his back – a lucky escape'. This conforms to the stereotypical traveller narrative where an encounter with a wild animal was considered mandatory to represent a true colonial experience but like many events on tour, it manifests as an unconvincing version of the colonial experience. Primary material reveals that some of the cricketers were disappointed by the paucity of their encounters with wild animals and ironically when such a meeting did transpire, it was in the somewhat-regulated environment of the Moin-ud-Dowlah's zoo.

A quick trip to Hyderabad, a large princely state that adjoined Secunderabad, was squeezed into the schedule. The Nizam of Hyderabad, Osman Ali Khan, was thought to be the wealthiest man on earth and Oxenham gossiped that he was rumoured to have £50,000,000 of gold in his palace vaults and an annual income of £12,000,000. The Nizam had an incredible number of wives and His Exalted Highness was dubbed his exhausted highness by the English cricketers of 1951/52. The Australians were intrigued to learn that he had his own currency and they made sure that they didn't leave with any notes or coins as they would be useless elsewhere. Despite his wealth, the Nizam was reputed to be exceptionally tight with his money so the players were surprised to see how clean and efficient the facilities in his state were. Roads, public transportation and state buildings were kept in good working order.

The next stop was Madras. Oxenham hoped he would be well enough to play as following Ryder's thousand run milestone, the lure of taking 100 wickets dangled before him. However, Oxenham noted that sport wasn't the only priority, as he acknowledged that the experiences on the tour had imparted the cricketers with an enlightened understanding of culture: 'An injured leg muscle has kept me out of a few of the games, and, of course, this has meant greater opportunities of seeing the various places at which we have been staying. I never realised so much before that the World — the world outside our own country, that is — held so much that is not only interesting but educational'.[5]

A distinct change in the landscape was observed through the train windows. They hadn't seen such a luxuriant growth of green vegetation since Ceylon and they worried slightly about the malarious rainforests yet despite some close calls no-one had died…..as yet! It was rather nice to be hot and sweating after the cold environs they had experienced further north.

They were treated to an especially fervent welcome to the city. The locals were enthusiastic about the arrival of the visiting XI and barricades were erected to keep the cricketers separated from the fans who flocked en masse to see them dismount the train. Cries of 'Aussie Sahib' rang through the air. They were photographed and garlanded *ad nauseam*. At the start of the tour, they had felt privileged by this type of welcome yet in Madras they were completely fatigued by the adoration and a lack of personal space just annoyed them. Oxenham estimated the crowd was well over a thousand.

He also noted how much darker the locals were than their northern counterparts. There was also a variance of height and body shapes—down south the locals were small and squat with tiny hand and feet yet up north bodies were elongated. It was a further reminder of the diversity of the Indian population across the massive country. The population shared neither language, culture or even physical uniformity.

Madras was a pretty city and the locals were generous hosts, yet the toll of touring continued to accumulate. Macartney wrote that 'the players were very tired and worn, and unable to give off their best, owing to the strain of carrying on with no relief'.[6] A week later he observed that 'the last month has been a very hard struggle—the same side playing match after match without reinforcements of any kind'. Ryder in a letter home remarked that he was exhausted; 'stale as a cucumber', and he'd 'had quite enough'. Ryder embraced the role of captain seriously and acknowledged that the illness and injury incurred by the other players, required him 'to keep going to the end – the sooner the better – "Oh for the boat"'.[7] Thank goodness they only had three matches left to play including the last unofficial Test and they were counting the hours….minutes…and…seconds until they would leave for home.

The Madras Club, a gentleman's club operating on the premise of exclusivity and privilege, provided the catering for the Madras Cricket Club and usually did so with great aplomb 'except' when preparing for the visiting Australians in February 1936. The author of the history of the Madras Cricket Club is no doubt expressing some irony when he observed that, 'the only time the Madras Club let down the Madras CC was during Ryder's tour in 1936. It was minuted, "The catering for the members and the teams was very efficiently carried out by the Madras Club, in spite of the unfortunate breakdown on the first day when it was found that the Australian craving for chewing gum had not been catered for"'.[8] No other primary material details the absence of gum on the first day in Madras. Such notation in the minute book nonetheless does re-emphasise racial imbalance and the locals' dismay that they would be critiqued harshly by the oversight.

The programme for the team's visit to Madras is located in the Bill archive at Cricket New South Wales. This programme is slightly dissimilar to others as it identifies the clubs that granted the visitors' honorary membership during the duration of their visit. It also nominated where the cricketers would stay and included the hosts' contact details (including phone numbers). Ryder, Macartney and Bill resided at Government house with Lord and Lady Erskine. It is logical that the captain and vice-captain of the team would be accommodated at the most prestigious lodging however to include Bill in this arrangement suggested that he was placed there on the presumption that his double-barrelled surname (which was an inaccuracy perpetuated in India) equated to him being aristocratic. Ryder in a letter to his wife revealed that he was uncomfortable staying at the prestigious residence and observed that we 'will have to be on our best behaviour at Madras'. The remaining team members were billeted amongst military men, members of the police force and other prominent British figures.

Early one morning at Government house, the Australian trio were abruptly woken to the sound of gunshots being fired in quick succession. Considering the precarious nature of late-Colonial India, they feared the worst and jumped out of bed half-expecting to find nationalist militants ransacking the residence. However, they were relieved to find Lord Erskine had spontaneously organised a crow-shoot. He took cheeky delight in how his behaviour unnerved his guests.

In Madras, the Empire was still mourning the death of King George and despite many social functions being cancelled Bill observed that the death did not totally suspend all pleasure as the players managed to locate 'gaieties in the pleasant surroundings of the many fine clubs which Madras possesses'.[9] Regarding their time in Madras, Ryder earlier wrote to his family from Secunderabad on January 31: 'We are looking forward to 8 days of a nice quiet spell, apart from cricket. All official functions naturally have been cancelled so we will have to enjoy a lot of the Gov's [Lord Erskine] company at home – most likely'. Ryder's hesitance at the end of the second sentence may be due to him questioning the likelihood of eight days, without external influences, of social interaction with Lord Erskine as enjoyable. Luckily (or unluckily) for the cricketers two games were back on the schedule at Madras. Seemingly, India had mourned the death of the King for long enough!

Oxenham lodged with Major Hildebrand, a rather apt arrangement as he was secretary of the Madras Racing Club. Oxenham was a non-drinker yet keenly observed the racing industry and loved a punt. Oxenham couldn't believe his luck when he realised that the Major lived in a comfortable house adjacent to the racecourse. Newspaper articles reveal that it wasn't just Oxenham who spent time at the racetrack as the cricketers were acutely aware that they'd soon be Australia bound, and some wanted to devotee as much time to activities they enjoyed and possibly couldn't pursue so freely at home. A few also had surplus funds that they wished to spend. I'm sure they argued that there was no reason to take it home with them. Bill reported on further evidence of gambling and wrote about a delightful day spent at the Madras Race Club. He observed that 'it was a great day in one sense, but not so good in another, as the majority of us went back to town well out of pocket, the bookies no doubt thinking that that we might be good cricketers, but bad punters!'.[10]

Tarrant stayed at the Connemara Hotel that, according to Macartney, was 'one of the best hotels in India'. Now part of the Taj consortium, the Connemara still symbolises luxury and is described in promotional material as 'colonial brilliance at its best'. In 1935/36, the players' commentary frequently observed the standard of accommodation and indeed the standard of everything, either good or bad, in India. Seemingly being 'the best' was important to the players personally and to the wider reputation of the tour, however the Australian's concept of 'the best' did not always correlate with that of their hosts.

Hendry's lodging was a point of variance as he stayed with the Zamindar of Kumaramangalam. He was the only team member staying with a local family which suggests a gradual relaxation of racial stipulations and points to the progressive nature of the tour. The Zamindar was the Chief Minister of the Madras Presidency from 1926 to 1930 and he later served in the Nehru Ministry. The Kumaramangalams were a prestigious family with numerous members being significant political agitators and military men who made a significant contribution to Indian history.

Hendry's perspective on being billeted with an Indian family can be reprised in detail as it identifies his ability to reconfigure theories of racial difference through the experience of the tour: 'I was far from happy when I was told I was to stay with an Indian family at Madras and asked why I was picked out. It appeared that my host had read so much about [Jack] Hobbs that a name beginning with H was his choice. It turned out to be very fortunate for me because I enjoyed my stay greatly'. The serendipity of Hendry's surname enabled him to be placed in an environment that challenged his racial perspective. Hendry describes an incident, concerning the same Indian family, where cultural inequality between the colonisers and the colonised led him to question the dominant order:

> There were two young boys and a girl in the family I was staying with, and at breakfast on the first day of the test, I asked the boys were they coming to the cricket. On their reply they were looking forward to it eagerly. I said "Good, well come down to the ground with me". "We can't, sahib, because we are not allowed in the Members' Reserve". "Come with me nevertheless" I said. On arrival at the Members' gate, I said I wished to bring my two young friends in "Sorry, Mr. Hendry, it is not possible" "Get the Secretary to whom I said "if your authorities think these boys parents were good enough to house me then these lads are worthy of being with me. If they don't come in I don't either". Eventually it was

> agreed that they could come everyday. I considered I had done something worthwhile and it thrilled me to sit with them in the Members' Reserve to the utter astonishment of all present.

This passage reveals that Hendry's racial perspective modified throughout the tour. He observed that initially he was 'far from happy' to be billeted with an Indian family however after staying with them his irritation was re-directed at the British Raj who insisted on imposing the regressive rules of racial segregation.

The match Hendry referred to was described by the playing personnel and the press as the 'most exciting match of the tour'. The Australian team competed against the Madras Presidency at Chepauk stadium. Despite the visitors' lack of enthusiasm, they managed to stave off defeat despite only managing a paltry 47 in their first innings with five of them making ducks. Defeat looked inevitable on the final day before Leather and Oxenham added 77 for the final wicket to snatch a one-wicket victory. Bill acknowledged that 'our chances were a million to one against us, as Leather's habit' was 'to hit wildly at every ball and get out in quick time'.[11] When Leather went out to bat, the police were preparing the ground for a local's victory, the ground staff were getting their hoses ready to water the pitch; and 'garlands of flowers were in readiness to be placed around the necks of the Madras team in recognition of their victory'. However, on this occasion 'he [Leather] again hit wildly, giving several easy chances which were not accepted; then the luck seemed to be "in his pocket", as everything went right, and every ball hit into the air fell just out of reach of the fields men, and, aided materially by Oxenham, who played a grand innings, he pulled the match out of the fire amid tremendous excitement'. Bill further explained:

> All these plans were upset, the game being unexpectedly prolonged; then, in the wild excitement of the finish—the policemen were so carried away themselves that they cheered instead of keeping the crowd off the ground—in a twinkling the entire oval was alive with people. Across the wicket they swarmed, ignoring the groundsman brandishing his hose, sweeping him, indeed, with the crowd to the pavilion gates, where Leather and Oxenham, together with the other members of our team, were garlanded with the flowers intended for the Madras players. What a finish it was! — something to be remembered long after our tour is over.

Group shot, Madras. February 1936. Leather archive

The next match was the last unofficial 'Test' played at Madras and it was a comparatively uneventful and routine event—played on a 'treacherous' wicket. The locals won a low-scoring game by 33 runs. Wazir Ali captained the side as he had in Lahore and on both occasions, he was victorious which attributes him an impressive record. The principal architects of the Indian win were once again Nissar (11 wickets in the match) and Amar Singh (7). Again, Nayudu didn't play – however this time it was attributed to him being dropped for disciplinary reasons. The Australians had incurred more injuries and setbacks and Tarrant had requested that Southby and Johnstone, two British gentlemen living locally, play for the Australian team. These two had played for the Madras Presidency side in the previous match– Johnstone had led the Madras side and Southby had opened the innings with him. It is unknown if Tarrant's request was accepted or not however, he managed to field an all-Australians team despite Joe Davis having to play. Davis only managed to scramble a few runs, but it was reported that he showed promise as a fielder. Alexander somehow managed to bowl, albeit somewhat unsuccessfully, with a broken bone in his hand. He didn't take a wicket in the first innings in his six overs and was not bowled in the second innings.

Madras 'Test', Tom Leather batting. February 1936. Leather archive

Australian team, Madras. February 1936. Leather archive

A photograph from the Salahuddin archive enables a local's interpretation of events. The text that accompanies the image is charmingly subjective and revealing of the occasion and the author. Echoing orthodox photographic practice, the image authenticates the experience, in this case a victory. Salahuddin titled the photograph *Struggle for Booty* and the image depicts the excited Indian cricketers racing to acquire the stumps as a symbol of victory. Strangely, the crowd in the background sits calmly and does not appear to be overawed by the victory and the occasion. Despite the Australian players' frequent commentary about the Indian's enthusiasm for the game, in which they employ clichéd rhetoric describing an unbridled passion for cricket, the crowd is surprisingly sedate. Seemingly the crowd does not acquiesce to Western expectations and popular-culture clichés. Traditionally the stumps were souvenired to celebrate a win. The stump and the photograph were valued as trophies that verify the experience; this echoed the Australian cricketers' acquisition of objects to validate an occasion. Salahuddin noted the names of his fellow cricket countrymen depicted in the image identifying that he acknowledged the importance of the photograph, the event and the individuals' performance. Ironically, he uses the word 'struggle' in regard to the acquisition of the stump rather than applying it to the three days of arduous cricket played in the heat. The Australian players' accounts, in accordance with wider tourist narratives, frequently reference the oppressive climatic conditions endured in India, yet no mention of the weather appears in the Indian descriptions.

Indian team following 'Test' victory in Madras. February 1936. Salahuddin archive

The photograph, rich with the symbolism of Indian victory as a nationalistic accomplishment, also provides a visual representation of the ground. The concept of photography as a colonial tool of authority is inverted as the photograph empowers the locals by depicting both the Indian cricket victory and the triumph of acquiring the 'booty'. It depicts a cricket scene that is devoid of Westerners, which visually implies the Indian's proprietorship of the game and of cricket. It also suggests broader indigenous hegemony of the political, cultural and geographic landscape. The Australian cricketers are not present in the frame revealing that they have transited through the pictorial narrative. Such an interpretation encourages the tour to be viewed as heralding the growing Indian appropriation of the game. The Australian cricketers, as superfluous participants to the events taking place, do not occupy a position of racial hegemony as prescribed by colonial hierarchy. The image alludes to the historic narrative that was to ensue, as the image portrays an absence of Western figures.

With the tour coming to a close, Tom Leather decided to an accept an invitation to join a joy flight in a Tiger Moth. Little is known about the circumstances, yet a photograph of the event survives. It was the first time he'd ever left the ground and, nearing the end of the tour, in Madras he had the courage to take the risk.

Leather in a Tiger Moth, Madras. February 1936. Leather archive

The Australians were palpably excited about the prospect of arriving home and only had to get through one more game! The final match of the tour was a non-first-class encounter against Mysore at Bangalore and resulted in a draw on a magnificent wicket. Possibly one of the best on tour, the cricketers noted. If only they'd all been so well curated. Oxenham was fit enough to re-join the team and took five wickets, enabling him to achieve the impressive record of 101 wickets on tour.

Following the last ball of the match, the Australian cricketers in a demonstration of *esprit de corps,* scrambled to secure it as a memento of a historically significant tour. I'm unsure who was successful. Possibly it was Tom Leather as two balls are located in his archive yet it's impossible to identify which matches they came from. The crowd enjoyed the players' enthusiasm to acquire the souvenir. More than anything, the visitors were relieved that cricket was over. Ryder gave a speech congratulating the playing personnel and then called upon his team to give three cheers to the Indian public. Despite Macartney being one of the shortest players on the field his bellow was the loudest. Despite his age and the taxing nature of the tour, Macartney batted in an elegant and graceful manner that belied his years. The *Hindu* described his innings as 'sparkling'.[12] It was a great way for him to conclude the tour. Although no one knew it at the time, he would not play first-class cricket again after this visit to India.

---

[1] *Daily Examiner* February 24, 1936.
[2] Roy 1947.
[3] *The Telegraph* February 18, 1936.
[4] *The Sydney Mail* March 11, 1936.
[5] *The Telegraph* February 3, 1936.
[6] February 26, 1936.
[7] Undated letters 1935/36.
[8] 1998, 478.
[9] March 18, 1936.
[10] March 18, 1936.
[11] *The Sydney Mail* March 18, 1936.
[12] February 12, 1936.

MEGAN PONSFORD

23 SNAPPING AND SHOPPING

'Today everything exists to end in a photo'

With their final game completed, the cricketers were counting down their time in India and rushed to collate traveller knick-knackery and other mementoes conforming to the tourist narrative. Seemingly, physical objects were necessary to authenticate the Indian experience. The players were increasingly cognisant that India was undergoing a changing cultural and political landscape and they knew that their experiences would not be repeated.

Jack Ryder, in a letter to his wife, requests that she keeps track of the photographs and curios that he sends home, emphasising the importance of these objects to him personally—to evoke memories and to authenticate events. In a similar vein, Ron Morrisby, prior to departure, was presented a Kodak Junior 620 revealing societal pressure to fulfil the tourist narrative through documenting the tour.

Importantly, images and keep-sakes authenticate that events took place and enable insight into the cricketers' perspectives of their Indian experiences. The tour photographs reveal an intensely subjective response that, in light of the absence of living participants, is otherwise unobtainable. In many ways, the images alongside the players' writing present a faithful rendition of their attitudes towards their colonial experience. The images suggest that the Australian visitors, despite the initial novelty of wearing a topee and a strong desire to take aim at game, didn't conform to the stereotype of touring white cricketers.

As a photographer, it was the images located in Tom's archive that immediately appealed and encouraged me to retell the story with a strong reliance on visual analysis. The different genres of photography include official team portraiture, journalistic action imagery and personal snapshots taken by the cricketers. These encompass diverse objectives and are aesthetically distinct. The snapshots enable insight into the subjectivity of the image-maker whereas the formal images depict the occasion yet can be limited in the messages they transmit and suggest how the authorities desired the tour to be memorialised. Following the tour, official photographs were circulated amongst the team to celebrate and commemorate the occasion, however these were sanctioned images and therefore the cricket authorities held jurisdiction over the messaging. Identical images are located in various players' archives, highlighting the reproducible nature of the photographic process, while the personal snapshots are customarily one-offs.

Cecily Dougan, (Ron Morrisby's daughter) noted: 'For as long as I can remember a framed portrait of Bhupinder Singh, the Maharajah of Patiala hung over our dining room fireplace'.[1] Research has resulted in locating imagery eighty years later—in family albums, in frames and sometimes in shoeboxes—which reflects the prestigious, if at some times forgotten, reputation of the tour to the individuals (and the ensuing generations) and celebrates the potency of the photographic medium to retell history.

Some images pay homage to the cricketers' ethnographic encounters as a highly exoticised cultural collision. Simultaneously other images depict a familiar British setting yet, as argued by critical theorist Homi Kharshedji Bhabha, the British Raj were frequently unsuccessful in trying to emulate home in an Oriental setting.[2] Sara Stevenson, a curator and scholar, critiques the role of the photograph in relationship to British soldiers stationed in a colonised region of China and writes, 'They wished to send back these pictures of themselves, both exotic and familiar, to remind their families and lovers of their continued existence – to replace themselves in facsimile in their home setting'. The cricketers' attitudes to these environments, both the exotic and the familiar, were changing as through their Indian experience they embraced a more nuanced and learned perspective to racial politics and cultural identity. The tour images do not represent the stock-standard tourist gaze and reveal a level of engagement between the visitors, the locals and the Indian landscape.

Photography is an intensely subjective process as image making does not solely replicate what is visible through the camera's viewfinder. The photographer's choice of composition, editing, lighting and supplementary text, along with technical aspects such as shutter speed and aperture are coded messages that constitute extensions of the degree of emotional attachment to the subject matter. The photographs provide a rare and previously unobtainable glimpse into the everyday cultural life and practice of the tour. The snapshot images are raw and intuitive. They are predominantly taken outside, using an ambient light source and demonstrate an instinctive point-and-shoot approach. The images are not pre-imagined nor consciously contrived; they represent an intuitive response to a moment in time and photographic accessories, such as a flash or backdrops, do not impede the process. The images are personalised and the photographer as novice is apparent. The key images capture the dynamics, cultural relations and the nature of the *mise-en-scène* in ways that other historical sources haven't and reveal a deeper level of identification that goes beyond customary tourist documentation.

The role of the viewer is integral to the interpretation of photographs as the observer occupies a receptive role and disseminates the imagery in a subjective manner. In 1936, auteur film director Alfred Hitchcock observed that when 'watching a well-made film, we don't sit by as spectators; we participate'.[3] The role of the active viewer applies equally to the 1935/36 photographs as the potency of the response elicited by the images has, in many ways, gained currency over time. Despite the images portraying a frozen moment, our knowledge of subsequent Indian history, the dissolution of the British Empire and the development of cricket as a professional entity impacts the way we interpret, and collaborate with, the events documented.

Hendry's manuscript refers to a treasured alabaster miniature of the Taj Mahal 'with electric light attachments which could light up the entire building' that he purchased in Agra. Hendry observed, 'I had it for years until my dear old Aunt aged 95 who stayed with us 20-odd years, broke it whilst dusting'. Ignoring the gender stereotype that his aged aunt was still responsible for the dusting at ninety-five years of age, the diminutive object, just like the photographs, served for years as a physical reminder of the experience. Through observing the miniature Taj Mahal, Hendry is constantly reminded of his Indian experience and after his elderly aunt broke it, it ceased to function as a faithful prompt of the experience. Photographic imagery, like the miniature model, eulogises the destination and the tourist experience itself. Photographic theorist Susan Sontag observes: 'Ultimately, having an experience becomes identical with taking a photograph of it, and participating in a public event comes more and more to be equivalent to looking at it in photographed form. That most logical of nineteenth-century aesthetes, Mallarmé, said that everything in the world exists in order to end in a book. Today everything exists to end in a photograph'.[4]

Charlie Macartney's perspective on the relative worth of a reproduced image in comparison to directly experiencing it differs from that of Sontag. Macartney wrote, 'Most readers have seen pictures and photographs of the Taj Mahal, and while they portray it perfectly, they cannot compare with even one fleeting chance by human eyes'.[5] The merit of the value of photography compared to a first-hand account is open to interpretation however the exhaustive documentation by the cricketers reveals that they revered the newly accessible process as a symbol of affluence, and the subsequent collation of the imagery, as it verified the experience. The images provide an intensely personal insight into the cricketers' experience, revealing their convoluted attitudes to the cultural dynamic they encountered and to the changing political landscape. However despite their ambiguity, their empathy for the locals and scenes they document is evident and exceeds the typical exchange embedded in the tourist gaze.

Imagery located in the cricketers' archives illustrates the cultural collision that took place and emphasises the 1930s fascination with the Orient as a culturally elitist subject of study. Tourism and photographic documentation have long been researched. Sontag, in her widely influential collection of essays titled *On Photography*, proclaimed that 'taking photographs fills the same need for the cosmopolitans accumulating photograph-trophies of their boat trip up the Albert Nile or their fourteen days in China as it does for lower-middle-class vacationers taking snapshots of the Eiffel Tower or Niagara Falls'.[6] Sontag's, somewhat cynical, assessment accurately reflects the portrayal of the tourist, armed with a camera, as a recurrent stereotype in popular culture which could apply to the Australian cricketers. However, the images from the tour identify a deeper level of engagement with the subject matter. The cricketers are paid employees (as are their Indian counterparts) and their images demonstrate an unconscious affinity and respect between the cultures.

Unfortunately, photographic analysis has been largely overlooked as a methodology to interrogate sport. Yet it plays a pivotal role in the re-telling of the 1935/36 Australian cricket tour of India. Huggins and O'Mahony observe the paucity of photographic analysis in sporting studies. They argue that 'it was only a few years ago that historians, most especially those of the modern and early modern period, still clung rigidly to text, too often treating visual images with reluctance or even condescension'.[7] The embrace of visual analysis in sport scholarship gained traction in the 1980s coinciding with the expanding global saturation of imagery. However, it remains an unorthodox methodology. Historian John Hughson identifies the potency and authenticity of the visual while critiquing Ken Burns' 1994 documentary, Baseball. Hughson argues that the documentary, as an intersection of cultural and social history, uses period photography, artwork and newsreel footage to place 'sport within a vernacular landscape'.[8]

Many of the 1935/36 tour photographs include text written by the cricketers. Popular theory argues that text adds currency to a photograph and without it the image can be misinterpreted. Such analysis perceives text as a superior conduit of information and historically it has been prioritised over visual imagery. It is impossible to separate the text from the aesthetics when analysing Leather's imagery as he frequently wrote over the image. Leather's text, possibly written years after the event, contains inaccuracies and numerous grammatical and spelling errors. As time passed, and Leather's memory faded, he possibly felt that the images required text to actualise the events. Leather added biro text to the imagery at a later date to memorialise his presence in colonial India. Maybe hindsight made him value the political and cultural significance of the time. Leather's captioning of the images situates him in a position of hegemony, controlling how he desired the image to be interpreted (especially in later decades following the tour). The process of image making (and the subsequent captioning of the image) empowers the photographer and the photographic process becomes a tool of control.

However, it wasn't only the Australian cricketers that documented the tour. As mentioned earlier, in 2015, I was invited to Pakistan by the Australian High Commission and the Australian Federal Police to attend cricket events in Lahore and in Islamabad to raise money for The Fayyaz Sumbal Foundation and to reinforce the goodwill between the two countries. Travel to Pakistan was particularly fruitful in locating significant private archives relating to the 1935/36 tour of pre-independent India. These artefacts enable insight into the local cricketers' perspective. It also reveals that the Indian and Australian cricketers were similar in their desire to memorialise and remember the experience through documentation. The research trip unearthed valuable archives although, interestingly, similar archives have been noticeably absent or undetectable in India. Interpreting the 'Pakistani' imagery is fraught with ethical complexities, however the Indian voice is irrevocably clear, and the unambiguous messages embedded in the material culture are evident.

Crucially, the photographic material located at the Lahore Gymkhana Cricket Club Museum and in the archives of Indian players Mohammad Nissar and Masood Salahuddin provides a point of comparison with the Australian documentation of the tour. The images (as a physical representation of events) and the accompanying text reveal how the local cricketers interpreted late colonial India and the role of cricket within it. Research gathered through conversations and exchanges with families associated with the 1935/36 Indian cricket team has revealed that in many ways the Indians' experience shared similarities with that of the Australians. Both countries acknowledged the importance of victory yet also viewed the cricket encounter as a conduit to facilitate cultural harmony and racial cohesion with resultant political overtones. So, stereotypes of difference, such as Kipling's late-Victorian imperial conceit of the incompatibility of the East and the West, are undercut by the shared experiences and motivations of the two opposing national cricket teams.

The Salahuddin, Saeed and Nisar family narratives reveal that like the Australian cricketers, the Indians were thrilled to be involved in this inaugural venture. Some images in the Pakistani archives are press photographs that have been duplicated globally however the Nisar archive contains many previously unsighted photographs detailing the fast bowler's revered career. The images comprehensively chronicle the growth and professionalisation of cricket in India during a period of rapid change in India's political circumstances. The Nisar archive, now held by the cricketer's son Waqar, contains high-quality restored and reprinted images that emphasise the prominent reputation of the events they portray and reveal the manner in which the subsequent generation re-articulate and memorialise Indian cricket and history.

An image from the Nisar archive shows Nissar and fellow batsman Salahuddin exiting the field and the elongated shadows suggest that it is at the end of play. The Indian batsmen occupy a central position in the composition and the Australian players feature as subordinate cast members. The depth of field holds the batsmen in sharp focus and the Australian cricketers range from barely identifiable to indistinguishable blurs. Jack Ryder can be identified on the far left of the image and on the right the willowy Nagel and the squat Macartney can be recognised (their physical disparities encourage them to be interpreted as comedic light relief). Seemingly Macartney is desperate to keep up with the long strides of Nagel. His swinging arms are blurred which suggest he is moving hastily. The difference in height between the two cricketers is inflated by the camera angle and perspective. The remaining Australian players form part of the landscape and, just like the trees, they morph into the background and become a decorative backdrop, no more important than the blurry cricket devotees in the distance. The composition of the photograph racially inverts the semiotics in the Australian archives, as the Indians dominate the landscape. The Indian batsmen are central in the image and caught in sharp focus. The centrality of the Indian cricketers to this sporting scene, and the visual subservience of the Australians, could be interpreted as suggesting that cricket was experiencing a political and racial restructure that heralded that of other cultural spheres. The Indian and Australian cricketers adopted the liberal attitude of Tarrant and the Maharaja and these images conform to the progressive interpretation of cricket demonstrated throughout the tour.

Salahuddin and Nissar exit the field.. Nisar archive

The Salahuddin scrapbook depicts him engaged in various sporting activities, yet the iconology of the portrait on the front cover reveals that he wished to be seen as a gentleman who played cricket as he his dressed in formal attire. The words "the owner" on the front page is written in large capital letters placed within quotation marks. The words are heavily underlined which highlights the importance of the scrapbook and the cricketer's pride in being involved in the sporting narrative. They infer the adventurous and clandestine nature of Salahuddin's sporting narrative and suggest a youthful indulgence. Superficially, both countries interpreted aspects of the tour as a *Boys Own* narrative. The Australians and the Indians used photography to make sense of their tour experiences, which in turn becomes another similarity between the competing players.

As was common with all journeys to the East, the players returned home with an array of trophies and memorabilia to verify their experience and to serve as a reminder of the luxury, exoticism and sophistication they had experienced. Ethnographic items were of particular interest and my father, Geoff Ponsford, recalls the tiger skin, complete with head, which sat, incongruously, on his uncle Tom's floor in his modest unit in suburban Melbourne for many years. As a child, Dad was always intrigued by it. Jack Ryder's granddaughter also described the animal skin which lay on the living room floor. She remembers as a child thinking it would be soft like a cat but can still recall its rough bristly texture. Ryder referenced the skin in a letter to his wife and wrote: 'May [Jack's daughter] mentioned about the panther skin, it is a sort of brown colour with nice black markings. You are sure to get the wind up when you see its vicious head'.[9] Ryder observed that the skin would shock his wife however for him it would eternally recall his Indian experience. The players' writings suggest that although these confrontations (with wild animals) were limited, they inevitably occupied a major role in the player's imaginary. As earlier noted, Hendry returned home with a treasured lamp replica of the Taj Mahal. Macartney in a newspaper article observed that 'most members of [the] team secured miniatures of the Taj Mahal, which for years to come will grace their homes in memory of a day never to be forgotten'.[10] Seemingly the memory of the event was as important, if not more so, than the event itself.

Ryder frequently referenced the purchasing of gifts to bring home. He had cricket boots made for his son, bought napery and clothing for his wife and purchased various locally made goods for his family. In one undated letter he stressed the high cost of living in India and his paucity of money. This is the only indication that the £3 spending money per week was insufficient. Ryder mentioned that a coat he has purchased for his wife cost him 'three weeks wages'. He revealed to his wife that he had very little money left and would have to be cautious with the purchasing of additional gifts and wrote, 'As far as other things [purchases] are concerned I will do my best. I will have to make a call on Frank Tarrant, you know what that means if you want these things'. This reference to Frank Tarrant is ambiguous however it suggests that Jack could borrow money from Frank in order to buy additional gifts for his family. It seems that having an outstanding debt to Tarrant sat uncomfortably with Captain Jack, as he appears reluctant to engage in the arrangement. Research suggests that Jack Ryder and Frank Tarrant were vastly different, and possibly incompatible, characters.

The players were keen to engage in bartering with the sellers of goods and chattels, which was and is common practice throughout the subcontinent. Success at acquiring a bargain was as important as the actual physical memento. Nearing the end of the tour, Bill described the flurry of retail activity at the Chandni Chowk bazaar in Delhi, which he identified as a 'filthy place':[11]

> It was really amusing to see the different methods adopted by the members of our team to purchase articles at prices about 100 per cent lower than those asked by the crafty Indian storekeepers, and every evening a post-mortem of the day's purchases and prices would be held, with many lamenting the fact that they had paid too much for their goods. One never pays the price asked for things in India, but usually about two-thirds less. To obtain your object it is necessary to bargain, for hours sometimes. If one has plenty of spare time it is very amusing and entertaining.

Oxenham also viewed the buying of tourist knick-knacks as recreation:

> the Australians were seen in the role of bargain-hunters. It is a known fact that the natives set themselves out to catch the strangers in their midst; but I am sure they must have thought when we were done with them that Palestine was one of the suburbs or Sydney or Melbourne. They asked a price. We offered them half the amount, and in most cases got the article for less. My nose felt inches longer by the time I had bought all I required![12]

Hendry's manuscript reveals that he missed out on buying a 'bargain price' Persian carpet because he feared he would have to pay customs tax on it on arrival back in Australia. He later expressed regret that he did not make the purchase as when the team returned home the Australian authorities turned a blind eye to the purchases and no-one had to pay additional taxes on their luxury goods. I guess after all they were the sporting elite on the inaugural cricket tour to India and being an international superstar had to have some perks.

---

[1] Dougan 2012.
[2] 2011, 142.
[3] Manlove 2007, 83.
[4] 2008, 24.
[5] February 20, 1936.
[6] 2008, 9.
[7] 2011, 1091.
[8] 2009, 121.
[9] January 3, 1936.
[10] February 20, 1936.
[11] March 11, 1936.
[12] *The Telegraph* February 18, 1936.

24 HOME, AT LAST

'India is rather a hub of Empire than an outpost, yet before it was my good fortune to visit India and play there with Frank Tarrant's team I was, like many other Australians, quite unaware of the extent and the color *(sic)* of Indian cricket.'[1]

At midnight, the team boarded the train at Bangalore following their final game and within fifteen minutes they were all asleep, dreaming of home. This was their last train journey and in just shy of forty hours they would arrive in Bombay. Unfortunately, the cricketers' dreams were disrupted when they were abruptly woken as the train pulled into Hubli where it would wait for four hours. Despite this being their final time on the Indian railway system, Macartney couldn't hold his tongue and complained vehemently. He couldn't understand why the train system was so inefficient and why all the journeys took so long. Sometimes he thought it would be quicker walking! However even he had to acknowledge that the situation improved when they arrived in Poona and changed trains.

This time they boarded the ultra-modern, ultra-luxury, ultra-fast *Deccan Queen*, a famous train that was established in 1930 and still runs to this day. Historically it was used to shunt the British Raj between Bombay and Poona. In 1936, it was famous for numerous reasons including being the first long-haul train to be powered by electrics and being India's first super-fast vestibuled train that contained a 'Ladies Only' car and a dining car. The cricketers were delighted to complete their Indian journey on such an efficient and luxurious train. They boarded at 6.00am and completed the 118-mile journey to Bombay in record time. Macartney toned down his criticism and referred to the *Deccan Queen* as the 'finest train in the country'.[2]

The team was back at the now well-known Victoria Terminus and caught taxis to the similarly familiar Taj Mahal Hotel which the players now perceived as a home away from home. They viewed the hotel even more fondly due to the fact that soon they would be entering it for the last time. A concierge greeted Hendry in the foyer and informed him that the Maharawat of Pratapgarh had earlier been enquiring as to the whereabouts of the team. The Maharawat was planning a farewell function for the team and he asked the concierge to invite the cricketers to attend drinks at the cocktail bar at 5pm. They had previously met the Maharawat in Indore and had been quite taken by his charisma, charm and generosity.

Through the hotel windows, the team was additionally excited to see the *Strathnaver* sitting in the harbour waiting for them to board later that evening. Seeing the ship made their departure feel very real.

The cricketers bathed, cleaned their teeth and changed into fresh clothing. They counted their money to see what remained to be spent on curios and trinkets.

They were delighted to learn that Arthur Allsopp had almost recovered and was well enough to board the *Strathnaver* and would accompany the team back to Australia. It was only when Ellis and Hendry collected him from St Georges hospital that they realised how sick he had actually been. He looked grey and emaciated and much older than his twenty-seven years. A doctor informed the cricketers that he was lucky to survive and the hospital staff were reluctant to let him leave, but the sweet-talking cricketers managed to convince them. Allsopp was so relieved to re-join his teammates and leave the facility. He hadn't played cricket for close to two-and-a-half months and had been hospitalised for almost as long.

It was their last day on Indian soil and what should they do? Time was tight, and the cricketers realised that they could only fit in a few good-byes and some last-minute purchases. Suddenly despite all their complaints, they were really rather sad to be leaving and already viewed India nostalgically and fondly.

Hendry spent the afternoon visiting a few friends he'd made over the journey and sadly realised it may be the last time he would ever see them. He went from household to household to pay his respects and was treated to many farewell drinks. He didn't have the stomach for alcohol yet didn't want to be rude, so he joined in on the *bon voyage* toasts taking tiny sips. Returning to the Taj just after five, he and Alexander, Nagel and Bryant adjourned to the cocktail bar. Hendry was rather embarrassed as he knew that the royal would insist on picking up the tab and the cricketer really wanted to do something sincere, as a token of their appreciation, as he really had been the most generous and obliging host. The cricketer felt that earlier in Indore some of the team members had taken advantage of his generosity and accepted gifts including animal skins when they really shouldn't have. Hendry explained the Australian concept of 'botting' to the royal and apologised on behalf of the team.[3] The Maharawat laughed it off—nothing seemed to bother this fellow. Hendry expressed his appreciation to the Maharawat and suggested he join them as a guest that night to dine together. Hendry didn't really expect that the royal would have the time but much to his surprise he said yes, and the cricketer quickly arranged a private dining room at the Taj and ordered the finest champagne to celebrate.

The Maharawat disappeared for half an hour, saying he had urgent business to deal with, but he promised he would be back. Somewhat predictably, on his return he was armed with gifts. Hendry protested loudly, saying in light of their previous conversation, he couldn't accept the gifts. The cricketers were all gifted a gold trinket box with fine filigree work illustrating a tiger hunt. Such intricate craftsmanship was a speciality of his state. During dinner he removed his eighteen-carat gold watch and handed it to Hendry who was incredulous. He really didn't think he could accept it, yet the royal insisted and said, 'Please put it on your wrist and think of me in Australia'. The Maharawat then turned to Jack Ellis and said 'And you have a smoke with me' as he handed over his gold cigarette case to the gob-smacked cricketer. He was evidently not expected to give it back. The royal then excused himself, as he had another matter of some urgency that he had to attend to, but promised he'd return to the docks to see the team before the *Strathnaver* set sail.

True to his word, on the team's arrival at the dock at 9.30pm, the Maharawat was sitting waiting for them in the smoking room. By his side sat another bottle of champagne and crystal glassware to celebrate their departure. Thinking back to their arrival, they couldn't count the bottles of champagne they had consumed. Even tallying the bottles opened that day was staggering. As the players climbed the gang plank, the Maharawat and his valet stood on the dock and waved them goodbye until they were only small dots on the Bombay Harbour. It was unprecedented for a royal to behave so obsequiously. But I guess such was his affection for the travelling Australian personnel.

As they waved to the Maharawat they also bade farewell to Frank and Eva Tarrant. The couple had worked tirelessly throughout the tour and it certainly wouldn't have eventuated without their investment. The younger boys were especially grateful to Eva who had filled in as 'mum' when required. Bert Tarrant was travelling back home without them and although he'd enjoy the liberty of being away from parental supervision, he did rather question what was in store for him when he returned to Victoria. The situation back at home for him wasn't too rosy ... maybe staying in India would be an easier option he imagined.

Jack Ryder had earlier been handed a telegram from the Nawab of Bhopal, president of the Indian Board of Control. It read:

> On the eve of your departure from India I write, on behalf of us all, to wish you all bon voyage, and to convey to you all our grateful thanks for your visit. It has been a great education for our players to meet a team such as yours, and I assure you that both players and spectators will retain happy and grateful memories of your tour of India. I am afraid your tour has been very strenuous and the illness of some members of your team has added still further to the strain on the players. We trust, however, that you will forget the discomforts and weariness of long journeys and crowded engagements and remember only that everyone tried their best to play the game and to make your stay in India enjoyable. We hope that your tour will lead to a regular exchange of cricket'.[4]

Jack thought the missive summed up the tour accurately. He too hoped that the tour signified the conception of a regular cricket exchange between the two countries. Maybe they really had made history, he surmised.

Little is known about the cricketers' return journey. However, Hendry's manuscript reveals that he met up with his wife in Colombo where they bid farewell to the cricketers and holidayed for few weeks. He was seemingly happy to extend his Eastern sojourn despite his many complaints about the Orient. The *West Australian* observed that Nagel hadn't completely recovered from stomach issues and spent much of the return voyage in the ship's sickbay. Despite the team being thoroughly tired of cricket they spent hours on the *Strathnaver* playing a modified version of the game. Enthusiastic tourists joined in—delighted to be playing with the Australian cricket elite. A newspaper article detailed a trick played on Ryder. According to Oxenham, Ryder bragged to a few women on the boat about the extravagant jewels he had received from the Indian royalty. He wasn't completely fibbing, yet he was exaggerating the facts. The team had been given extravagant gifts yet there is no evidence to indicate that they were given jewels. Oxenham noted that Ryder almost began to believe the lie and trying to impress the girls he was 'laying it on pretty thick'.[5]

When the ship arrived in Perth, Oxenham decided he'd go along with Ryder's white-lie and purchased a fake diamond necklace and a matching pair of earrings from a 'cheap retail establishment'. He posted them airmail to Ryder's address in Melbourne with an accompanying note: 'With Kind Wishes, the Maharaja of Patiala'. In Melbourne, a week or so later, Ryder received the parcel and for a few days didn't say anything as he smelt a rat. Eventually, the other team members heard of the gift and some naively thought that the Maharaja had sent the jewellery to Ryder to celebrate his 1000 runs on tour. However, some did question why Oxenham wasn't a similar recipient as surely 100 wickets should be equally rewarded!

To compensate for their earlier oversight, the West Australian Cricket Association arranged a luncheon for the returning cricketers at the Palace Hotel. Mr. H. Edmondson, one of vice presidents of the association, toasted the tourists and Mr. A. H. Christian, acting chairman of the executive, also officiated at the function. In reply, Jack Ryder declared that the welcome was in keeping with the spirit of the West Australian Cricket Association. I wonder how much he laced the speech with irony. Most likely, he was having a dig at the earlier disrespect shown to the travelling personnel. During the luncheon Ryder was called the last of the old guard yet it was duly noted that his work rate had been excellent, and he achieved one of the highest batting averages for the tour.

The West Australian press described the playing group as 'A mere shadow of the high-spirited party which left Australia last October'.[6] The media chose to dwell on India's lack of hygiene and sanitation, the unbearable heat, the rickety roads, the devious staff, the poor-quality food, the abysmal standard of umpiring and they just wouldn't stop moaning about the coir matting.

Bryant, the only player to put on weight in India, was delighted to be reunited with his family. They were happy to have him back and rather surprised how well-nourished he looked.

It seems that it wasn't just the cricketers who had missed their families, as their families had also missed them. Mrs. Oxenham from Queensland and Mrs. Love from Sydney travelled by train to Fremantle to be reunited with their respective husbands. They imagined that they could join the Strathnaver in the West and travel back to the Eastern states with their husbands, yet the Sun observed that they were 'not permitted to travel on the boat' and both had to return by rail.[7] Considering they both travelled over two and a half thousand miles, it's difficult to imagine that they hadn't checked the feasibility of their plans before they set out for the reunion.

The next stop was Adelaide. The majority of the remaining team members attended a match between Tasmania and South Australia at the Adelaide Oval where they were entertained at a luncheon hosted by the South Australian Cricket Association. Ryder, in the absence of Tarrant, was the designated spokesman and was interviewed by the press. He talked up the talent of his young stock especially Morrisby and Leather and claimed that Test cricket was their future if they desired it. He described Leather as 'a whale for work' and acknowledged that he would greatly benefit from some 'careful coaching'.[8] The subject of Morrisby's move to Adelaide was again flouted and Ryder observed that 'Morrisby is a very sound young batsman with a great future'. Ryder added 'He has strokes all round the wicket and is particularly sound with his cover shots. What he needs now is to be taken in hand and given the opportunity to play in good company. A season under Bradman's captaincy would be of great value'.[9] Morrisby himself was slightly more circumspect regarding the move and despite confessing that 'I would like nothing better than to be able to play with Don Bradman' he noted that 'Arrangements have not been completed yet and I will not decide anything definitely till I get back home'.

Mrs. Bert Tarrant and Mrs. Jack Ryder woke hours before dawn to meet the *Strathnaver* in Port Melbourne. Despite gossip circulating about the unhealthy state of domestic affairs in the Tarrant household, both wives couldn't contain their excitement about reuniting with their husbands. They managed to convince customs officials to allow them to board the small customs launch which travelled out to meet the ship before it docked. What followed was described by the Herald as 'a comedy of errors.' On arrival at the designated spot in the bay, the excited wives were dismayed to learn that women were not permitted to climb 'the Jacob's Ladder' which officials and pressmen used to board the ship and they had to remain on the launch.[10] On the morning of the *Strathnaver's* arrival, the port was particularly congested and four international ships were waiting to be guided into their loading bays. Seemingly hours passed and the women had to be patient and wait in turn for the launch to return to the dock at Port Melbourne. The *Talisman*, a Norwegian ship, took pity on the waiting wives and lowered down Norwegian coffee and biscuits for morning tea. The launch finally made its way back to the shore. There, the women were united with their husbands in an unimagined fashion as the men were waiting on shore as their wives approached from Port Phillip Bay.

With the cricketers and their families safely back on shore, a welcome home celebratory lunch was arranged. In attendance was the team (minus Frank Tarrant, Hendry and Bryant) and a cast of local sporting and political celebrities including Mr. Justice Evatt (a politician and high court judge) and the great Hugh Trumble, former Australian off-spinning legend and current secretary of the Melbourne Cricket Club. Ryder spoke of a hard but successful tour and stated that 'India has become cricket mad. They play it everywhere, and one of these days it will be a formidable stronghold of the game'.[11] How prescient he was. Ryder was confident that the Australians had left a wonderful impression behind them of skill, sportsmanship, and good companionship.

It was straight back to cricket for Tom Leather who played in the final game of the home-and-away season for St Kilda on the Saturday following his arrived home. He had a few more weeks of cricket ahead of him as St Kilda made the finals but wasn't successful in winning the premiership.

Macartney announced to the press on arrival in Sydney: 'I have had a wonderful innings and I enjoyed the Indian tour immensely, but I am putting my cricket togs away for all time'.[12] Macartney stated that he would not even play club cricket. It was a sad announcement, but it was hardly unexpected.

Morrisby returned to Tasmania, a few days later, a state hero. The Lord Mayor (Alderman J. J. Wignall) tendered a welcome to Morrisby in the Mayor's Reception Room, at a function that was attended by his father and representatives of sporting bodies and public and commercial life. During the evening he revealed that he would not be transferring to the mainland but rather assist cricket in Tasmania. He said: 'I hope the experience I have gained will be of some benefit to the State in the future'. Seemingly he was already getting cold feet by the prospect of an interstate move.

The Tarrant family reached a decision about their future plans too, as reported in The *Herald* on March 13:

> After refusing managership of the Indian Test team to tour England, he [Frank Tarrant] has accepted a position to supervise the erection of the huge new stadium, or sports ground, at Bombay. It will take three years to complete, and Tarrant will work in co-operation with the architects and contractors, advising chiefly from the sporting side. That information is contained in a letter just received from his father by Mr A E Tarrant, who left Melbourne with the Australian team as assistant-manager and scorer, and returned with them. At the request of Frank Tarrant, his son will leave for Bombay in April to help him in

> the stadium work. Mr A. E. Tarrant says that, when completed the stadium will accommodate 75,000 people. Cricket will be largely played there. This will shift Indian cricket headquarters from Delhi to Bombay.

Despite Bert's romantic reunion with his wife and his excitement about being back at home, the lure of Patiala and India, again, called. Seemingly the Tarrant-Patiala partnership in nurturing Indian cricket onto the world stage, and into the future, wasn't going to cease anytime soon.

The construction of the new sporting facility, Brabourne stadium, was another project emblazoned with the Patiala stamp and was assisted by Patiala money. The Patiala pavilion was Maharaja of Patiala's final gift to Indian cricket before he died in 1938. Between 1948 and 1973, seventeen Test matches and six Ranji finals were held at Brabourne. It was a built on a nationalistic ideology as it provided a space for locals to watch and enjoy cricket in response to the many private clubs which still had signs at the entrance prohibiting access to 'dogs and Indians'.

---

[1] *Sporting Globe* February 26, 1938.

[2] *Newcastle Morning Herald and Miners' Advocate* February 26, 1936.

[3] Bot is an Australian derogatory term which means to take or to scrounge.

[4] *The West Australian* February 26, 1936.

[5] *The Telegraph* March 13, 1936.

[6] *Western Argus* March 3, 1936.

[7] *The Newcastle Sun* March 2, 1936.

[8] *The Telegraph* February 29, 1936.

[9] *Recorder* March 2, 1936.

[10] March 2, 1936.

[11] *Table Talk* March 5, 1936.

[12] *The Daily Telegraph* March 6, 1936.

25 A DISMAL ENGLISH SUMMER

The primary purpose of the Australian tour was to help prepare the Indian team for their Test encounter in Britain later in 1936. Despite the overall win/loss ratio in 1935/36 not flattering the locals and some inconsistent performances, the locals were mostly satisfied with how they performed and were especially upbeat about their 2-2 unofficial 'Test' record. A few Indian players had excelled and, as a team, they showed enough and knew that they were inching along a learning curve. They were confident that they would be better prepared for the English tour.

During the Australian's visit, cricket officials in India were voting on who would captain the Indian Test team to tour England and they scrutinised the performance of the potential applicants. During the process, the Maharaja of Patiala withdrew the candidature of his son, the Yuvraj, from the race. Possibly he was prescient of things to come. He authoritatively noted:

> The controversy about the selection of a captain and vice-captain has been extremely unfortunate. With all my love of cricket and eagerness to develop the game in India I cannot let the name of Patiala be associated with what is happening now. It was never my intention that my son, the Yuvraj, should either be captain or vice-captain of the Indian team to England through canvassing or without consideration of his cricketing ability. In view of the misunderstanding that seems to be prevalent I wish to withdraw the name of my son from being proposed either as captain or vice-captain.[1]

The Nawab (I. A. K.) of Pataudi also withdrew for multifarious reasons, ill-health was primarily nominated. Seemingly, he made a habit of rejecting invitations to play, as evidenced during the Australian tour. Vizzy, an unexceptional cricketer yet an influential and wealthy sovereign, won the vote (10 to 4 in his favour) against the increasingly out-of-favour C.K. Nayudu. Vizzy wielded his influence and, campaigning with gusto, was successful in persuading cricket administrators around the country. Nayudu really had no chance against the aristocrat. The squad selection panel consisted of Pataudi, who was called away on the day the meeting was scheduled in Delhi (he left his nominations in an envelope, and the historical narrative suggests that his choices were disregarded) and the Nawab of Bhopal who really just functioned more as a figure head. Players from regions that had supported Vizzy's captaincy were pretty much guaranteed of selection.

Vizzy arrived in Blighty with thirty-six items of luggage and two manservants which was uncommon cricket practice! He was not accompanied by a vice-captain or a selection panel and thus he was the sole decision-maker—the only other administrator was Englishman Captain Brittain Jones who occupied the role as tour manager following Tarrant's rejection of the position. Jones, an ex-ADC, had been an employee of Lord Willingdon and he possessed a coloniser's sensibility through and through. He had been employed in colonial diplomacy but possessed minimal cricket experience.

On arrival on April 22, 1936, newspapers reported that the Indians were shocked by the icy winds of England. It would prove to be a long bleak English summer.

Vizzy's autonomous control over the team led to a few questionable and seemingly illogical decisions being made including field positions, batting orders and bowling changes. Despite his lack of cricket experience, he revelled in rubbing shoulders with the social elite of England. He was thrilled to receive an invitation to visit Buckingham Palace and even more ecstatic when it was announced on June 24 that he would be knighted. The ceremony took place on July 15 at the Palace, yet the occasion was filled with mixed emotions. Vizzy was thrilled to be rewarded for his 'invaluable services to the crown' yet was upset as the service coincided with a match against Lancashire. During the match, C.K. Nayudu assumed the captaincy role and took seven wickets. He oversaw an emphatic victory—the only one of such magnitude on the tour.

As the chilly and damp summer progressed, Vizzy became increasingly agitated by the insubordination of some of his stock as his authority over them diminished. Much to Vizzy's chagrin, Nayudu's sporting aptitude and his capacity to rally and inspire the troops became increasingly evident. Annoyed by his failings and the success of other team members, Vizzy unofficially adopted the motto 'Conquer and Divide' for team governance. He enlisted the unwitting assistance of Lala Amarnath, arguably one of the most promising and in-form cricketers of the side, to psychologically combat Nayudu. This was the start of the end for Amarnath as Vizzy's vitriol quickly moved from Nayudu to Amarnath.

Team morale and team congeniality unravelled pretty quickly. The Indian XI had been comprehensively beaten in their early matches. Vizzy insisted on making frequent bowling changes while his own performance on the field was poor. During the match versus the MCC at Lord's Vizzy, an inexperienced bowler, came on to bowl when John Human was on ninety-seven. His first ball was walloped for a six. Vizzy firmly congratulated the batsman on their century and one had to wonder where his loyalties lay.

On June 11, the Australian press reported on the dismal state of the Indians' performance. Without a win, talk in Bombay was circulating that Vizzy wasn't up to the job as captain. Wazir Ali and C.K. Nayudu were proposed as possible replacements in the leadership role. Googly bowler, C.S.

Nayudu (the brother of C. K.), was sent urgently to London from India on an aeroplane in an attempt to strengthen the attack. Jahangir Khan, a young Indian student at Cambridge with considerable cricket talent, was also enlisted to assist on-field performance.

Team spirit was also at a low ebb and the cricketers' antagonism towards Vizzy intensified as he and Brittain Jones stirred the pot—further inciting communal and personal tensions.

Amarnath started the tour promisingly yet during a match verses Cambridge he suffered a back injury. Vizzy questioned the legitimacy of the injury and insisted that he was well enough to keep playing despite the protestation of the talented all-rounder. Amarnath usually batted fourth or fifth yet during a match against the Minor Counties on June 18 he was instructed to pad up yet was left to wait for hours until he was finally sent out to bat at number seven. His back hurt and it was aggravated by waiting around. He was eventually used as the night-watchman which was an insult for such a talented batsman. At the end of play, Amarnath returned to the change room and threw his bat and pads into the corner of the room. He uttered some grievances under his breath in Punjabi which were heard and understood by only a few team members. The gist of the conversation got back to Jones and Vizzy. A letter was drafted and signed by some of the players in the pro-Vizzy camp stating that they could no longer play alongside Amarnath.

The situation became untenable and, on the eve of the first Test match, Amarnath was given his matching orders by Captain Brittain Jones and Vizzy. He was placed on a train to Southampton and then bundled onboard the *Kaiser-i-Hind* and sent back home to India without the consultation of the Indian cricket board. Up to date, Amarnath's record in England had been impressive: he'd scored (a team high) 613 runs at 32.26, including three hundreds, and had taken thirty-two wickets (the second highest of the Indian team) at 20.87.

Without Amarnath, the first Test proved to be even more disastrous for the Indians who lost easily by nine wickets. They only managed to score 147 in their first innings and 93 in the second.

Questions were raised whether India was ready for Test cricket.

Vizzy continued to meddle, further fuelling team malcontent. Gold watches were gifted to players who didn't complain while others received the cold-shoulder from him and Brittain Jones. The opposition players and administrators were also recipients of gifts and money. Vizzy, seemingly, thought his money and generosity could buy people, approval and cricket success.

Back in India, Frank Tarrant and the Maharaja of Patiala sat at Moti Bagh Palace gossiping about the state of affairs. As previously discussed, the Patiala camp vied fiercely with Vizzy in their desire to control Indian cricket. Frank

Tarrant couldn't contain his displeasure and weighed in publicly on the disintegrating tour. According to the South Australian News, Tarrant admitted that Amarnath was 'impetuous, but members of the team should have been humored *(sic)* in every possible way and not drilled like recruits'.[2] Typically Tarrant, who was perpetually conscious of the amateur/professional divide, was vehemently critical of Vizzy and stated that a team of amateurs should be treated accordingly.

Amarnath's arrival home on July 9 was tightly choreographed by the Indian Board of Control. Hundreds of supporters waited for him at the docks including Frank Tarrant who anticipated he would be able to speak to his friend yet was prevented from doing so. Amarnath was whisked away by the board member Anthony de Mello. Rajinder Amarnath revealed that his father was upset at not being allowed to speak to his supporters, especially the Tarrant family. According to his son, Lala said: 'I spotted Frank and his family in the large crowd and wanted to thank them for making the long journey. I couldn't exchange any words or shake their hands, which depressed me. I noticed tears in the eyes of Mrs Tarrant and felt bad as she treated me like her son. I couldn't do anything to comfort her'.[3]

Local opinion protested that Amarnath was Vizzy's scapegoat and that action against him had been enacted to cover up the captain's own failings. Public pressure mounted for Amarnath to be sent back to England to re-join the tour. The Viceroy Lord Willingdon entered into the debate and spoke out in full support of Vizzy et. al. and maintained the decision was 'justified'.[4] The press around the Empire editorialised the fiasco and events were followed like a riveting soap opera. The Australian Advertiser referred to additional sensitivities amongst the team:

> If his [Amarnath] petulance was the only instance of dissension and indiscipline, doubtless a serious warning would have been sufficient but the Indian tourists since their arrival have been frequently at loggerheads with the captain and the management owing to their supersensitiveness. Some feel that they are not sufficiently consulted on the selection of teams and others have objected to travelling in tubes and motor coaches. One was slighted because he was omitted from a photograph.[5]

The Indian cricket community furiously debated the situation and tried to come up with scenarios that would best resolve the situation. Board decisions seemed to be made according to pressure applied by various political and sporting bodies rather than what was best for Indian cricket. The reputation of Indian cricket was shot.

The Indian cricket board went in to panic mode—meetings were held, decisions made and then they were hurriedly reversed. At one stage, Amarnath had his bags packed and loaded to return to England and at the last minute he was advised that the board had changed their mind.

Unfortunately, Amarnath's luggage was in transit on the mail boat to England without him.

Amarnath was eventually permitted to travel to Chail (one of Bhupinder's country residences) where he revealed to the Maharaja the sorry state of events in Britain. Bhupinder and Tarrant advised him on how to proceed. I'm sure the Maharaja of Patiala was thankful that he, or his son, had played no part in the shambolic tour. In retrospect, he possibly also questioned if his financing of the Australian tour was worth the financial and logistical input.

The Indian team returned home on the *Elysia* having played twenty-eight first-class games. They won four, lost twelve and twelve were drawn. Of the three Tests they lost two and one match was drawn. All in all, it was a disastrous series on and off the cricket field. The Beaumont Committee, established by the Nawab of Bhopal, led a full investigation of the debacle. The findings were eventually delivered to the board in January 1937. Amaranth was exonerated of all charges laid and rules were implemented to prevent future dictatorial control of a cricket tour. Never again would a few (or in this case one) influential individuals hold so much power over a team.

Vizzy finished the tour with a Test batting average of eight and he vowed to step aside from cricket.

---

[1] *Tweed Daily* May 23, 1936.
[2] June 27, 1936.
[3] *Lala Amarnath* 49-50.
[4] *Examiner* June 24, 1936.
[5] June 23, 1936.

26 THE AFTERMATH OF THE INDIAN EXPERIMENT

Following the tour, the Australian players settled back into the routine and monotony of home, which provided them with everything they had missed in India: familiarity, security, safety and predictability. India slowly became a distant memory.

None of the team would subsequently play Test cricket or Sheffield Shield. There are several likely explanations for this including the impact of the Second World War on sport, the players' illnesses and injuries incurred in India, financial impediments and I strongly suspect that the cricket establishment punished them for their participation on the Indian tour although this is impossible to prove. Maybe they were placed on a cricket blacklist.

Newspaper reports reveal that throughout the 1930s, the Indian independence movement continued to gain momentum while stability in Europe became even more precarious. The inevitability of another world war set in. Comparatively, Australia was a safe haven.

Ron Morrisby's return to Tasmanian was marred by the unanticipated death of his father. Ron, as the only son, took over the family business, an orchard in Tasmania. It put an end to Ron's ambition to play Sheffield Shield or Test cricket. Possibly, he didn't possess the ambition and personality to play cricket at that level anyway. He certainly starred in state cricket and was the only touring player to compete against India when they played in Tasmania in 1947. He led the state side in both the matches against the tourists and scored 130 in the second encounter.

My great uncle, Tom Leather, returned home having acquired Pyorrhoea (inflammation of the teeth sockets) resulting in the loss of his teeth. With a full set of false teeth, he continued to play cricket for St Kilda, yet he really didn't fulfil the potential that he, the cricket community and the press had imagined. Certainly, he didn't reach the cricket heights that Frank Tarrant and Jack Ryder had promised. He was however successful in pursuing a football career where he played for Williamstown in the VFA, most likely driven by the remuneration offered. He would receive greater payment through the VFA than he did at the VFL competition where he had previously played. The *Williamstown Chronicle* on May 13, 1939 details how, through injury to a fellow player, he achieved selection. Two weeks later Leather's reputation appeared to have grown and the same newspaper acknowledged that, 'Tom Leather should never have been out of the side, and showed, although a big man, that he can play in all conditions. Leather is a half forward and is prepared to play in that position, not roam all over the ground, and for this reason, together with his accurate passing, makes his retention in the side essential'.[1]

Tom was simultaneously employed by the MCC as a member of the ground staff. He worked in numerous capacities and his duties were diverse. Club records reveal that at times he was employed as a ground bowler. He commenced this casual form of employment for the Club sometime between October 15, 1938 and August 5, 1939.

An article in the *Daily Advertiser* described sportsmen that enlisted en masse in 1940 reflecting the success of campaigns that promoted the call to war: 'Following a Saturday afternoon football match in Melbourne, the Imperial Rovers decided to enlist as a team joining many other local sportsmen from various groups including the Richmond Amateur Swimming Club, the A grade water-polo team, four members of the Melbourne Cricket Club (MCC) staff including Tom Leather, D. Courtney [first XI scorer] and Watterson'.[2] The article concluded that Clive Fairbairn, a footballer and cricketer of note, had enlisted a few weeks prior. Army records reveal that Tom, when he attempted to enlist in the Second World War on May 29, 1940, nominated his occupation as 'professional cricketer' and 'groundkeeper', indicating that by 1940 cricket was the sport that Tom viewed as professionally viable. However, my research indicates that the only significant payment he received for cricket was for the 1935/36 tour to India.

After sixty-three days of service Tom was deemed medically unfit to serve. My father, Geoffrey, claims that army x-rays detected pleurisy leading to Tom's expulsion from active service. Following his short-lived career in the army, Tom was employed at the Commonwealth Explosives Factory in Maribyrnong in an administrative capacity. Paperwork pertaining to this role is scattered throughout Tom's box.

Following the war, Tom was granted a permanent position in the office at the MCC. My grandfather Bill had joined the staff at the MCC in 1932 and he would have been instrumental in assisting Tom's employment at the club as, they weren't just related by marriage, they were firm friends. Tom was the inaugural secretary of the MCC's *XXIX* Club which was a social team formed in 1956 by a group of MCC senior players. The club's objective was to foster cricket generally, but particularly in the country, by playing mid-week and Sunday games in addition to the normal Premier Cricket fixtures.

Arthur Allsopp returned to Australia still gravely ill and was sent to recuperate at Mr. A.A. Beck's property at The Gap where his medical team advised him to stay for many months. He recovered sufficiently to play district cricket for Richmond in Melbourne during the 1936/37 season yet like Tom Leather he didn't have great success at the game. It's been difficult to establish exactly why he didn't succeed armed with the talent he had. He did however commence playing baseball and softball and he gradually devoted more time to these sports. In 1950, Allsopp acquired his Victorian softball umpire's badge and four years later his Australian umpire's badge. Allsopp was instrumental in encouraging the growth and popularity of the game and coached into his early 80s. In the early 1990s, the Australian Softball Federation decided it was fitting that the Allsopp name be permanently linked with an under-age championship. In 1991, the Australian U16 Boys' Championship was initiated with NSW winning the inaugural Arthur Allsopp Shield. Arthur died two years later.

Ron Oxenham is another team member who has been difficult to research, attempts to locate family members have failed. He was involved in a car accident in 1937 on the way to cricket practice in rural Queensland. Suffering a fractured skull, the *Morning Bulletin* wrote that he was unconscious 'for a long time'.[3] Two years later he died of an unrelated illness aged forty-nine.

Following the tour, Jack Ryder became a national selector and cricket administrator. His grandchildren and daughter-in-law contacted me shortly after a newspaper article appeared in The Age regarding my research trip to Pakistan. The family had collated his memorabilia in an organised and professional fashion and having access to his letters, photographs and material culture was a windfall.

Throughout the tour, Lisle Nagel was very much at home with the ragtag team yet following wartime service he returned to Australia and his circumstances changed when he married society-girl Gwendoline Tolhurst, a Victorian golf champion, in 1942. The Tolhurst family were Melbourne sporting and business establishment. Later he acquired a position on the Melbourne Cricket Club committee.

Harry Alexander also went to war. His daughter maintains that his enthusiasm for touring India with the cricket team was matched by his desire to enlist. Both, she believes, were driven by the inducement of danger, excitement and the camaraderie of travelling with the boys. On return home, Harry settled in rural Victoria and championed the local cricket and football competitions. The Memorial Oval Pavilion in Euroa adorns his name. According to his daughter, one of the young boys in the area couldn't afford to buy football boots so Harry loaned his cricket boots to the family and they were painted black.

We are a close family and my grandfather moved in with my parents in rural Victoria, in 1977, following the death of his wife. The Leather and the Ponsford family frequently socialised. I certainly wish that I had taken the opportunity to discuss the tour with Tom Leather prior to his death in 1991 yet I was really a child and remained ignorant of his participation on the tour until I located the box.

A photograph found in the Leather archives reveals that a few of the Victorian players met to celebrate my grandfather's retirement from the MCC in the late 1960s and certainly some of the members reunited at the Centenary

Test in 1977 but who knows if the Indian tour was ever mentioned.

Ironmonger, Ryder, Ponsford, Leo O'Brien and Ellis celebrate Ponsford's retirement from the MCC. Late 1960s. Leather archive

In the 1970s, Hendry and Bill wrote in detail about the tour. Fortunately, I located versions of both manuscripts: Hendry's at the Bowral Museum and Bill's at the Macquarie Library. Both gentlemen resided in New South Wales and it is feasible that they discussed the retelling of their shared adventure although no evidence can be found that corroborates this theory. For some reason, they felt the necessity to write about the tour after years of remaining quiet about it. Interestingly, the writing of these memoirs coincided with an overhaul of global cricket and the increasing professionalisation of the game. Kerry Packer and his brains trust gave birth to the biggest story of cricket in the twentieth century with the formation of World Series Cricket and the emergence of a truly professional global competition.

In my opinion, the 1935/36 tour to India is a revealing case study which should be evaluated in a wider political and cultural context. The tour should be viewed as a precursor to the subsequent trajectory of the modern game and one that highlights the growth of the subcontinent within it.

---

[1] *Williamstown Chronicle* May 27, 1939.
[2] June 7, 1940.
[3] August 17, 1939

27 THE REAL FRANK TARRANT

A few years back I was fortunate to meet Andrew Toruk—the only person I've encountered who knew Frank and Eva Tarrant. Meeting Andrew was fortuitous and assisted a new chapter of my research.

In 2015, my father attended his annual school reunion. They were celebrating sixty-six, or was it sixty-seven, years since completing their matriculation. Dad was unsure. Dad noted that they were all getting older and the number of attendees fewer each year. He hadn't really known the youthful looking Andrew at school, yet they sat together at the celebration. As parents do, they talked about the successes of their children and remained quiet on their failures. My older brother, the medical doctor, was discussed at length. Andrew had been a patient of his. 'He was very good', Andrew congratulated. Dad looked smug. Conversation trickled down to my sister and her recent executive appointment at the University of Melbourne and lastly to me. Dad spoke about my doctoral research and somehow the Tarrant name was mentioned. 'I lived with Mr Tarrant', Andrew announced.

Frank and Eva returned to live in Australia during the first few years of the 1940s. Residing in India had become increasingly precarious, as no one quite knew what would happen when sovereignty was attained. What would happen to the Europeans living there, the British Raj worried? Before his death in 1938, Bhupinder, in an authoritarian and knowing tone, promised that nothing much would change but Frank, despite being a risk-taker, felt too much was at stake to stay. Acknowledging that he and Eva weren't getting any younger, they returned to their safe yet somewhat dreary existence in Melbourne. Frank had to adjust to again being a nobody and to a distinct absence of luxury. They had to cook and keep house for themselves. Eva had to re-learn those skills. Finances were tightening and Eva didn't understand what had happened to their fountain of cash that had flowed so abundantly for years. In Australia, Frank wasn't invited to functions and if he did scrounge an invite somewhere, he certainly didn't sit on the head table. He didn't spend his evenings at glamorous functions, elite clubs and high-end events like he had in India. If he went to the cricket, he purchased his own ticket and sat with the masses. He even caught public transport in Melbourne—something he hadn't done for years. In India it had been Rolls Royces and elephants.

I quiz Andrew as to how he came to live with Frank.

'Well, I didn't really. My father did. We arrived in Australia as refugees from Hungary following the war. I was bright so I managed to get a part scholarship or maybe it was a subsided rate to attend Wesley College where

I met your Dad. We knew another Hungarian family who luckily were able to rent a house in Camberwell, but they just had room for one more. It was a tight squeeze, yet I went to live with them. Dad was confident that I was in safe hands, so he applied to rent a room in nearby Hawthorn East. It was walking distance and Dad could just afford it so was happy with the arrangement. Frank Tarrant had placed the advertisement'.

The Tarrants lived at 37 Tourello Avenue, Upper Hawthorn (now known as Hawthorn East). It was a typical, upper middle-class, house in an attractive tree-lined street in a well-heeled, yet not too flashy 'old money', suburb. Seemingly, the property has only witnessed minor cosmetic revamps over the past eighty-odd years—unlike the construction of neo-Georgian manors or modernist monolithic structures, which have popped up alongside in recent times. Now, a cream picket fence hems a neat garden and a well-maintained red-brick, late-Edwardian, or maybe it's a Californian, bungalow. The manicured garden has all the hallmarks of the Tarrant family's nurture and it's lovely, albeit romantic, to imagine that Frank and Eva were involved in its construction. It's also interesting to conjecture how Frank and Eva's Blue Blood neighbours welcomed the arrival of the avaricious professional cricketer from Fitzroy, and his German consort.

I wondered aloud why Frank was taking in tenants? I guess for the extra money, Andrew answered. 'Times were tough, and money was scarce', he explained. My understanding of Frank and Eva is vastly different to the duo that Andrew knew. 'They were simple people', Andrew said. 'Mrs Tarrant loved to cook and would spend hours in the kitchen labouring over a weird repertoire of Indian, Aussie and European fare. She worked wonders within the confines of rationing. She also loved cards and we would spend hours and hours and hours at the kitchen table playing Gin Rummy. We would use old buttons and foreign coins to gamble with'.

I ask Andrew about Frank, as I was really there to discuss him.

'He was really old and a little unstable on his feet, but he still insisted on teaching the young foreign whippersnapper about cricket. He used the asphalt footpath that ran behind the house down to the washing-line as a wicket. He taught me about spin. He scientifically explained the technique and like a good student I understood. I asked lots of questions. For hours he'd bowl to me. I showed some promise as I could deflect the cricket ball where I wanted it to go with a degree of proficiency. When I expressed some interest in learning more, he took me by my hand and led me to his bookcase. His actions were always hard to deduce and I was unsure if I was in trouble or not. He said I was welcome to read his beloved Wisdens. I wasn't allowed to remove them from the house, but I was always welcome to read them, providing my hands were clean, he warned'.

Years of fossicking through newspaper articles and cricket books hadn't enabled me to really get to know Frank. The readily available material on him portrays him in a one-dimensional manner. Traipsing through the narrative of cricket through the Western canon I realise he is almost mocked by commentators. The statistics and scorecards tell me that he was an extraordinarily good cricketer, yet the Australian sporting world refused to acknowledge him and overlooked his exceptional batting and bowling records. He's been pushed aside in cricket historiography, it seems. I guess it's extra difficult to research people who seemingly don't really want to be discovered.

As research progressed, I learnt about Frank's involvement in the racing industry. He was an agent for the sale of horses across the Empire. It was connections made through the equine industry that accessorised him with the accoutrements of wealth, yet Andrew suggests that by the late 1940s there is no evidence of it: somehow it had seemingly been lost or maybe hidden. I know of his substantial wins but like all canny punters they don't disclose their losses. Clues are located about his legendary love of gambling. Maybe it was his downfall, I imagine. Comments, alongside the clippings in his scrapbook, observe odds and winnings. Letters from Indian royalty compliment Frank on his exceptionally good eye concerning horse stock. Andrew is certainly aware of Frank's cricket triumphs yet unaware of his financial ones.

Andrew clearly remembers the first Indian Test tour to Australia in 1947/48. The visiting Indian team was a permanent fixture in the Tarrant house. They squeezed into the small formal parlour and didn't seem to ever want to leave, recalls Andrew. Frank kept them entertained with conversation about home and updates on the development of recently attained Indian independence. They played cards and listened to radio broadcasts on the political situation in India—from a distance they watched the unravelling of the Empire. The players were sad that they weren't at home to experience the birth of the new nation yet were equally proud to contribute to the first Australia-India Test series.

Eva laboured in the kitchen and would emerge carrying her *vindaloos*, *masalas* and *kormas* to the dining room to satisfy the seemingly starving cricketers. The cricketers loved the curries she cooked. The kitchen staff at their hotel attempted to accommodate their culinary requests but failed dismally. The Tarrant family knew all the team members, as Frank had been largely responsible for their cricket tutelage in India. It was like a big family reunion, Andrew observed. Frank's pride in their launch on the Test arena in Australia was overwhelming. I locate a photograph of Frank, Eva and a few Indian cricket administrators sitting at the MCG. Frank and Eva look deliriously happy. It was inevitably a welcome escape from the drudgery of their Melbourne existence. Andrew recalled being gifted Lala Amarnath's guest ticket to attend the match when India played Victoria at the MCG. It's his first time at the ground and the first time he attended big cricket.

I ask Andrew about the jewels that the Indian royal families bestowed on Tarrant. Did Eva wear them, I enquired? Andrew was certain, 'no, absolutely not, she definitely didn't'. The thought of a bejewelled Eva is alien to him. He chose his words slowly and carefully, 'Mrs Tarrant was a very Spartan woman. She dressed in a very homely manner and her only accessory was a simple gold wedding band'. I wonder what happened to her jewels and accessories as I've seen photographs of her wearing them, so I know a glamorous Eva is not a figment of my imagination. However, I guess these images reflect an earlier chapter in her life—one that Andrew didn't know. Certainly, by the late 1940s she wears a dirty apron, a look of exhaustion and a worried expression. She tallies the housekeeping budget at the end of each week and frets about their financial future.

I also enquire if Andrew ever met Frank's two sons: Bert and Frank. Middle son Loris had died whilst in transit from Bombay to Melbourne. He mysteriously fell sick on the boat and was buried in Fremantle. I've had difficultly locating additional information regarding the circumstances and now it seems incredulous that such things happened. Andrew is oblivious to the existence of the Tarrant boys. I mention that they would have been about three decades older than Andrew. I also know that at this time there were five grandchildren slightly older than Andrew. Again, Andrew promises that, to his knowledge, there was none. 'No photos, no phone calls, no Christmas cards, no discussion of Frank's family', Andrew promises. I ask him to rack his brain yet again he can't recall Tarrant's blood relatives and I don't question his memory—he's sharp as a tack. However, I am surprised as up until the time of the tour, Frank's children are frequently included in discussion about him. I wonder how and why they are erased so easily from Frank's life. Andrew mentions the only family members that visit the house are Eva's two sisters and their families. Andrew's fondness of Frank and Eva does not extend to the sisters. I try to make sense of the story, yet I think I have invested too much creative energy into the scenario. Andrew evades my further questions about them.

Andrew finished school and moved interstate. A few years later he's back in Melbourne for work. His father had passed away and with no close contacts in the southern state, he called the Tarrant house on the off chance that they had an available room. He was in luck. Frank had died in 1951 but Eva was still in the same house in Hawthorn East and still eager to supplement her pension with cash payments for rent. Andrew lived with the widow in a tenement capacity for a few uneventful but happy years. He recalls Eva's death and her sisters' visit to the house shortly after the doctor's official proclamation that she had passed away. 'They arrived really quickly—were around there in a flash', observed Andrew. I secretly wonder if they knew the whereabouts of the jewels. It's not a nice thought and I choose not to share it with Andrew.

Immigration records reveal that Frank sponsored Eva's two sisters to migrate to Australia from Germany which is further evidence of Tarrant's commitment to his second wife and his progressive stance regarding racial acceptance and inclusion.

I fill Andrew in on some details about Frank that I can guarantee are true, gleaned through almost a decade of research. I tell him about the enormous finances accrued, the high life in India and Frank's unequivocal love of Eva. We both have learnt a lot about Frank and Eva on this Melbourne summer morning. We've drunk multiple cups of coffee and we promise to stay in touch. Frank is now a far more tangible character.

Following the tour, Frank continued to agitate the Australian cricket community and the cultural sensibility of the era. In 1940, he proposed another Australian cricket tour of India following the success of the 1935/36 tour. In anticipation of not receiving support from the official Australian cricket authorities, Tarrant declared that he would take a team because he 'knows of no laws which prevents cricketers leaving Australia if their passports are in order'.[1] The journalist, Onlooker, editorialised: 'Mr. Tarrant is right; there is no law. But I believe that it will be a poor argument to advance to the sportsmen who play cricket. There is much more than the law to he considered. The country is at war. While tours are fine things for the game during the days of peace, there is no place for them while the country faces such responsibilities as it does now'.

In a 1950s press article in his scrapbook, Tarrant lists his hobbies as 'cricket, tennis, bridge and racing' and refers to his membership of the Cricket Club of India [Bombay] and the Rajindra Gymkhana in Patiala.[2] Considering he had been residing back in Victoria for a decade it is unusual that Tarrant, as a sporting enthusiast, would not be a member of a local sporting club. He attended the Indian Test match in Melbourne as verified by a photo in the Tarrant scrapbook however Melbourne Cricket Club archives reveal that he was not, or ever was, a member. Possibly this equally reflects Tarrant's rejection of the establishment clubs in Melbourne as it does their rejection of him.

Historians and cricket commentators from India viewed Tarrant's role as an administrator, player, umpire and promoter of cricket in Britain, India and Australia auspiciously yet appraisals from the West are pejorative. The India cricket writer Sujit Mukherjee declared him to be a 'legend' of the game and the greatest contributor 'to the betterment of Indian cricket'.[3] Another Indian cricketing great and commentator of the time Deodhar, likewise superlative in his assessment, claimed, 'Tarrant arrived in India with a big reputation, as one of the best all-rounders produced by Australian cricket till that time. With his vast experience in England, as well as in Australia, in the highest class of cricket, Tarrant literally made merry while toying with his opponents in India'.[4] Deodhar later observed about the match between the Europeans and the Muslims, at Deccan Gymkhana Ground, in 1915/16, '[i]n the previous year, Tarrant had blown off like chaff a good Islam side at Poona for the lowest total of 21 runs, with nine blobs, only two batsmen had 8 and 4 and the extras 9 was the top-scorer!'[5]

Lee Semmens commences his publication with the observation that 'Frank Tarrant might seem an unusual choice of book in a series on great cricketers' which reflects Australian public sentiment.[6] Semmens booklet is the only significant document detailing Tarrant's achievements and was published in 1991, over 110 years after his birth and forty years after his death.[7] His entry in *The Oxford Companion to Australian Cricket* is brief yet he receives great acclaim in Indian writing of cricket history.[8] The downplaying in the Oxford Companion appears to be a hangover from the game's more conservative past.

Death notices published following Frank's death in 1951 are revealing. Acknowledgements in the *Argus* are from son Albert and his three children, from wife Eva and her two sisters and their families (Rupp and Priday). Many close family members (including youngest son Frank, with a wife and two children) and the sporting world ignore Frank's passing. The death notices reveal that he possibly died without significant friendship. Customarily tributes would appear from sporting teams for whom the deceased had played, especially involving a sportsperson as talented as Tarrant.

His will decreed that his possessions were left to various family members. The four properties in leafy upper middle-class suburbs of Melbourne, shares, stocks and cash were divided between his surviving blood relatives. Provision to provide for Eva for the rest of her life was made.

A close reading of the Tarrant family history may seem unnecessary in the context of retelling the story of the 1935/36 inaugural cricket tour to India however research has revealed that Frank embarked on all negotiations with aggressive determination and the utmost clinical application. Seemingly, Tarrant relished the political and radical nature of the tour however primarily his motivation was self-serving.

Tarrant's constant relocation, lifestyle choices and his reputation as an outsider and chancer did not fit the stereotypic notion of the dour, single-minded Australian cricketer whose only ambition was to represent his country in Test cricket. Certainly, he wasn't the only cricketer in this category. There were others who did not quite earn laurels for Australia but were very successful elsewhere such as Bill Alley, Bruce Dooland, George Tribe and Cecil Pepper. This, in itself, is revealing of the deep conservatism of Australian cricket throughout the earlier years of the twentieth century.

Over his lifetime, Tarrant constantly upset the cricket establishment and is one of the most misunderstood, elusive yet charismatic, characters in cricket history. He was castigated for his unorthodoxy by the conservative world of cricket primarily because of his unrelenting ambition and the nonconformist, unequivocal, measures he implemented to achieve success. These included initiating collaborations with Indian potentates for financial and professional advantage: a union some from Australia and England found problematic. Despite Tarrant belonging to the West, signified by the colour of his skin, and partially adhering to the colonial elite, his cutthroat ambition, philosophical irreverence and Australian heritage led to him being portrayed in a disparaging light.

Likewise, the three generations of the Patiala family demonstrated an unwavering commitment to the promotion of Indian cricket as players, administrators and financiers. They were largely responsible for fostering the professionalisation of the game. Tarrant's contribution to India-Australia cricket and the nurturing of wider transnational sporting diplomacy is integral to, and became entangled with, the Patiala story. The relationship between Tarrant and the Patiala family can be viewed as a microcosm representing the broader bond between Australia and India in the dying days of British colonisation. Tarrant's progressive ideology minimised the ethnic division between the Australian tourists and their Indian hosts on the tour. The Maharaja of Patiala and Frank Tarrant were key protagonists in the inauguration of Indian-Australian cricket and both men transgressed the increasingly fragile racial line that blurred the division between the East and the West.

The ICC now schedule the Indian and Australian teams to meet frequently, often multiple times a year, in all forms of the game. I hope all those involved tip their caps in homage to the tenacity of Tarrant and the Maharaja in making the competition what it is today. I'm sure both fellows would take immense pleasure in that gesture.

---

[1] *Newcastle Morning Herald and Miners' Advocate* March 14, 1940.

[2] Both subsidies were most likely paid by the Patiala family.

[3] 1968, 13.

[4] 1948, 52

[5] 1966, 32.

[6] 1991, 3.

[7] This manuscript was written before the publication of *Cricket's Forgotten Pioneer: The Frank Tarrant Story* by Mike Coward in 2020.

[8] Both authored by Semmens suggesting that other sporting historians have ignored him.

APPENDICES

A. Brief Scores

Ceylon v Australians
Colombo, 25-26 Oct 1935
Ceylon 96 (Ron Oxenham 9-18) and 111 lost to **Australians** 334 (Wendell Bill 101, Charlie Macartney 53, Jack Ryder 67, Lisle Nagel 40) by inn and 127 runs

Western India v Australians
Rajkot, 5-7 Nov 1935
Western India 154 (Oxenham 5-40, Frederick Mair 4-63) and 95 (Oxenham 5-28) lost to **Australians** 197 (Mair 42, Ladha Ramji 4-68, MS Gurtu 4-77) and 54-4 by 6 wickets

Jamnagar v Australians (misc)
Jamnagar, 9-10 Nov 1035
Jamnagar 158 (Ogadhashankar Manilal 42, Oxenham 5-32) and 128-6 (Manilal 40) drew with **Australians** 315-9 dec (Bill 47, Macartney 106, Frank Bryant 53)

Gujarat v Australians (misc)
Ahmedabad, 12-13 Nov 1935
Gujarat 121 (Ryder 4-14) and 93 (Tom Leather 4-11) lost to **Australians** 300-4 dec (Ron Morrisby 90, Ryder 139*) by inn and 86 runs

Rajputana and Central India v Australians
Ajmer, 15-17 Nov 1935
Rajputana and Central India 131 (Oxenham 7-31) and 118 (Hansraj 42*, Oxenham 7-13) lost to **Australians** 149 (Morrisby 72, Ziaul Hassan 5-25) and 101-3 (Stork Hendry 48*) by 7 wickets

Sind v Australians
Karachi, 22-24 Nov 1935
Sind 79 (Nagel 5-24, Oxenham 5-28) and 125 (Oxenham 5-7) lost to **Australians** 294 (Morrisby 59, Arthur Alsopp 51, Hammy Love 46, Oxenham 44*, Mohammad Ibrahim 4-91) by inn and 90 runs

Maharashtra v Australians (misc)
Poona, 28-29 Nov 1935
Maharashtra 205 (MM Naidu 124, Nagel 7-53) and 42-1 drew with **Australians** 349-4 dec. (Hendry 62, Bill 70, Ryder 101*, Bryant 60*)

Bombay v Australians
Bombay, 30 Nov - 2 Dec 1935
Australians 468-8 dec. (Bill 107, Morrisby 40, Bryant 155, Jack Ellis 53*, Grimley Richards 4-133) drew with **Bombay** 241 (SM Kadri 41, LP Jai 59, DR Havewala 71, Mair 5-101) and f/o 171-7(Jai 115)

India v Australians**
Bombay, 5-7 Dec 1935
India 163 (Yuvraj of Patiala 40, Mair 5-50) and 163 (Lala Amarnath 41, Bert Ironmonger 5-70) lost to **Australians** 268 (Morrisby 67, Ryder 104, Mohammad Nissar 6-72) and 59-1 by 9 wickets

United Provinces v Australians (misc)
Allahabad, 11-12 Dec 1935
United Provinces [12 men] 137 (Maharajakumar of Vizianagram 40, Mair 4-46) drew with **Australians** 89 (Masood Salahuddin 4-25)

Central India v Australians
Indore, 14-16 Dec 1935
Central India 380 (Madhav Jagdale 55, CK Nayudu 50, CS Nayudu 42, JN Bhaya 106, Mair 4-117) and 55-1 drew with **Australians** 223 (Love 46, Oxenham 40*, Ziaul Hussain 4-53, CK Nayudu 5-48) and f/o 272 (Morrisby 51, Hendry 77, Leather 41)

Maharaja of Cooch Behar's XI v Australians (Misc, 1-day single innings)
Woodlands Ground Calcutta, 26 Dec 1935
Australians 211-6 dec. (Morrisby 80, Macartney 63) drew with **Maharaja of Cooch Behar's XI** 101-2(Phiroze Palia 57*)

Bengal v Australians
Eden Gardens Calcutta, 27-29 Dec 1935
Bengal 136 (Kamal Bhattacharya 48, Mair 5-43) and 184 (G Arratoon 56, Leather 4-31, Oxenham 4-40) lost to **Australians** 308 (Bryant 50, Morrisby 76, Macartney 85, Shute Banerjee 5-53) and 13-1 by 9 wickets

India v Australians**
Eden Gardens Calcutta, 31 Dec 1935-1 Jan 1936
India 48 (Macartney 5-17, Oxenham 5-7) and 127 (Leather 5-29) lost to

Australians 99 (Nissar 6-35) and 80-2 (Bill 45*) by 8 wickets

Southern Punjab v Australians
Amritsar, 5-7 Jan 1936
Australians 340 (Bryant 48, Ryder 115, Love 82, Murawwat Hussain 4-123) beat **Southern Punjab** 163 (Mohammad Saeed 80) and f/o 115 (Lall Singh 53, Oxenham 7-14) by inn and 62 runs

India v Australians**
Lahore, 10-13 Jan 1936
India 149 (S Wazir Ali 77, Nagel 4-72) and 301 (Banerjee 70, Wazir Ali 92, Leather 5-102) beat **Australians** 166 (Nissar 4-72) and 216 (Ryder 70, Nissar 4-80, Baqa Jilani 4-16) by 68 runs

Patiala v Australians
Patiala, 15-17 Jan 1936
Patiala 352 (Wazir Ali 152, Baqa Jilani 59, Harry Alexander 5-64) and 77-3 drew with **Australians** 484 (Bill 118, Morrisby 145, Ryder 78, Amir Elahi 6-164)

Cricket Club of India v Australians
Delhi, 19-21 Jan 1936
Cricket Club of India 167 (Amarnath 50, Mair 4-40) and 81-6 drew with **Australians** 268 (Bryant 42, Ryder 47, Hendry 45, Amar Singh 5-91)

Nawab of Moin-ud-Dowlah's XI v Australians
Secunderabad, 29-31 Jan 1936
Nawab of Moin-ud-Dowlah's XI 413-5 dec. (Amarnath 144, SM Hussain 73, Palia 61*) beat **Australians** 144 (Nissar 4-56, Amar Singh 4-51) and 154 (Amar Singh 6-36) by inn and 115 runs

Madras v Australians
Madras, 2-4 Feb 1936
Madras 142 (Cotar Ramaswami 48*, Oxenham 4-42) and 165 (Ramaswami 82, M Baliah 44) lost to **Australians** 47 (MJ Gopalan 6-23) and 262-9 (Hendry 49, Leather 46*, Gopalan 5-62) by 1 wicket

India v Australians**
Madras, 6-8 Feb 1936
India 189 (Mushtaq Ali 43, Amar Singh 45) and 113 (Macartney 6-41) beat **Australians** 162 (Mair 48, Nissar 5-61, Amar Singh 5-54) and 107 (Ryder 41, Nissar 6-36) by 33 runs

Mysore v Australians (misc)
Bangalore, 10-11 Feb 1936
Mysore 216 (Ken Hosking 95, Oxenham 5-84) and 127-3 drew with **Australians** 392 (Love 91, Macartney 43, Nagel 80)

** Denotes Representative matches.
There were 4 matches against the representative Indian teams and the 'series' was tied 2-2.
All the matches other than the ones marked (misc) are considered first-class.

B. Tour Averages for the Australians (all first-class in India and Ceylon)

	M	R	Ave	100	50	Wkts	Ave	5WI	10WM	Ct/St
HH Alexander	11	42	4.66	-	-	16	27.93	1	-	3
AH Alsopp	3	122	24.40	-	1					4
OW Bill	12	623	41.53	3	-					7
FJ Bryant	15	613	25.54	1	1					5
JH Davis	2	4	1.66	-	-					-
JL Ellis	10	162	20.25	-	1					10/17
HTSL Hendry	16	408	18.54	-	2	7	29.71	-	-	15
H Ironmonger	3	4	2.00	-	-	10	21.20	1	-	-
TW Leather	14	214	14.27	-	-	47	17.25	3	-	6
HSB Love	13	369	20.50	-	1					9
CG Macartney	11	336	24.00	-	2	32	17.75	2	-	2
F Mair	15	252	16.80	-	-	58	20.44	3	-	6
ROG Morrisby	15	813	38.71	2	5					3
LE Nagel	11	147	11.31	-	-	22	23.55	1	-	5
RK Oxenham	12	247	20.58	-	-	86	6.81	9	5	7
Maharaja Patiala	1	15	15.00	-	-					
J Ryder	17	843	38.31	2	3	8	28.00	-	-	10
FA Tarrant	2	39	13.00	-	-	4	29.25	-	-	1
LBN Tarrant	1	16	-	-	-					2
FB Warne	3	27	16.00	-	-	2	15.50	-	-	-

INDEX

ABOUT THE AUTHOR

In 2005, Megan Ponsford's career as a documentary photographer took a sharp turn when she located a box of long-forgotten archives whilst working at the Melbourne Cricket Club. This led to researching the first Australian cricket tour to India in 1935/36 which combined her greatest passions: sport, photography, cultural history, travel, the subcontinent and family. Megan completed her PhD in 2016 and has published extensively as a writer and photographer.

Printed in Great Britain
by Amazon

20705426R00159